Echoes of Exile

A Palestinian Journey

Younes Freajah

Edited & Translated By

Firas Freajah

Dedication

To my people, deeply rooted in their land, who defend their honor and existence. To my family, both immediate and extended, whose roots stem from this people and from this land, the land of Palestine.

To every individual born and raised on this land, whether living in exile and estrangement, remaining steadfast on their land, in their prisons, or buried as martyrs under its soil.

To every free person in this world who has refused injustice, believed in this most just cause, and defended it.

Acknowledgment

As we enter this world, our beginnings are not ours to choose. The time and place of our birth, our parents, our siblings, and the people of our homeland are all determined by fate. From the moment we are born, we are enfolded within a family and a community that shapes our earliest experiences, guiding and supporting us as we grow, develop, and find our place in the world.

However, being born Palestinian casts a distinct light on this universal journey. It sets us apart in a profound way, shaping our lives under the weight of unique circumstances and challenges. This reality instills a deep awareness of the world's injustices, influencing us from birth and shaping our paths in profound ways.

My own journey has been deeply impacted by many, each leaving an indelible mark on my character and the course of my life. Foremost among them are my parents, the cornerstone of my existence, and my family - my brothers, sisters, and the community of my birthplace. From an early age, they presented me with challenges that fueled my determination to strive for something greater, to emerge from the confines of a narrow reality into a world of broader possibilities and brighter horizons.

I owe a debt of gratitude to many others who have

influenced my journey, altering the course of my life, sometimes intentionally and at other times inadvertently. This includes my wife, my steadfast partner, who has shared the ups and downs of my life, enduring changes in our circumstances and the fluctuations of my mood. My small family, beginning with my son Firas, has been a wellspring of inspiration. Firas first planted the seed of this endeavor in my mind and ardently supported its fruition, just as my other children have offered their unwavering encouragement, urging me to bring this work to completion.

Contents

The Introduction and Origin of the Story

As I sat in my car next to my eldest son Firas, who we had celebrated his nineteenth birthday just a few days earlier, heading to perform the Fajr prayer at the Islamic Center in Columbia, South Carolina, I did not envision that a discussion would lead to the beginning of writing my modest words and history. A history I consider not only my own but that of every Palestinian born and lived at the beginning of their life in Palestine after being awakened to injustice, oppression, occupation and displacement from the land of their birth. Unable to return to it even after reaching the age of 18 when I was uprooted from its embrace.

As I was nurtured and fed from the soil of this sacred land.

I had few choices when I left; I was forced to leave quickly or face imprisonment by the occupation.

I chose to leave then, not knowing I wouldn't be able to return to my homeland until I obtained American citizenship and could return only as a visitor, not as a citizen, 19 years after my first departure.

I hesitated a lot before starting to write, wondering for whom and what to write and what benefit would come from it. But my son's persuasion and his insistence that I at least write for them and their future children about what happened and how we, as children and their children, came here.

This made me start to carve out these memories, knowing my children and probably their future generations will not be able to begin their lives on Palestinian soil or live the life that even my generation started.

A life that was often difficult and arduous, chiseled in stone, because these generations came into a world where everything is available to them, unlike our times... However, each generation has its own challenges.

The Introduction and Origin of the Story

What should I remember and what should I leave unmentioned? Those bitter moments in my life or those few smiles that also passed. Do I consider myself fortunate or miserable in this world? Am I that person mixed with those collective moments? Do these combined moments have any significant value? Or am I like the rest of God's creation, most of whom are born, live, grow, and die without making any noticeable difference and without anyone knowing anything about them in this life. And even if they are known, it wouldn't add or subtract anything?

My life is that of a child born in a village to peasant parents whose foreheads would embrace the land, sometimes in the heat of the summer and sometimes in the biting cold of the Palestinian winter. Many questions flooded my conscience before embarking on writing...

What to write and for whom. As someone who didn't live long under the care of my parents, circumstances that I created myself forced me to migrate several times and to be independent with my own being, personality, and history, and to have my father and mother die while I was far from them, unable to even bid them farewell, may God have mercy on them and grant them paradise… They are always in my mind, conscience, and prayers.

Despite that, I decided to start writing. But in truth, I don't know where I will end.

Chapter 1 - Abwein: My Birth & Childhood

My Birth

Abwein…

This village, located northwest of Ramallah, about 30 kilometers away.

Here, in this village, I was born and witnessed my earliest moments of life, where I grew up. Regarding my birth, my late mother recounted its initial details:

One day, labor pains began very early, around the time of Fajr prayer. Then, she screamed for one of my brothers to quickly fetch the midwife, Umm Aziz, who lived not far from us. To witness the first breaks of dawn on June 5, 1960, heralding the arrival of a boy and the loud ululations that broke out with the crowing of the rooster that morning, announcing the great news that Younes had come into this world.

To give the good news to my father, that simple self-made farmer who was preparing to go to the fields, that it was a great occasion...

How could it not be?

With the trio in the stories of Al-Zeer Salem, which my father admired so much that he decided to name his sons after its heroes.

And now it was complete with Younes, the last to arrive. My father, in his love for the stories, would narrate them every day to the farmers who joined him for what is called the 'harvest,' meaning gathering wheat sheaves from the land my father cultivated extensively, as he owned much land which he bought with the sweat of his brow, having been orphaned and his mother passing away when he was 9 years old. He lived as an orphan, building himself up and buying land until he became one of the major landowners of the village.

All this during the harsh summer of Palestine in flaming June. As for Younes, the most beautiful of them as the story goes...

Which says that his birth came after his brothers Yahya and Murai and that the ambassador Aziza loved him dearly, as mentioned in that narrative.

In our family (as my mother, God rest her soul, told me), there was great joy and the news spread among the people about the arrival of Jameel Freajah's third knight... It was, as my late mother once said, a day everyone danced and sang joyfully, after everyone gathered at our modest family home.

Everyone said the legend was complete, and Younes was born and my father's deep love for the story of Al-Zeer Salem spread throughout the village. It was often the subject of conversation and sometimes the jest among our villagers.

Here ends my mother's story about my birth.

Childhood

I don't know... but as I recall, my childhood was very special...

How could it not be when that little child had all hands reaching out to tickle his cheeks.

And then they would say, "Masha'Allah."

The beginning of school was in a girls' school.

I don't know why the school officials decided that the first grade, the beginning of a long academic journey, should be co-ed and in a girls' school.

It was a challenge from the beginning of my life. I believed that my role in life was to be exceptional, not like the other children. To be the boy who everyone pointed out, not the one sidelined in a corner of the class.

I believed I had to be number one in everything and the center of attention. That's how I was or tried to be throughout my life. I stood out in class. I was the one who knew everything and who answered everything.

My appearance gave me a lot of confidence, and being number one made the school principal at that time (a noble lady who dedicated her life to educating many generations and later became the mayor of our village) chose me to be the class monitor. So I was in charge of the class containing boys and girls.

I believe this gave me the confidence from an early age to take on leadership roles through the last class of my high school years, despite the changes in schools and locations.

Because this experience gave me leadership qualities and opened my eyes to aspects of my personality I didn't know existed and hadn't noticed over the years - self-confidence, a trait that made my life much easier and helped me overcome many difficulties and problems.

That year, I believe, for the first time as a child, my heart whispered. Yes, I was seven years old... There was a girl two years older than me. I don't remember exactly, but my brothers were also friends with her brothers, which made me see her in class and outside it. Her being in the same class had a special melody that touched the strings of my heart.

I was very fond of her and, due to her older age as she entered school two or three years late, she often stood in line, always beside me... And we always spent the break together. We shared the small loaf of bread that either I brought or she brought. I don't remember what it contained, but most likely, it was oil and za'atar, the things we usually brought most days.

The special relationship that connected us remained even after we moved to higher grades, me to the boys' school and she remained in the girls' school. We always met, she would tell me what was happening in her school, and I did the same.

June 5, 1967 (The Setback)

The sun in Palestine was blazing that day, especially in Jabal Gharabeh (an area) in Abwein, where my father owned many wheat fields.

I was sitting on a small hill, my eyes gazing far into the distance at the paved road stretching between Nablus and Ramallah, with cars speeding by, sometimes fast, sometimes slow. This road passed by the village of Al-Libban, visible from my perch on the small hill. I thought to myself that there must be another world...

That the people in these cars lived a different life, and I, who had never ridden in a car.

Certainly, there is another world beyond what I see and different from what I see in my father's face and the faces of these farmers in front of me, harvesting wheat from the red earth mixed with the shimmering heat waves.

My father, that hardworking, faithful, patient man, was encouraging these simple harvesters, singing Palestinian songs to them, and recounting the story of Al-Zeer Salem and the ambassador Aziza, bringing joy and laughter despite their exhaustion, sweat, and the intense heat... A remarkable paradox.

Of course, I was that boy loved by everyone, bringing lunch prepared by my mother - whose face time had been etched with the most beautiful images of resilience. Like my father, she was like the Roman olive trees with deep roots through time.

This amazing contrast and comparison deeply influenced me, realizing there's another side to the world apart from toil and heat.

Riding in these cars that I saw when I turned to my right, I believed their occupants didn't tire or sweat like my father and these good people.

I didn't want to toil and struggle like them. I wanted to ride in a car like those people on my right. At that moment, I felt I would never settle for a life of hardship, which my father, God rest his soul, and these people endured.

On that day, which I still remember well, June 5, 1967, which was supposed to be my birthday, we didn't really know what birthdays meant. After sitting at the top of the hill watching my father and the farmers harvest wheat, my older brother came to bring more water and food for these people. My father, God rest his soul, said to me: go back home with your brother instead of staying under the sun.

So, we returned, both riding a donkey, traversing the rugged path back to the village... People we met along the way were spreading the news that the Jews had come.

They spoke in haste and fear, saying things like, "They've taken the rest of the country..." or "The Jews have occupied us now." These were some of the phrases we heard from those we met. My brother stopped everyone he met to ask what had happened, each describing the situation in their own way. I could see the astonishment on his forehead as he continued to ask, "I heard so and so..."

I held my brother's hand, scared, and asked him the innocent question I still remember in detail.

Me: Brother, what are the Jews... Are they humans like us... or big animals... Do they have hands and eyes like us?

I bombarded him with questions as our Cypriot donkey swayed us, trying to find even ground on this rugged path.

My brother tried to silence me and ease my fear, which I noticed in his movements and voice.

"Yes, they are humans... and no…"

He smiled a worried smile, watching everything... and continued, "If we're lucky, they won't kill us like they did before..."

Intense fear gripped me, and I wanted to continue asking, but the severe worry I saw on my brother's face made me silent, and I began repeating the questions inside.

What if... and what if???

Especially since the people we met later said that many Israeli tanks had been entrenched in the back (a region in the country), a mountainous area where people had started building their homes away from the lower areas of the village, known as the town until it became the center of the village after people left the town.

After that, the news spread, and everyone returned from the wheat fields and the wilderness to their homes, watching and fearing what the Jews would do...

Especially since the massacres the Jews had committed in their first occupation in Deir Yassin and other areas in the 1948 occupation were fresh in people's minds, and what made things worse at that time was the talk among the people that the Jordanian soldiers in the West Bank had abandoned the battlefield.

Rapid Growth

I believe I grew up quickly, or at least, that's what I thought. After learning about the Jews' arrival and their occupation of our land, everyone realized that life must go on. The Jews hadn't massacred us or killed anyone, contrary to what people had feared. This realization opened my eyes to the need for initiative in life. People were compelled to seek different sources of livelihood due to financial necessities.

I noticed people picking sage and thyme, which grew wild in our mountains, during the summers. Curious, I asked my brothers what they did with these herbs. They simply sold them. This sparked a thought in me: why not do the same? At eight years old, I went to my father, may he rest in peace, and proposed that I, like others, pick sage and thyme to sell.

Laughing, he suggested that I work with them on the land instead. But I found that option unappealing; it was unpaid and arduous. My father toiled tirelessly through all seasons, drenched in sweat. I resolved never to do such work. Picking herbs and olives during the olive season seemed easier and more manageable with no one overseeing me. It would also allow me to afford things I wanted but couldn't ask my parents for, as they'd consider it wasteful.

I decided to join people and children older than me in this endeavor. Initially, I didn't know the ropes or where to go. Accompanying these people, who treated me like a child among them, I learned about the places where these herbs grew – part of the Palestinian people's collective memory and their daily sustenance – and where to sell them.

Eventually, I ventured out alone, discovering new places no one else had been to before. The shopkeepers I sold to looked at me with a mix of admiration and curiosity. It surprised them that Younes, son of Jameel Freajah, who hired people to work for him, was doing this job. They remarked on my hard work, saying I worked harder than many adults.

I kept this activity hidden from my father. If he had known, he would have insisted I work with him on the land, dismissing my efforts as frivolous. But it wasn't trivial to me; I was earning money, changing my circumstances, and affording many things with my earnings. I hid my savings outside the house, burying them in the ground in our almond garden so my father wouldn't find them.

However, my secret didn't remain hidden for long. One day, the shopkeeper, a friend of my father, casually mentioned to him how well I was doing selling sage and thyme. Surprised, my father hid his reaction from the shopkeeper, but he didn't keep it to himself for long. That evening, he called me aside, gently patting my shoulder and smiling. He asked how much I had saved, then advised me to stay sharp at school and take care of myself, expressing confidence in my future success in business. He left me with a warm smile, preparing for evening prayers.

From then on, at eight years old, I never asked my father for pocket money. Instead, I sold olives, pumpkins, sage, thyme, and other produce of the Palestinian land.

Grapes

I wasn't yet ten years old when I noticed some farmers coming to my father, may God have mercy on him, paying him five dinars and saying:

"Hajj, we want a load of grapes!"

Then my father would bless their endeavor with "On God's grace."

I wanted to find out what they were doing but didn't dare ask my father directly; instead, I went to my older brother. What do these people do? He explained to me that these people go to our grapevines in the Ghuraba area. They pick the grapes themselves during the season and go to sell them in Sinjil, a village about 10 km from us.

I thought about it.

Why couldn't I do the same? I said to my father: "Okay, let me do as they do... I'll pay you five dinars like them... and go sell the grapes in Sinjil..."

Everyone laughed at my words and said: "These are grown men... they can load the burden and put it on a donkey... and you are a boy who cannot do that."

I pleaded with my father... to take the donkey and work like them... He laughed and said: "Okay. I'm sure you'll come back because you won't be able to do it..."

That instilled a challenge in me... and the next summer morning, I rode the donkey to Ghuraba... Before I started picking, I told myself... If I put the boxes on the ground, I won't be able to load them onto the donkey's back after they are filled. So, I decided to keep the donkey next to me and filled the boxes without setting them down. I carefully picked the grapes and arranged them in these boxes... and continued this way until they were full...

Of course, I chose the most beautiful bunches of grapes, for which our land was renowned... and covered the top of the box with grape leaves to protect the grapes, as I had seen others do...

And I headed with my load, riding my donkey, to the village of Sinjil on a rugged path that passed through the mountains... covering about 10 km in the summer sun... through wilderness areas rarely visited by many people...

After finally reaching the square next to the mosque, just before the Dhuhr prayer, I asked some men standing there to help unload the burden... They looked at me in amazement... How could a boy not yet ten years old come from another village with a load of grapes like this!!!

Indeed... they helped me unload, and I began selling... and I was almost done selling everything shortly after the prayer... Everyone was eager to buy from me...

I remember that about a third of the box remained... when an elderly man came and said: "I want to buy these leftovers in one go."

At that time, I didn't understand exactly what he meant... The man explained that he wanted to buy the remainder for two dinars... I looked into that man's eyes at the moment and thought: If he wants them that much, I can get three dinars instead of two. I told him: "No... for three dinars." In the end, we agreed to meet in the middle... at 2.5 dinars... and this deal was a new milestone in my life...

Some men helped me load the wooden boxes back onto the donkey... I rode back to my village happy, counting the roughly 12 dinars I had collected that day. I was thrilled because I had succeeded in the challenge first and foremost... and also in my first selling mission outside my village...

In the evening, I went where my father, may God have mercy on him, and his friends sat on stone chairs placed at the mosque doors where they sat after the Maghrib prayer until the Isha prayer time. I went there with signs of victory on my face... and said "Salam" and sat next to him. He asked, somewhat mockingly as he thought I had given up and returned halfway: "Ah... what happened with you today?"

Confidently, I said: "First, here are the five dinars like those who pay you..." He looked at me, surprised, wanting to know the details. I told him exactly what happened and how I had managed to sell the entire load for about 12 dinars... My father and his friends were very pleased, laughing and saying "Masha'Allah," and at that moment, my father said... "I will never worry about you again... You are truly a man... You will manage your life."

What's funny is that he refused to take the five dinars... saying, "Keep it for yourself, add it to your capital." Then, this story became one my father would recount when he sat in front of the mosque with his friends after prayers.

But this story did not just pass by...

My father started entrusting me with the task of milling wheat in the neighboring village of Aarura whenever we needed flour, meaning I had gained experience in these tasks. This also gave me experience in dealing and getting to know many boys in that neighboring village, especially the son of the mill owner, with whom I developed a strong friendship... even as we grew up...

The way villagers would socialize in front of mosques between prayers, as a custom.

School Days in Abwein

The school in our village was perched atop a hill in an area that was almost devoid of houses at that time. It was about 7 kilometers away from our home in the old town. As usual, with the passage of time, urban expansion reached the area, turning it into a neighborhood surrounded by many houses, which were once sparse.

Nowadays, the school lies in the midst of the new town, after urban sprawl reached and exceeded it, and after people in our village abandoned the old town. They started building their homes in this area known as "Al Dhahr," which eventually developed into a kind of suburb.

My daily journey to school during those times was not easy, especially since most of the school days were in winter. And what a winter it was in a region already significantly elevated above sea level! When there were strong winds, it felt like they would carry us away as we struggled to ascend the rugged, muddy mountain path, sinking in mud and water streaming down the mountain slope, resisting the ascent towards the school.

The climb up the mountain from the valley was our daily challenge. Our boots (plastic shoes), already riddled with holes, often filled with water and mud. The khaki trousers we wore as part of the school uniform became a bizarre mix of mud and water. This, coupled with the biting cold that continuously made us sick during winter - we hardly had adequate clothing to shield us from these daily trials, not to mention the roughness of the path.

Upon finally arriving at the school, after much struggle, we were met by the school principal, who was actually from the same village. His greeting often included swearing and harsh words, not to mention the stern and serious faces of the teachers, who seemed even stricter than usual.

It wasn't easy, but at the same time, it fueled my determination to excel... I had to be an outstanding student. Indeed, I managed to be the first to learn to read and write. I always solved my problems and homework in class before going home because I devoted the time outside school to reading, revising, and learning. For instance, I would ask my brother, who went to Ramallah for high school every day, to buy me the Al-Quds newspaper. I would give him the money for it after he was initially surprised by my request. I would immerse myself in reading it daily to understand what was happening in the world. I voraciously read, gathering topics and enjoying the novelty of seeing the news and subjects change every day.

Echoes of Exile

The Ministry of Education distributed stories for us to read and take home, to be returned at the end of the week. I took not only my share but also collected the stories from students who disliked reading. I returned home after stopping by the shop to buy some snacks for leisure instead of playing with the other children after school.

I would go to a place dear to my heart called Al-Musrara, away from residential areas and remarkably quiet, dense with apricot, almond, pear, and fig trees. There, under a large pear tree, I cleared an area of stones to create a reading spot, using the tree trunk as a backrest. I read with great eagerness, often finishing the stories I had with me on the same day before the sunset, when its disk began to hide behind the mountain. Then, I would gather my things and return home. This almost daily journey drew much teasing from family and friends, leading to a sort of estrangement between them and me. Of course, this bore fruit. My academic achievements in school were positively reflected. When the Arabic language teacher wanted to ask who had read these stories and discuss them, I was always the first to explain, discuss, and elaborate in detail.

Thus, my cultural knowledge became known to everyone in the class and even the whole school, even though I was in the lower grades. Therefore, I was tasked with editing the school's wall newspaper. I was also given the responsibility of reading poetry and stories to the students every morning. This laid a wonderful foundation with the stern principal, who began smiling at me, even praising me regularly. The teachers, too, always put me at the forefront of everything good happening in the school. This was natural, given my near-perfect grades.

I was the top student in class throughout the early grades, and being the class monitor in these grades gave me significant popularity among the students and teaching staff.

This distinction was not well-received by my elder brother. He disliked school, teachers, and the principal, and he was uninterested in his studies, unlike me. So, the school principal and teachers, when anything happened, would ask him in complete astonishment: "We can't believe you are Younes's brother," especially since he was always subject to punishment and beating due to his behavior and lack of interest. Therefore, he took the matter seriously. When we went home, I would face daily beatings from him, saying, "Do you have to be smart so they keep teasing me with you?"

I would always go to my father and mother, complaining, and they would scold him, saying, "Be like him, smart, don't make him become like you." This brother of mine didn't continue in school for long. One day, he was absent from school and home and went to work, deciding that the life of education meant nothing to him.

There's a story I still remember from when I was in the third grade of primary school. One day, an education inspector visited us with the teacher and informed us to line up as there was an inspection. When the inspector entered and wanted to test us, he asked, "Do you know how to read?" We all said yes. Then, he wrote a sentence on the board. I stood up, raising my hand eagerly, and he asked me to read it. I read it easily and then he asked me to read from the book in front of me, which I did comfortably.

I saw signs of satisfaction in the inspector's eyes, his clear smile. I also looked at the teacher and found him almost flying with joy. I was holding my head high. How could I not when I had made him proud? Then he praised me a lot. If the inspector had asked many of the students, especially those sitting in the back rows, he would have been quite displeased, as many of them knew nothing.

Chapter 2 - Ramallah: School, Growth, and Work

The Major Tremor

As I said before, this surge in my young personality, whether on the academic side or even in non-academic activities, gave me a sense of self-esteem, confidence, enthusiasm, and polite boldness. In our village, the criterion was that the clever one was the only beloved and popular person, receiving many appreciative attributes, especially since the teachers and the principal used to go daily to the village's only café, where they would begin categorizing their students even in front of the village men who played cards with them. Strangely, all the students would scatter in the streets when they saw the teachers coming, but I was the opposite; I made it a point to show myself and greet them often.

Why not? There was nothing I was afraid of, as I was the top student in the class, and they always loved that, praising me in class the next day. I said I was highly rated by the teachers in the café or outside, and this gave me fame since our village was small and everyone circulated news about it.

My excellence wasn't limited to this level only. We used to make our own toys back then, for instance, building cars out of iron wires, which were plentiful in the village. As I recall, I built the nicest cars, which many boys envied and asked for my help to build their cars. I also took the initiative in activities all the time. Behind our house, there were many gardens planted with almond trees. I made space, surrounded it with stones, and named it 'Younes's Restaurant.' The tables and chairs were also made of stone. My sister and other friends would come to the 'restaurant,' where I served food from home, pretending I had prepared it in my small kitchen. It was usually za'atar with oil and taboon bread. I don't remember what they paid me or what I earned for this service.

The important thing is that I played the role with elegance and capability, and many other similar games that awakened in me the spirit of initiative during those days and it has not been extinguished to this day. I still learn towards innovation and make the impossible possible, turning ideas into reality over time, shining brightly.

As I said, the type of fame I had given me a kind of vanity. I was the one pointed out with fingers, and I also noticed that girls started looking at me differently, especially when we went for evening walks in the summer in Al-Ain Street, which was frequented by girls at that time to fill their water jars from the famous spring, the main water source for the villagers. I noticed admiring glances from these blossoming girls. How could I not when I was the smart, attractive boy (the 'personality') as they called me, and also because of the distinguished clothes I wore. I was the one who wore everything new that came out in fashion, especially, as I said, I depended on myself to amass wealth at that time, which allowed me to take the bus to Ramallah and buy new clothes. That bus, which has another story, was part of our village's heritage for many years, a village that was isolated from the world, and this bus connected us with the rest of the world.

As I said, my eyes were opened to seeing the other side, especially the friend of that girl who was older than me in the first grade. As for the same girl who was older than me, she had grown noticeably, which somewhat removed her from my imagination, as she was three years older than me. True, my admiration for her was great in the early grades, but she had become a young woman and the focus of men's attention when I was thirteen, especially since she was charming and attractive. I heard that her cousin or one of her relatives was going to propose to her, so I tried hard to keep her out of my mind. Of course, this admiration was one-sided; she would talk to me and ask about school when she saw me, just because of the friendship between our families.

As for the other girl, the one who caught my eye, her friend, who was about my age, she would always smile at me. How could she not? I had become a star in our small village, with the eyes of many young girls turning towards me, and things continued in this way.

One day, I was carrying a book and going to the Lower Al-Ain area, which held many meanings for me, especially since this area was known for its tall, dense trees and lush greenery due to the flowing water from underground. We would sit on the green grass there, where some friends would come, and I usually went there to read. As usual, I went there one afternoon, and there was that girl with our friend from the first grade, walking together in the area where I usually sat. When she saw me, she smiled as if they were expecting my arrival. I shyly approached them, turned to the girl who was also shyly looking at the ground and spoke to our friend, who wasn't really a barrier between us. I turned to the girl, who wasn't looking at me, greeted her, and it was the first time I talked to her. We stood for more than five minutes talking, trying to steal this precious time from the world, then they hurried off as they heard someone talking near us. They were afraid it might be someone from their family (their families) and that it would be a disaster if someone saw us, even though we were just talking and despite our young age at the time.

But the strict traditions of the village forbade us from having anything but a secret relationship. Our meetings were regular in this area and very secret, ending whenever we heard people talking nearby. One day, a friend from the first grade shyly told me, despite being older, that the other girl, her friend who was with her and whom I thought I loved at the time, wanted to ask me for something. Excited, the small knight in me ready to fulfill all requests, I asked what she wanted. She said she wanted a letter from me expressing my love, and I, the writer who had written prose and poetry, of course, agreed. This was what I had hoped for at that moment to craft my words into a letter to send to her. I asked how I would deliver it to her, and she said to give it to my younger sister at school, and she would give it to her.

I was happy with the idea. Why not? How could I not show my beloved that I was the inspired, sensitive poet in writing? And so it was. After they left, I began to squeeze my thoughts and pen to write a letter. It was full of innocence, spontaneity, and true love. I drew flowers and blossoms around it, pouring out all my wild imagination at the time. At night, I went to my younger sister and said, "Look, this is a letter; give it secretly to so-and-so tomorrow." I think my sister was in fifth grade at the time, and I was in the second preparatory grade.

Indeed, the next morning, as the girls lined up for morning assembly, my sister quickly and loudly went to the girl in front of all the schoolgirls and said, "This is a letter from my brother Younes." Naturally, the girl was embarrassed in front of all the students, and the teacher who saw what happened took the letter from her and gave it to the principal. This marked a turning point in our lives.

The girl's family found out about the letter, and it became a major honor issue starring her and me. The girl's family and relatives gathered at her father's house, who decided unanimously at the time to attack our house, Jamil Freajah's, i.e., our house, and kill or beat me with sticks and stones. The villagers gathered at that time, and we had no idea except that the school administration knew about the letter. News reached us that the girl's family would attack our house and pounce on me, as I was wanted dead or alive.

At that time, we had just engaged my older sister to a family related to these people. This new family quickly came to stand by us before the crowds of the girl's family that were going to attack us arrived. Some of our family also came, and we formed a kind of defense front. They ordered me to stay inside and not leave my place, no matter what. Surprisingly, everyone scolded me for this dark deed I had done as if I had committed an unforgivable crime, especially my older brothers, who used to beat me for being smart in school and were known for their manliness and ferocity at the time. They threatened me, accusing me of causing this problem that would happen. My father calmed everyone down, ordering them not to come near me, while I sat in the corner, waiting and wondering:

What is happening? My young mind couldn't comprehend all this commotion over a letter I had written. I was thirteen years old, writing to a thirteen-year-old girl. What was happening, and why were these people behaving like this?

It wasn't long before crowds stormed the road in front of our house. Everyone was carrying a stick or stone, and we were on the brink of a war between the two families because of my letter, like the wars we heard about. Everyone was showing off in their own way, or let's say dueling. My brother, who used to beat me for being smart in school and was known for his manliness and ferocity at the time, was showing off to them, saying, "Anyone with hair on their chin, step two steps in front of our house." Our new relative, also known for his love of trouble and problems in those days, was threatening them with my brother, saying the same thing. All this while my patient, silent father didn't utter a word, just repeating, "God is sufficient for me, and He is the best disposer of affairs." Eventually, a group from the town came and separated the two families, pulling their men away from our house.

Then, the village elders gathered in the attic, i.e., the Mukhtar's house to discuss the situation and reach a solution between the two families. My fear was intense, especially since it was certain that there would be a clash between the two families, and if one of my family members got hurt, it would all be because of me or because of that damned love letter. It didn't take long for them to meet these village dignitaries, as they are called. In the absence of anyone from my family, the dignitaries unanimously decided to exile Younes Freajah from Abwein for a year.

Ramallah: School, Growth, and Work

What???!!! To be expelled from my parent's house, my village, and among my friends into the unknown for a year, all because of that damned letter, under the pretext of cooling down tempers. My young mind couldn't bear all this. Exiling a child of my age out of the country for a year, never to return, all to extinguish the fire of shame and disgrace for that family caused by that damned letter. This verdict was to drop the demand to attack our house and my family. There were not many options for my family but to comply with this decision, which made my mother cry and scream, "Where is the mercy for a child of this age? What will he do, exiled from his home?"

My family and our new relatives chose Sinjil as it was the closest to our village, and I would join its school for the third preparatory grade, which was like the Tawjihi at the time. We would take the exam for all of Palestine. Anyway, I would join the school next year for secondary education, as it was the only high school around us. So our relative at the time, who owned a taxi and was well-known, went to the village of Sinjil and, through his acquaintances, found me a house with one room and an outside bathroom. He rented it for me, and one of my brothers went with me, along with a small mattress, a small quilt, and some small things to live on for a year, like a kerosene lamp and other simple things.

This was my first exile and my first departure at the age of thirteen. When I got in the car, saying goodbye to my family and village, I felt the world closing in on me, almost crushing me. I am not exaggerating when I say this was my feeling when my brother and our relative dropped off the stuff in the room rented for me. They headed towards the door, returning to the village, and asked, "Do you need anything?" I almost went mad. What was this? My new prison where I would be jailed for a year away from my family? Away from everything I lived for, all because of that damned letter? I felt that moment was a turning point in my life.

How could these people think this way about a child? How could the village elders come to the conclusion of imprisoning me in that room? This is sheer ignorance! From that moment, I stripped my heart of any tenderness for my village and its elders. But as I said, the bitterness in my throat had solidified, and the intense resentment I felt, especially since I would be taking the Matriculation exam alone between these cold concrete walls that held no meaning. A deep feeling of bitterness was born in me, a feeling that I should stay away from these people as much as possible. I had to carve into the rock to adapt to the new situation. What more could happen to me?

These scars that formed deep in my spirit made me distance myself from my village for the next 19 years without batting an eyelid, hardening my heart to many actions I later took to avenge myself for this unjust verdict. Indeed, it wasn't long before I adapted myself to the school, easily emerging at the forefront. I carved a place for myself at the top. I got to know people in the village of Sinjil and made friends who visited me, and I visited them. I gained popularity in the school grades.

The experience wasn't that bad. It stimulated my spirit of challenge, gave me the ability to adapt, endure hardships, and also opened my mind a lot. My surroundings expanded a bit. It was hard for me to explain to people in that village why I had come from Abwein, and those who knew the reason laughed for a long time at the despair of the people of Abwein, as they called it, for issuing this verdict.

The picture was completed in the first year of high school when the rest of the students from our village joined the school. As I said, it was the only high school around us, giving me a special place among them, especially since I knew these students as I was their class monitor in Abwein and knew all the Sinjil students, having spent a year among them.

The past year, which I spent alone, was very difficult, especially when I locked the door on myself, especially in winter with the harsh cold and strong winds that frightened me as I stayed up studying for the Matriculation exam. I would hug the lamp that ran on kerosene, which often went out when strong winds blew. I heard the sound of trees swaying on windy winter days, thunder and lightning, and even the dogs outside howling loudly, which I think was due to the severe cold. This made me feel very scared, but despite all this, I excelled that year. My mother, God rest her soul, would cook for me and send it with our relative, who would bring it and leave it in a store on the street that I would pass by every day, jokingly asking if there was any supply from Abwein.

The important thing is that I returned to our village after the year ended. I felt like I had aged a hundred years, as I thought. I studied the first year of high school, as I said, enjoying popularity among the grades and my excellence granting me the opportunity to join the Hashemite School, the only scientific school in the Ramallah area, which accommodated students from all the surrounding villages and towns of Ramallah.

Of course, this set me on the edge of a second departure and a second exile at the age of sixteen to Ramallah, which was much easier this time. Firstly, because I had matured, and secondly, because it was my choice and desire, something I was looking forward to. One of the experiences I had in Sinjil in the first year of high school was direct contact with Jewish settlers. I didn't know much about Jews, except that they passed on the main road, heavily armed in armored military vehicles. I also read about them in newspapers or novels I was fond of at the time, which talked about the Palestinian struggle, especially Ghassan Kanafani, Emile Habibi, and others.

The boys came to me, as I was the class monitor, and said that tomorrow was a national anniversary and we should strike. We would not study; we would organize a strike for everyone before we headed to the main road between Ramallah and Nablus, where the village of Sinjil was located in the middle of the distance between them and on the main road, close to three settlements, particularly the Shilo settlement, which is historic for Jews, built on the land of the nearby village of Turmus Aya, adjacent to the land of Sinjil.

So, the next morning, the students gathered, many refusing to study and organize in the classes despite threats from the principal, who was from the same village and had a strong friendship with his son, with whom I shared the front seat in class. Despite threats from the teachers, which did not scare the students, and they paid no attention, we organized the students and went to the main road linking Ramallah and Nablus after some of us carried tires and put kerosene to burn these tires, in addition to stones. We indeed closed the main road.

It was only a few minutes before the settlers' cars, which were in contact with the Israeli army, arrived. It didn't take long for the armored military vehicles to come, and the skirmish began with them with stones. The battle of attack and retreat with the army began; they would open the road on one side, and we would close it on the other, interspersed with bullets and tear gas grenades. We threw stones over their heads, and they fired tear gas grenades that made me dizzy, along with tears and a runny nose, which I was experiencing for the first time. They also fired bullets everywhere.

It was also my first experience of a live bullet fired by the occupying soldiers passing by my ear, its loud noise deafening me, making me and the other students run in every direction, chased by the Israeli occupation soldiers in the mountains. The school day went in every direction because the chase continued even among the village neighborhoods, and some students were arrested that day. It was a day when I was lucky not to be caught or hit by a bullet, despite its proximity to touching me.

August 25th, 1975 - Me (age 15) and friends visiting Al Aqsa Mosque & Dome of Rock

Ramallah

My arrival in Ramallah is an indelible memory. This transition from a visitor to a resident in this city was a significant shift. Initially, the challenge was to find a small room to live in. Soon after joining the Hashemite School, I entered a larger community, a vast contrast to the environments of my village and the larger village of Sinjil.

This was the second exile in my life's journey. The Hashemite School housed a large number of students, the elites from all the villages and regions of Ramallah, all vying for distinction. Among these students, it was my task to stand out and make my name known. Only three students, including myself, were from my village, but I soon made friends from various villages, emerging from the large crowd of students.

My new friends from Al-Bireh, adjacent to Ramallah, helped me find a room, sparing me the daily commute from Abwein, which consumed most of my day. I moved into a small room attached to a large, mostly empty house owned by an elderly Palestinian woman from Al-Bireh, Um Mahmoud. Her family had migrated to America, a common destiny for many Palestinian families scattered between the Gulf countries and the West.

I found myself obliged to assist her in every way, which provided me with a semblance of the familial warmth and affection I missed. I helped her with her chores and minor house repairs. Although she consistently struggled to remember my name, calling me something different each time, I quickly adapted to life in my new homeland.

I learned to live alone, content with the small things, and adapted to the modest allowance I usually had. I made many friends in the area, who often visited me or invited me out. On Thursdays, I would visit my family in my village, returning to Ramallah on Saturday mornings.

My experiences and exile from my village had given me a certain fame and reputation as a survivor and a lover. This exile not only boosted my confidence and broadened my cultural and intellectual horizons, but it also marked the beginning of my maturity and a shining youth. Everywhere I went, I could hear echoes of my growing reputation.

The Hashemite School

The Hashemite School was a bright spot in my early history. Indeed, how could it not be? It enriched my experience, where I met many friends who later became prominent figures in the history of the Palestinian struggle, such as Marwan Barghouti and Bassam Salhi, among others. One of the most memorable stories from this period:

From the beginning, my personality leaned towards leadership. Being the class prefect in secondary school section (B) for students from various villages around Ramallah, with Marwan as the prefect of section (A) and Bassam Salhi of section (C), we had our share of significant days. On one such day, the anniversary of the Balfour Declaration, when the British minister promised to give the land of Palestine to the Jewish people and the Zionist movement, we decided not to enter our classes. Instead, we gathered in the schoolyard, planning to join other students from various schools in central Ramallah for a protest condemning this event and reminding people and the world of this unjust promise. Our intention was to meet at the circle known as the "Expatriates' Circle" at that time, later renamed Yasser Arafat Circle.

As students gathered in the yard, chanting and singing, the school principal, Hamdi, accused by students of being an agent for the authorities, came with a microphone, urging us to enter our classes, warning that the army would intervene. He was later executed by young men who were subsequently sentenced to life imprisonment, along with the infamous and notoriously spoken Israeli deputy governor, Morris. But only ten minutes after the students disregarded the principal, armored personnel carriers and light tanks surrounded the schoolyard, and a clash with soldiers ensued, starting with stone-throwing.

The police station next to the school, housing both Arab and Jewish police, also came under a barrage of stones. Soldiers began firing live rounds close to us and tear gas canisters, causing choking and nosebleeds. Resourcefully, students used onions provided by vegetable cart vendors to mitigate the gas's effects on nerves. They also countered tear gas by placing canisters in water buckets, neutralizing them.

It soon became evident that the soldiers did not want us leaving the school to meet other students in the field. At that moment, Morris reappeared, declaring himself the deputy head of the military governor for the Ramallah area. We knew him well, as he had once gathered us in the schoolyard, threatening and boasting fluently in Arabic about his master's thesis topic, which was offensive towards Ramallah's girls. He coldly gave us ten minutes to enter our classes or face consequences. Despite his threats, students responded with more songs, chants, and stone-throwing.

After the ten minutes elapsed, it was clear Morris wasn't bluffing. Armored vehicles breached the school's barbed wire fences, and soldiers began firing and lobbing tear gas as if in real warfare. We scattered, some managing to escape, others injured. As we ran towards the main gate, we found it blocked by soldiers' vehicles, arresting anyone who emerged.

We retreated to our classrooms as the yard emptied, save for the occupation forces. Some students had escaped through holes the vehicles made in the walls, but most of us took refuge in the classrooms. We braced for what would happen next, watching from large windows overlooking the main yards and corridors as soldiers methodically attacked each class, dragging students out and beating them with notorious batons. They herded them to an unseen location, their fate unknown.

We decided to barricade our classroom door with wooden desks, resolving not to open it for the soldiers. Eventually, it was our turn. Soldiers attempted to break in but couldn't, so they resorted to inserting tear gas through the keyhole, causing us to sneeze and tear up. Even opening all the windows didn't help much, and the soldiers kept hurling insults from outside.

"Open the door, you filth!" they yelled.

We looked at each other, knowing I had to make a decision. After hearing shots at the door lock, we feared for our safety. I shouted, "Stop, we'll open the door!"

We removed the desks, and the soldiers burst in, grabbing me first. One soldier seized my long hair and began beating me with his baton. I tried to escape, but he pushed me towards the door, where other soldiers took turns hitting me. Descending the stairs, every three or four steps, another soldier would strike me. The first blow to my left hand left a pain that lasted years.

My situation worsened when my high-heeled shoe—a fashion among young men at the time—broke, complicating my escape. I don't recall how many blows I received that day; I just thought it was over for me. But then soldiers herded all students to the front yard. Seeing me arrive, they signaled me to stand with others. Morris strolled among us, selecting certain students to be taken away in waiting armored vehicles. He smelled students' hands and checked their clothes for signs of involvement in the day's events. I spat on my hands, trying to clean them as much as possible, believing I had somewhat succeeded. Finally, it was my turn.

Morris first asked Marwan, standing next to Bassam and me, for his name.

"Marwan," he replied.

"And your father's name?" Morris prodded.

Marwan gave his father's name, then his family name—Barghouti.

Morris smiled, "You should have said straight away you're Marwan Barghouti... Instead of making us come to your house at 2 AM to take you, right? Take him away!" Soldiers seized Marwan, beating him until they put him in an outside armored vehicle.

Bassam's turn came next, and he suffered the same fate.

Then Morris asked me my name. I gave my full name, and he inquired, "Younes! Have I met you before?"

"No, I haven't had the honor," I replied.

He smiled slightly. "Are you joking? Have I ever arrested you?"

"No," I answered.

Morris tapped his forehead, repeating my name, trying to remember. Fortunately, his memory didn't serve him well, and he finally said, "Younes, go, go..."

I silently praised God and was about to leave when the school principal, Hamdi, emerged from the main door, shouting at me, "Younes, how many times did I tell you to go inside!"

I whispered desperately for him to be quiet, lest Morris hear and change his mind. But the intelligence officer at the gate, a well-known Druze named "Shahada," noticed the commotion. He was a large, broad-shouldered man. I left Hamdi talking to himself and headed for the main gate. Shahada grabbed my shoulder, asking my name. I repeated my story about Morris's dismissal, and Shahada glanced at Morris, who gestured that I wasn't on the wanted list. Shahada pushed me away, saying, "Leave."

I exited the gate, relieved, passing many onlookers watching the events unfold. I felt reborn.

Later, I learned that the approximately 50 youths taken that day were imprisoned for a month after suffering torture, and their families had to pay hefty fines for their release.

Growth and Work in Ramallah

I had to adapt to the new, larger society of Ramallah, as well as Sinjil. The city environment shows you everything and offers you everything. After settling in terms of housing and forming a group of friends, my concern was finding a job in this city, which I had learned everything about. I started asking friends if they knew any place to hire me. A friend from my new friends suggested that he was leaving his job at a women's fashion store on Salah al-Din Street in Jerusalem, especially since the summer vacation was approaching. He proposed that I go with him the next day to meet the shop owner, who is from a well-known family in Jerusalem and the shop is very well-known.

Indeed, the next day, I went to Jerusalem, which is only 15 km away from Ramallah and the borders were open, without the presence of the separation wall that exists now. That's how it was, and I was employed in place of my departing friend, which was a completely new experience for me.

My mornings were slow; I would wake up at 6:30 AM to prepare myself to head to work, which, as I mentioned, was located in Jerusalem on the famous Salah al-Din Street. After waking up at 6:30 AM, I would leave my small apartment after making myself a cup of tea and eating something small, a habit I maintain to this day. I would leave at 7:00 AM and walk 4 km, the distance from my residence to the Jerusalem bus station.

I always walked this main street, which links the city of Al-Bireh to the main market. Al-Bireh and Ramallah are two adjacent cities, indistinguishable from each other, and this street starts to get busy as shops begin to open. I had gotten to know many people there, greeting them in the morning until I reached the bus stop, then boarding the bus. I was usually one of the first people who always allowed me to choose a front seat after greeting the driver, whom I had gotten to know from my daily commute. A bus would leave every half hour, slowly making its way through the main street to Jerusalem.

The trip was about 12-15 km, taking about half an hour, including the time it took for passengers to get on and off; in addition to the Israeli military checkpoint, we had to pass ten minutes before reaching Beit Hanina. There, we would stop at the checkpoint, and an Israeli soldier would board the bus and check each passenger's ID against their faces. If he didn't like someone, he would ask them to get off, and the bus would leave them behind to be interrogated.

At 17 years old, during those days, I never had any problems at that checkpoint. After the soldier finished, the bus would sluggishly continue until it reached the station at Damascus Gate, where everyone would go their separate ways. I usually arrived half an hour before starting my job and before the doors of the clothing shops where I worked, Fair Lady, which still exists today, was opened.

I would buy a bagel from a vendor at Damascus Gate, which has now become very famous, along with an egg or some falafel, and sit on the steps opposite the gate, watching the diverse array of people passing through. I also watched Palestinian women from rural areas come to take their places to start selling the produce that the Palestinian land generously offered at that time, along with bagel carts and everything else, with vendors loudly advertising their goods—a tradition still practiced at this location to this day.

These remaining thirty minutes occurred daily, and five minutes before work, I would head to my job, which was opened by one of my colleagues. I would cross Salah al-Din Street after walking past Solomon's Quarries and the great walls of Jerusalem. At that time, I did not realize the significance of this city, these streets, and the stones the world fights over. For me, it was just an ordinary day at my workplace, moments I enjoyed and reflected on, sipping from the historical and sacred aura of the place.

I worked until 6:00 PM, then closed up and returned to Ramallah the same way I had come in the morning. My job at the clothing store taught me a lot during those days, as women require a special kind of treatment, particularly regarding clothes. The store attracted many different nationalities and colors, increasing my interactions with a world beyond my own showing me the need to learn another language. I would ask another colleague to handle foreign customers, whether they spoke English or Hebrew, but I started picking up words here and there.

At that time, I developed a desire—one of my wishes at that stage was to learn English. When asked what I wanted to do, I would answer without hesitation that I wanted to be able to read the newspaper in English or have a conversation with these foreigners without fear.

Days in Ramallah

The second year of high school passed wonderfully after I established a foothold in this city, especially with my work experience that lasted three months during the summer in Jerusalem. I had to visit my village at the end of each week to see my family, after which my personality changed, and my outlook on things differed. I often skipped many weeks without visiting, spending the entire time in Ramallah instead.

However, the picture wouldn't be complete without romantic adventures, which were a part of my life and often emerged. Still, the echo of what had happened to me two years earlier in Abwein made me reject any serious attempt at these endeavors. I displayed indifference and revenge in all my interactions, representing the unborn child that was killed and buried while still in its mother's womb. Thus, I convinced myself to meet as many girls as possible with a kind of recklessness that, at the time, placed my conscience on the shelf, prioritizing material benefit above all else.

In this journey, one of our neighbors caught my eye. She lived in the villa opposite my residence and was named May. She was in the same grade, the Tawjihi, but at a different girls' school. I noticed her watching me as I arrived and departed.

One day, I followed her, and a relationship that she believed was the most romantic in the world developed between us. However, I did not take this relationship seriously for the reasons I mentioned earlier. For me, these relationships were a challenge, merely proving to myself that I could obtain anything, no matter how precious.

Thus began the messages and phone calls whenever possible... We started meeting during our third year of high school in a park in Ramallah. She would come with her Christian friend and neighbor, who would then leave us alone. Unlike the girl who was smitten with me, I never felt serious about the relationship. It was merely completing the image I had crafted for myself among friends who looked at me with great surprise.

Ramallah: School, Growth, and Work

My friends, especially the young men from the neighborhood, wondered how the new guy could steal the heart of the neighborhood girl who had never paid them any attention, especially since she was from a prestigious family in the city and her father was a well-known judge.

Therefore, the boys looked up to me, especially those close to them who knew I wasn't serious... It was I and the judge's daughter who loved me, and they greatly respected her father and her family. These relationships were merely a way to satisfy my whims and ego.

The days passed.

One day, as we were walking along Al-Irsal Street in Ramallah, which later became one of the main streets in the city but was almost empty in those days, she held my hand like lovers do at sunset, laughing together when suddenly a green Volvo stopped abruptly next to us. A man got out of the car; her father had been sitting in the back seat while the driver sat behind the wheel.

Seeing him approach with his large body and bald head, she trembled with disbelief and fear. I stepped aside as he went to her and commanded in a stern voice, "May, get in the car." She began to utter a few words, "Dad... I swear we aren't doing anything... we study together..."

He scolded her again with his gruff voice, insisting, "I told you to get in the car." She headed to the car and sat down. He then turned towards me, puffing up his chest, but I remained unshaken by this display.

He asked me, "What's your name, son?" I told him my name. He then asked, "What are you doing with my daughter?" I coolly replied, "What did you see us doing? We're just walking on the public street in front of everyone. What could we possibly be doing? We're walking and reviewing lessons, and we're discussing with each other in the same grade."

I happened to be carrying my school books at that moment. He asked, "You're in Tawjihi?" I confirmed, "Yes." He arrogantly said, "Do you know I could jail you?" I smiled and responded, "And for what would you jail me? What wrong have I done? I'm not your son, and I didn't force your daughter to walk with me on the public street."

He continued, "Listen, son, do you know who I am?" I said, "Yes, I know." He asked again, "You know, and you still walk with my daughter?" Surprised, I replied, "I didn't force your daughter to walk with me, and you can deal with your daughter as you wish." Adding, "Do you need something from me? I'm leaving."

I turned my back on him and walked in the opposite direction. He shouted, "I didn't say you could leave," but I looked back while walking away and said, "I believe I'm not in court. I'm leaving."

I continued my way, leaving the scene while he muttered words I never understood. This incident was an opportunity for me to distance myself. For several weeks, I did not call or send a message until I received a new message from her apologizing for her father's behavior and explaining the nature of our relationship to him, which he now understood. The relationship was officially sanctioned, but I wasn't serious about it. I replied to her that there was no future for us because her father would continue to pursue me, and I did not need the trouble or headache.

Thus, this relationship ended, and even after many pleas and messages asking to meet, I saw no reason to return to the past, and to this day, I don't know what happened to that girl.

"School days of Tawjihi in the Catholic school & Graduating with Hilarion Capucci"

Chapter 3 - Consequences of Occupation

Curfew

It was one of the national events that I can't quite recall. At the time, the West Bank, particularly the streets of Ramallah, had witnessed intense demonstrations. There were protests, tire burnings, and road blockages, which led the occupying forces to impose a curfew in the areas of Ramallah and Al-Bireh.

During those days, I was living in Al-Bireh. One day, I decided to defy the curfew and go to the post office in Ramallah, where I had a post box. I wasn't exactly sure what I was expecting there, but I wanted to challenge the oppressive measures—a form of Palestinian defiance at that time. The post office was about 4 kilometers from my house.

I took side streets and got within about 50 meters of the post office on the main and famous street in Ramallah, which we called Rukab Street. This street contained a well-known shop that is still famous today. Back then, we would spend late nights hanging out around it.

As soon as I walked on the street, an Israeli patrol jeep spotted me speeding along. They shouted through loudspeakers for me to stop and hurled insults typical of the occupation soldiers. Naturally, I didn't stop; instead, I ran faster, and the vehicle started chasing me.

Suddenly, without any warning, a friend named Saleh, well-known across Ramallah, appeared. He was riding his Vespa, a type of fast Italian scooter popular at the time. He drove up beside me and yelled, "Jump on, Abu Al-Ans, jump!" So, I jumped on and rode behind him while the Israelis behind us continued shouting and demanding us to stop.

But stopping was out of the question; we knew that to stop meant arrest and a beating for at least a week since we had violated a military curfew order and because we were young men.

Saleh knew the streets very well, allowing us to lose the soldiers chasing us through the old streets of Lower Ramallah. Eventually, he dropped me off at my residence in Al-Bireh. He stayed with me for a couple of hours before heading to his home in the Sharafat area between Al-Bireh and Ramallah, taking back alleys and paths that were too narrow for the military vehicles to follow.

That day remained another memorable one in my life, often recalled with laughter about how we escaped arrest and bullets flying around us.

The school year ended, and I was in my third year of secondary school at the Hashimiya School. Truthfully, I wasn't very focused on my studies. I was confused between school, romantic adventures, work, and friends. I found myself in a place many sought to befriend, and the attention from women at that time led me to engage in many reckless adventures.

When it came to the Tawjihi exams, despite all my studying, I was not well-prepared, particularly in Chemistry, which I found uninteresting, unlike the humanities subjects like Arabic literature and history that I was passionate about. But my determination to excel and transition from a school in the village of Sinjil to the distinguished Hashimiya School in Ramallah—which catered to the top students in the region—kept my resolve firm despite my disinterest in the sciences.

As the final exams approached, I faced my academic reckoning. My score in Chemistry was 49 out of 100, which was considered a failing grade since Chemistry was a compulsory subject. Although I had an overall average of 70 percent, it wasn't enough.

I remember going to the school to check the result lists posted on the walls. I searched thoroughly, hoping it was a mistake and that my name must be listed among those who passed. But it wasn't there.

I left the school devastated, unable to walk, dragging the weight of my disappointment. People I knew asked me what was wrong as they passed by, but I couldn't respond.

They could see the answer written across my face—I had failed.

Wandering the streets of Ramallah, I didn't know where I was going or what I would do next. Where would all my pride and arrogance go? What happened, and why? I had been at the top of my class in previous years, only to fail in my final year.

I told myself, yes, why not? All signs indicated that my path and methods were wrong. I walked aimlessly, wondering what I would tell my parents and those who had high expectations of me.

Deciding I couldn't run from this, I faced it. How could I return to them as a failure? What would they say about me? Despite my reluctance, I resolved not to return that night, waiting until tomorrow. Despite my fears of my mother's extreme worry, I didn't know how I spent that night.

The next day, I decided to face the truth and head to the village, refusing to bury my head in the sand like an ostrich.

. As expected, there were questions on everyone's faces about what had happened to their brilliant son. Naturally, the city was blamed for my misfortunes.

My kind father, God rest his soul, reassured me not to lose hope and that I could retake the Tawjihi exams. My mother's reaction was different; though she tried to offer comfort, the disappointment was palpable in her every word.

Consequences of Occupation

I returned to Ramallah with a determination not to be defeated. My failure wasn't the end. I had to rise again, especially since a single point in Chemistry was the cause—an essential subject for the scientific track.

Thus began my journey back to Ramallah, determined to prove to myself first and foremost that my will must prevail despite the crushing blow. My first step was to find a job, asking around everywhere. A friend suggested I meet with the owner of the Al-Rafati car showroom on Al-Muntazah Street in Ramallah, where he worked. The idea was that I could work in the evenings, allowing me to attend a private school and retake the year while he worked the morning shift.

I got a job at the car showroom, tasked with being there in the evenings until one after midnight to guard the displayed cars and keep people from getting too close. The showroom was located on Al-Muntazah Street, a very lively area in the summer since Ramallah is known as Palestine's summer resort. This street was lined with parks and restaurants, inviting people to stay late.

I also began my search for a nearby school to enroll in and settled on the co-educational School of Our Lady of the Annunciation for the Roman Catholics, located less than half a kilometer from my new workplace.

I entered the school and immediately felt a resurgence of the old enthusiasm after shaking off the dust of failure and despair. Elected as the class prefect, but this time in a mixed-gender school, I found fertile ground to flourish. Within a short time, I became well-known at the school, which was a conservative Christian institution that didn't partake in external activities, especially nationalist ones. I felt it was my duty to change this insular and rigid atmosphere.

I stood among the students and spoke at every national event, declaring that Palestine belonged to all of us, not just to the poor or students from public schools. I knew that the wealthy and their children, who typically attended private schools, were wary of jeopardizing their interests, thus participating only minimally in any form of expression, whether peaceful or militant.

My speeches didn't always find receptive ears since these students were raised from an early age to focus solely on their education and nothing else. Naturally, those like me who had come to the school by chance were the ones who listened.

Such talk did not go unnoticed; it brought me into conflict with the school principal, a bishop of Lebanese origin, who repeatedly warned me against inciting students to demonstrate.

But my consolation lay in my academic excellence and control over non-academic activities, from editing the wall magazine to reciting poetry and short stories, some of which I sent to the Al-Quds newspaper for publication. My Arabic teacher and homeroom advisor, who was covertly nationalistic, found a voice for his silent patriotism in me.

My popularity was also bolstered by my friend Sami, who would pick me up in his car, which varied day by day. He never let me get out in front of the main gate; instead, he drove into the playground, where all the students were during the main break, showing off conspicuously. Many thought my father owned the car showroom because of this, and when they asked me about it, I never corrected their assumptions, especially not to the girls.

Indeed, those days were filled with enjoyment and irresponsibility with these new or rather numerous friends.

So continued my life between the car showroom and school—days spent with the vitality of youth, still vivid in my memory. Truly, everything in life happens for a reason. From the events and stories that occurred while I worked at the showroom, I learned lessons that have stayed with me to this day, and God willing, until the last day of my life.

It was just an ordinary summer night in Ramallah, characterized by the light summer breeze that the city is known for due to its high mountainous location. No matter how hot it got in Palestine, Ramallah always had this cool breeze, sometimes necessitating a light jacket at night.

We were used to this, and so were the friends who would place chairs in front of the shop and sit chatting away the night. We would watch people pass by, occasionally classifying them after buying and starting to eat seeds from our neighbor and friend, Khalili, who we always teased about his Hebron accent.

Across the street was the Bardouni Park and restaurant, one of the city's oldest, managed by Saadi, whom we often joked with, especially when VIPs, or "big fish," as we called them,

visited. He would be too busy for us, and we'd tell him it looked like he had important guests that night; he would agree with a nod. These evenings usually ended with the scent of alcohol mixing with the scents of roses and jasmine decorating the restaurant's gardens amid the dense trees. This fragrance would drift over to us, a scent we had become accustomed to.

The gathering of friends continued until one after midnight when the crowd thinned. They would take their leave, and I was supposed to lock up and head to my room to sleep and prepare for the next morning when I'd hand over the keys to Sami, who would drive me to school, as I mentioned before.

My primary job was to prevent anyone from tampering with the cars, inside or outside the showroom. The manager allowed me to bring my friends to keep the place "lively," ensuring no one dared damage the vehicles. He would sometimes check on us at night, often sitting with us and joining in our banter.

As usual, I was about to lock up and head to my room in Al-Bireh. I was carrying the iron rod I used to secure the high metal doors when a man crossed the street from the Bardouni restaurant towards me. He was dressed in a dark gray suit with a tie. Approaching me, he began to speak in a slurred voice, making it clear he was drunk.

"Hello, why are you rushing to close? I want to know the prices of these cars, especially this one," he pointed at a green Volvo, indeed one of the most beautiful cars on display.

I replied, "I don't know the prices of the cars, nor is it my job. You'll need to come back tomorrow if you want to know that. As you can see, I'm about to close the doors, and hopefully, we'll see you tomorrow."

However, the drunk man insisted, "I need to know now," and moved towards the Volvo at the back. I tried to push him away, but suddenly, I heard the exhaust pipe hit the ground—he had broken it by standing on it.

Enraged, I tried to remove him by his neck using the iron rod I was using to lock the doors. While I was attempting to do this, an Arab police car passed by. I signaled to them, and they stopped. The officer in the front passenger seat called out my name. When I approached, I recognized him; he often visited the showroom manager.

He inquired about the situation, and I explained what had happened with the drunken man who had broken the exhaust pipe. The officer looked over the situation and then instructed his colleagues to take the man. However, instead of taking him to the station, the officer directed them to throw him into a nearby dumpster. He said, "Now he'll learn his lesson."

The police did as instructed, throwing the man into the dumpster. The officer reassured me, "I'll talk to Taysir (the showroom owner) and tell him what happened. Don't worry." He then asked where he should drop me off, and I went with them after ensuring the showroom doors were locked. I reached my room around three in the morning.

I needed to return in a few hours, before 7:30 AM, to hand over the keys to Sami, who would then drive me to school. As I was about to get into the car the next morning, a municipal vehicle arrived to collect the trash from the dumpsters.

Just as the driver was about to empty the dumpster where the police had thrown the man the night before, I mentioned to my friend that the police had put someone in there last night. To our shock, a person jumped out of the dumpster just as it was being tipped into the truck. He looked around bewildered, not realizing where he was or how he had ended up there overnight.

Seeing us staring at him in disbelief, he jumped and hurried away, still disoriented. As I watched this unfold, I thought to myself about the destructive effects of alcohol, vowing never to let myself be degraded by it. I promised myself never to touch alcohol, a vow I have kept to this day.

The story didn't end there. A month after the incident, while I was sitting outside the showroom, a well-dressed man approached me confidently and said hello. I greeted him back, but when he seemed surprised at my lack of recognition, he asked, "Don't you remember me?"

I replied, "No."

He then referenced the night someone was thrown into the dumpster, pointing at it. My eyes widened as I realized he was the man from that night. I tried to explain that it wasn't me but the police who had handled him rather roughly, assuming they were taking him to jail. He cut me off, saying he had come to thank me because waking up in that dumpster had been a wake-up call for him. He cursed himself and swore off alcohol, a pledge he had maintained from that day to the present, he claimed.

This encounter was a profound lesson for both of us about the depths to which alcohol can drag a person and the potential for change in even the most embarrassing or low moments. And from that day to this day, God willing, forever, I will not drink it, nor will I go near it, and this was the greatest lesson in life for me.

1977 - Me with Saleh (left) & Bassam (right) next to Music Center in Ramallah

Jamal

I had a friend whose acquaintance I can't exactly recall how I made. This man was a force to be reckoned with—more energetic and lively than life itself—so much so that all of Ramallah seemed too small to contain him. He was a mix of everything: a student at Birzeit University and a Teachers' Training College graduate, meaning he was a school teacher. He knew everything; he was an electrician, worked with plumbing, and occasionally worked at a gas station. I even once saw him dressed as a sanitation worker working for the municipality.

Whenever we sat with friends, he quickly dominated the conversation, which could shift to any topic under the sun.

Whenever we walked through the modern streets of Ramallah, he would have already greeted the shopkeepers, many of whom knew him well. Many people would stop and greet him, and even passing girls were not spared his jokes and comments. I had a very special relationship with him as I knew he was involved in militant activities, organizing young men and women, especially teachers, within his group. He firmly believed his group had to be outstanding; hence, they had to be educated and cultured to avoid any mistakes in operational activities or if any developments occurred.

My connection with him deepened after I arranged for him to live in a part of the house I occupied, which also included an external room in a large house. This honorable lady allowed me to study on the house's spacious main balconies. In return, I would often fetch the items she needed from a nearby grocery store, asking her multiple times a day if she needed anything, and I would always hear her mumbling prayers for my success and good fortune.

A storage space had become available on the ground floor of the house, so I suggested to Aunt Um Mahmoud that I bring a friend to rent it. She agreed since he was my friend, and that was Jamal.

Jamal was relentless in trying to recruit me to join his organization. I distinctly remember one time he came in and found me having lunch before work, eating from a can of yogurt and bread. He looked at me and said, "Is that your lunch?" I replied yes that I couldn't afford anything else. He sharply suggested, "Why don't you join us? You would get a salary from us, your situation would improve, and other good things in your life would get better." However, I was aware that joining any party or group would mean being bound to that organization forever.

I had decided early in my life to remain free in my thoughts and mind and not to be subjected to any particular directives or patterns. To this day, I believe that freedom in thinking and autonomy in decision-making lead me in any direction I choose, away from coercion and predefined, predetermined decisions. This belief has remained my obsession and the master of my thoughts; to this day, I have not joined any organization or group.

Jamal knew this well and respected it, but I indicated I would help in anything I could without being listed as a member. I introduced him to many friends and relatives, whom he managed to recruit in his way without my knowing any details. His organization was part of the first Fatah faction on the Palestinian scene at that time.

I had taken time off work during those days as there were only a few days left until the general secondary examinations. I was studying intensely on my grandmother's balcony because the specter of my failure the previous year was haunting me.

Jamal, who, as I mentioned, lived in the ground floor storage, came up to see me. He was laughing, so joyful that the world could not contain him. "Today, Abu Al-Ans (my nickname among friends at that time), is the fifth anniversary of our group's founding, and we will celebrate in our way," he said. Out of curiosity, I asked how they would celebrate. "I won't tell you now," he replied. "Just listen to the Israeli radio news at six o'clock this evening, and you'll know about our celebration." Then he added, "Listen, Abu Al-Ans, a girl named Attaf will come in an hour. Give her the key and let her wait in the room until I go finish some things and come back." He also mentioned, "This girl is the last one in the organization to carry out an operation, making sure everyone has done something—that is, carried out operations." He said this as he went downstairs.

So it was; shortly after he left, the girl arrived, and I gave her the key to my room, where she waited for Jamal. I continued studying until Jamal came back, took her, and they left laughing as if they were going to a party. After saying goodbye to them after they had taken some items from his storage, I resumed my studies, reminding them not to forget the six o'clock news on the Israeli radio.

About two hours after Jamal and Attaf had left, I heard the sound of Jamal's car—a light blue Volkswagen—approaching, then suddenly stopping with a loud noise. He got out and headed towards the storage, or his room on the ground floor, while I tried to inquire what had happened. His usual playful demeanor was gone, replaced by a nervous seriousness. "We've been caught; our house is doomed," he said in a trembling voice, then hurriedly added, "Attaf got caught!"

I tried to get some answers about what he planned to do. He said he would leave. "Attaf will hold out for a few hours, then she'll confess about us, so I'm taking my stuff and leaving." He also advised me to leave and not come back for the next couple of days.

I told him I couldn't; I had my university entrance exams in two days, and the first test was in physics, a subject I disliked and needed to focus on. At that moment, I was torn between disappearing, as Jamal suggested, facing the situation, and the risk of being arrested and missing my exams. I decided to face the situation and stay.

"You are free to choose, but I strongly advise you," he said, then went to his room to move his things, which I later learned included weapons. He came to say goodbye, asking where he was going. He replied it was better for both of us if I didn't know. After this intense moment, I didn't see him for five years until after he was caught in a strange incident and sentenced to 225 years in prison for causing the deaths of 15 and injuring over 75 Jews. The PLO later released him before they left Beirut in a prisoner exchange deal and came to Amman, where we met. By then, I had married, and he had married one of the Christian teachers who had been in his organization after a love story with her from a very well-known family.

That night, I stayed up late, firstly because I was scared and secondly because I was studying physics for the first exam we were about to take.

Suddenly, as sleep began to overtake me, I was jolted awake by the sounds of many cars, soldiers yelling, military vehicles, lights, and commotion, turning the area into what seemed like daylight when I looked out the window. It appeared the area around our house had been transformed into a military barracks with troop carriers and Jewish soldiers running around as if we were on a battlefield after noticing that they were forming a cordon around the entire house we lived in.

Then I saw the soldiers rushing, carrying many weapons and heavy equipment, heading towards Jamal's storage room door. The moment the officer touched the door, an electrical shock threw him against the opposite wall, and he cursed Jamal Yasin. We later learned that Jamal had rigged an electrical circuit to shock anyone trying to open the door without a key. I continued to watch the situation from my dark room—they had cut the power to the house—and they were gathering the items Jamal had left behind, though he certainly hadn't left anything incriminating.

Then I saw junior officers, as I perceived them, spreading out to neighboring doors and beginning to knock on them for interrogations. Suddenly, I heard the sound of their boots on the stairs leading to my room and then a loud knock on my door.

I asked who it was in a shaky voice as if I were waking up. The officer behind the door shouted, "Open up!" I opened the door, and the officer pushed me so hard I nearly fell, then said, "Can we come in?" He was already halfway into the room when he quickly asked for my ID and bombarded me with dozens of questions about Jamal in a confused manner, not waiting for any answers from me.

Consequences of Occupation

Of course, I denied any close or distant relationship with him, saying I knew someone lived there but didn't know his name or what he did and that I was just a high school student and all my time was spent between school and work. He threatened me in broken Arabic, saying if he found out I was lying, he'd put me in jail. I insisted I wasn't lying. He threw my ID back at me and said we would see each other often. Then they left after turning my room upside down, finding nothing of concern.

This went on until dawn broke that day, and they finally left, apparently finding nothing valuable that night. However, it didn't end there; the officer in the military car would pass by every day, sometimes twice, and ask me, now that he knew my name if I had heard from my friend Jamal or heard anything about him. I always denied knowing anything and continued my studies.

The story I heard from Jamal after he was released from prison when we met in Amman five years later follows: Attaf was supposed to place a timed bomb at a gathering point for Jewish soldiers on the busy Jaffa Street in West Jerusalem, where they typically gathered to go to service in the West.

Bank, known as the Border Guard, or what we in the West Bank call "those with the green berets" (typically those who harass the people of the West Bank). The bomb was in a brown bag, also containing a kilo of cucumbers, and was supposed to be placed in the trash bin at the bus stop where the soldiers waited.

The agreed-upon signal was that Jamal, watching closely from afar, would signal her with a predetermined gesture with his finger. However, if there was another signal, she was supposed to hesitate and not place it. What happened was that Attaf, on her first mission, was very tense and fearful while under the bus shelter for soldiers going to serve in the West Bank.

Her Arab appearance also caught the attention of a Jewish religious person who noticed her, and Jamal saw this man looking at Attaf suspiciously. Jamal gave her the opposite signal, indicating that someone was watching her and not to proceed, but in her intense fear at that moment, she misunderstood and thought Jamal had signaled her to place the bomb. She decided to put the bag she was holding into the trash can, and as soon as she did, the Jewish man started screaming that she was an Arab and a saboteur. The soldiers at the shelter grabbed her. Jamal saw them seize her and fled the scene, returning quickly to his room as I described.

As for Jamal, after he left me in his car, he went to our town of Abwein, coordinated with his organization members, and, with the help of one of my brothers, managed to hide the weapons in an area outside the town, burying them underground.

The Jews did not uncover the weapons until after Jamal was captured, and four months after Jamal remained elusive, the occupation forces recruited hundreds of soldiers and agents to capture him. Despite the substantial monetary reward offered for his capture, announced in all newspapers and media, he managed to stay out of the occupation's grasp, so much so that I kept one of these advertisements after a friend brought it to me from Palestine for a long time, which I lost during my frequent travels around the world.

Jamal was eventually captured by sheer coincidence after many pursuits. Our friend, the motorcycle owner who had once saved me (Saleh), was imprisoned, and after prolonged interrogation and severe torture, another friend's name came up during the questioning. This friend was Bassam, who owned and his family a building next to Ramallah Park, and he and his mother lived on the ground floor. The upper floors were vacant and uninhabited.

When the occupation soldiers came one night to capture Bassam after completely surrounding the building, and after they stormed the house and turned it upside down without finding Bassam there, they interrogated his mother, who told them Bassam was in Jerusalem and was coming from there, so the soldiers decided to wait for him.

While waiting, the officer asked her what was on the house's upper floors. She told them nothing; it was empty, truly knowing nothing. The officer decided to send a group of soldiers to the upper floors of the building, and after they stormed the top floor, they found a man sleeping. They took him to the exterior stairwell of the house, and when the officer saw him, he recognized him from the widely circulated pictures.

Surprised, he asked, "Are you Jamal?" When he didn't respond, the officer took out a photo from his military trousers and compared it to the man's face. Then he started jumping for joy, shouting, "We've caught Jamal, we've caught Jamal!" He called his military command, which sent a full battalion and took him to prison, where he and his group remained until Bassam was also captured.

As for my rebellious brother, who had helped Jamal hide the weapons, he was arrested a week later after a force came to his house and took him away. His wife, pregnant in her last month with their sixth child and already a mother of five daughters, tried to prevent his arrest. The soldiers pushed her, and she fell on her back; she was taken to the hospital after delivering the baby boy they had eagerly awaited, all while her husband was in prison and after being sentenced to three actual years of imprisonment.

Me & Jamal in Jericho/Areeha.

1983 - Reunion with Jamal 5 years later after his release from political detention/prison due to a prisoner-exchange

My Father and Jamal

My father, may God have mercy on him, suffered severely from gallbladder inflammation, especially during flare-ups. He was seeing a doctor named Al-Sulti, who coincidentally was the director of Ramallah Hospital—the only major hospital in the area at that time. This doctor, quite renowned and a subject of many stories himself, had a private clinic attached to his villa, which was very close to where I worked.

Due to the hospital's busy schedule, the doctor continually postponed my father's gallbladder surgery, opting to give him painkillers instead. This went on for a long time until one severe inflammation episode. My father, known for his resilience and patience, could no longer bear the pain. We went to his clinic and were told he was at the hospital. Taking a taxi, we arrived at the hospital and met with a very arrogant gatekeeper who eventually let us in after I mentioned our appointment with Dr. Al-Sulti.

Upon reaching the doctor's room, he was furious to see us. He scolded us for coming to the hospital without his permission. Despite my father swearing he couldn't endure the pain, the doctor screamed at us to leave, stating the hospital was not a "doorless agency" where surgeries could be performed without an appointment. Even though we insisted our appointment was for that day, his rage blinded him. He ordered the hospital security over the phone to throw us out. Unable to control my anger, as I saw my father in agony, I grabbed the doctor by the neck and threatened him, ensuring he understood the consequences if we were forced to leave.

The hospital staff arrived and ejected us from the building. My father was in so much pain he could barely stand. By chance, one of the hospital employees who witnessed the scene sympathized with us and suggested we take my father to Rafidia Hospital in Nablus, where they could perform the surgery immediately. I called a friend whose father owned a taxi service, and they sent a car that rushed my father and me to Nablus. Upon arrival, the doctors immediately operated on my father after discovering that his gallbladder had burst, a potentially fatal condition. Thankfully, the surgery went well, and he was discharged after three days in the hospital.

However, Dr. Al-Sulti's disdainful treatment lingered in my mind. When Jamal visited me, and I shared the incident, he responded that all of Ramallah was suffering from this "dog" of a doctor and that he needed to be taught a lesson. When I asked him what he intended to do, he said I didn't need to know and to leave it to him. Nevertheless, I couldn't wait to see the doctor face his dark day.

Indeed, I later learned that three of Jamal's men had gone to his house and vandalized his car, which he used to parade around the streets of Ramallah. They smashed all its windows, slashed the tires, scratched it from every angle, and even damaged the glass fronts of his house. I only became aware of these actions when the police came asking if I had seen anyone committing vandalism at the doctor's house. I feigned ignorance, saying I didn't know any doctor lived nearby and hadn't seen anything. It's worth noting that they also spray-painted a warning on his car as a "first warning" to remind him of how to treat the people of Ramallah properly.

I believe his behavior must have significantly changed after this incident, especially since I heard that this force had also caught his son returning from the Friends School—a prestigious school in Ramallah—and shaved the middle of his head, leaving a stripe bare. They told him to message his father: "Next time, it will be different."

The Inevitable Night Under Strict Surveillance

As I mentioned before, I finished my Tawjihi exams under great difficulty because of the intelligence officer who would pass by our house daily, sometimes more than once. As I said, I would be studying on Aunt Umm Mahmoud's balcony, and he would stand in the street, calling out to ask if I had any news about Jamal. I kept telling him that Jamal was not my friend and I had not seen him return to the area or heard anything about him. The officer, seeing me studying in the same place each time, would end his interrogation by threatening to arrest me and prevent me from sitting my exams if it turned out I was lying about knowing anything regarding Jamal.

Thankfully, the exams concluded without incident. However, rumors and a tense atmosphere about Jamal and the rest of our friends became prevalent. Every day, we hear about someone being arrested, especially those associated with Jamal's group. Many of the teachers in the organization were detained, particularly Hanan, who I knew was married to Jamal. Hanan was a Christian from a distinguished Palestinian family. Nadia and other names were also mentioned. I was shocked to hear about the arrest of my uncle and friend, Jumah, after an intense chase in the streets of Ramallah. I was the one who had introduced Jumah to Jamal, and at that age, I didn't call him uncle because of how close in age we were.

I decided to go to our village to bid farewell to my family because I was certain that I would be arrested next as part of this unraveling situation. Indeed, that evening, I went to Abwein, and before heading to our house, I met with my friend—and Jumah's friend, whom I had also introduced to Jamal—Ahmed. Both were teachers and part of Jamal's group. As Ahmed and I walked together, he shared with me the full story of Jumah's arrest. We both expected that it was only a matter of time before the Israeli forces would come to arrest us.

It was well known that the endurance of these individuals would be temporary under the brutal torture they faced until they disclosed information about the rest. Here, they were arresting everyone associated with Jamal, who was still at large. They couldn't capture him despite broadcasting his photo as the most wanted and offering a substantial monetary reward for his capture, even announcing it in local newspapers.

As we walked through the old town, at the base of the mountain, military vehicles started appearing in the new area of the town called Al-Dahr. Ahmed said, "Here they come, just as we expected." I looked at him and asked what we should do—whether they came for him or me. He said, "It doesn't matter; we'll surrender ourselves whether they're here for you, me, or both. We can't run away; we're not going to be fugitives. We'll get arrested now rather than be chased and potentially end with a bullet in our heads."

I agreed with him. He said he would go home to face them to prevent them from damaging it, and I should go back to my family's house to say goodbye if we could. "Let what happens happen," he said. We hugged and bid each other farewell, and that was the last time I saw Ahmed until 19 years later when I returned from abroad, and he had become the head of the Teachers' Syndicate in the Palestinian Authority.

I went back to my family's old house, and there was my father. May God have mercy on him, returning from the Isha prayer. I told my parents to forgive me because the Israelis were coming to arrest me. I will never forget the questioning look mixed with sadness and reproach on my father's weathered face. In a sad, firm voice, he said, "Do not fear; nothing will happen to us except what God has written for us." My mother's tears betrayed my father's remarkable composure as she wept bitterly and embraced me, reproaching, "What have you done, Younes? Are you trying to kill me with your grief?"

I tried to calm her down, sitting next to her and wrapping my arm around her shoulder, telling her, "I haven't done anything, Mom. Since when do the Jews wait for someone to do something before they arrest him?" We watched the movement of military vehicles from our small house's window, heading towards Ahmed's house. They entered his house, turned it upside down, took Ahmed, and left without coming to the old town where we lived. That night, I heard nothing but prayers of gratitude from my father, and I felt that tomorrow would be another day. That night, I escaped.

The following day, I headed to Ramallah after saying goodbye to my family, with my mother's prayers not ceasing. After what happened, I decided that night to leave Palestine the next day without telling my family so as not to keep them worried about my fate.

As soon as I arrived in Ramallah in the morning, I decided that day to head to the bridge to leave the West Bank for Jordan. I gathered my few belongings in a shoulder bag and exchanged Israeli shekels for about 22 Jordanian dinars in my pocket. I headed to the bridge cars in Ramallah, and before reaching the car station, I met a friend from our village. I asked him for a favor, telling him I was headed to Jordan and gave him the keys to my room in Al-Bireh. I was heading to the bridge now and didn't know if they would let me cross or arrest me.

If the night passed and I didn't return to him or the house or café in the village, it meant I had either crossed the bridge or been arrested there. He was to wait just that night; if I didn't return, he was to go to my family the next day, give them the key, and tell them Younes had traveled to Jordan. If I returned, I would come back to him that night to take the key, and he wasn't to mention anything— as if nothing had happened. We agreed on this.

I continued my journey to the bridge cars, which I boarded with some passengers, traveling through the winding roads of the Jordan Valley to the King

Hussein Bridge or Allenby Bridge. This was the first time I was leaving our small borders.

I was lucky; they allowed me to pass, although they usually didn't let young men my age travel, especially when there was trouble. The officer scrutinized my identity and permitted intensively. I still remember when he commanded, "Go, go, move on from here," after stamping my exit permit.

I breathed a sigh of relief; all the while, I was anxious he would say I was forbidden to cross or that I was under arrest. But God blinded him in that moment, and I firmly believe that my parents' satisfaction and their prayers facilitated my passage, and God's will above all.

The next day, my friend went to my parents, as I later learned, gave them the key, and told them that I had traveled. Their grief was profound, especially since they weren't sure whether I had traveled or been arrested at the bridge.

All this happened on July 5. That day and date were pivotal in my entire life.

Just a few days before I began writing these words, when I was returning from visiting family in Palestine (using my American passport), I encountered an Israeli officer who spoke Arabic and tried to pronounce it without mistakes at the Sheikh Hussein crossing. Before stamping my passport for departure, he asked, "How long has it been since you first left Ramallah?"

Surprised by his question, I smiled a little and answered, "Exactly, on this day in 1979, I left Palestine for the first time." He was puzzled by my response and asked what I meant. I clarified, "Yes, like today, on July 5, 1979, which is today, 34 years ago, I left." He didn't appreciate that I referred to it as Palestine and shook his head disapprovingly.

I asked him if he wanted to ask any other questions, and he declined, seemingly regretting his initial inquiry.

Indeed, on that day, as I rode in the taxi headed towards the King Hussein Bridge, I had no idea they would allow me to cross or that this day would become a significant turning point in my life. Nor did I expect that 19 years later, I would return to this bridge as a visitor, like any foreigner from a distant land, no longer as a citizen stripped of my nationality by that cursed ID that had allowed me to pass back then.

And where was I allowed to go? To the unknown. Yes, to the East Bank, to Amman. And what was in Amman? Yes, it was a land I was entering for the first time, knowing absolutely no one. Where would I go? What direction would I take? What would I do? All these questions weighed on my mind as I rode the bus, passing from the Jewish checkpoint to the Arab checkpoint. I was lost in thought until the Jordanian officer boarded and ordered the bus passengers to disembark and line up beside the bus to check our passports.

When it was my turn, he asked if I carried a passport. I told him no, so he asked, in his Jordanian accent tinged with Bedouin inflection, "Okay, give me the Kushan." I had never heard this term before and was confused, not responding until the officer moved on to the next person. I asked an elderly man next to me what 'Kushan' meant, and he told me it was the birth certificate. I took it out and handed it to the officer.

He then instructed us to board the bus again, and we did, riding to the Abdali bus station in Amman.

Chapter 4 - Exile in Amman

The journey was long, the taxi climbing the ascent of Sweimeh with the Dead Sea stretching out beside us. I sat in the front seat next to the driver, who chatted away with everyone while I was lost in thought. I pondered how my parents would react when they learned I had left for Jordan without even saying goodbye.

They didn't know I was planning to travel, nor did they know if the Israelis had detained me at the bridge. I never thought that this departure might be the last time I would see my father's face.

Those thoughts tangled with the unknown fate awaiting me in this bustling, large city—a place where, as I said, I knew no one and didn't even know where to head next, especially with the mere 20 Jordanian dinars in my pocket.

I snapped out of my reverie only when the driver announced our arrival at the Abdali bus station. I didn't understand what that meant, and I didn't know that the bridge bus only dropped us off at the public station in Abdali, where we were then free to choose our destination.

As I stepped out of the car and grabbed my small suitcase, other taxis were lined up, drivers shouting destinations: "Amman!", "Irbid!", "Zarqa!". Truth be told, I didn't know where to go. Then, a taxi driver approached to end my quandary, asking, "Going to Amman?" I quickly responded, "Yes," and got in. There were other passengers, and he asked where I wanted to go in Amman. I told him I didn't know, but I'd go there if he could recommend a cheap hotel. He mentioned a decent hotel that only charged 5 dinars per night.

I thought to myself, I'll stay there tonight, and God willing, tomorrow will take care of itself.

Exile in Amman

True to his word, he took me to a hotel on Teliani Street in Amman, as he had told me. Exhausted from the early departure from Ramallah, I slept deeply despite being intermittently woken by the snoring of an elderly man sharing the room.

Early the next morning, as was my custom, I left the hotel and wandered the nearby streets, afraid of losing track of the place. By sheer coincidence, someone called my name. I turned to find it was an old school friend from my early school days in our village, surprised to see me there.

He asked, "What are you doing here?"

I replied, "I arrived from the West Bank yesterday."

He then inquired where I was staying, and I told him about the hotel. Surprised, he remarked on the expense, saying, "That's quite expensive." I explained that I had paid 5 dinars last night and didn't know where else to go.

He then kindly offered, "Come stay with us. We rent a room with four other guys in Jabal Al-Nuzha, Suburb Prince Hassan. You would be the sixth." Without hesitation, I agreed. I returned to the hotel to grab my things and joined him, grateful for the unexpected companionship in a city where I was a complete stranger.

Arriving Amman in July of 1979

Early Days in Amman

I must write about Amman, how significant it was to me,

Indeed, it was the starting point in a phase I consider to have been one of the most important stages of my life.

Why not, when it witnessed the major transformations in my mind during those days? It was then I truly understood life in this stage,

I learned what it means to be alone, what it means to be deprived, what suffering is, and everything that lies before you.

It was a starting point for manhood and the endpoint for childhood and adolescence.

Aren't all beginnings essentially the endings of something else?

I didn't realize I was laying the foundations for another phase... then, these are the steps of fate and the will of God that this life for a human is predestined with an arrangement and a wondrous scenario that even the greatest writers, had they wished to write it, would have found impossible, while we firmly believe that we are the ones who chart our paths. However, I fully believe that we merely play a role, already drawn and written by divine will, that guides us to the foothill of safety!

The decision to move to Amman was compulsory for me to avoid bigger problems that could have been much worse, possibly leading to a backlash or turning my life upside down, like certain imprisonment. I learned that the Israeli army had come to our house a few days after I left to ask about me, and surely, arrest would have been my fate had I been there. Then, I believe my family knew I had managed to escape to Amman and was not detained. In truth, I do not know how long I would have stayed in detention because all those associated with Jamal were arrested.

Exile in Amman

After my friend and I left the hotel, we headed towards Jabal Al-Nuzha in the Amman / Suburb of Prince Hassan. Then, we walked more than 500 meters on a dirt road after the bus dropped us off at the last stop. I found things to be different.

The room was small, especially with five to six people in it, creating a rare congestion since the room lacked the simplest things like a bathroom, which was built outside.

The bathroom wasn't the only problem; the room itself had a primitive kitchen with a manual gas stove and a washing basin, "Al-Lakn," which the six of us would use to bathe after heating the water on the stove or 'Primus' as it was called.

But now I had no choice, and it was still better than an occupation cell if I had been arrested.

I am now in a new world.

Even with those other five people, there was no common factor between us; we had never been friends, and there was nothing in common among them either, with each one engaged in something different from the others.

Yet, I also had to adapt to this new situation and behave as if I were one of them.

Oddly, I was the only one among them without a job or a profession!

The first step was to go out and get a passport to carry a document proving who I was and to start looking for a job to support myself after the little money in my pocket had evaporated.

But the question remained: what was I going to do?

I started going downtown with my friend, who had brought me to the room and knew the area well, gradually getting to know it a bit by bit. I used public transportation from one area to another, but more importantly, finding a job became crucial after the last dinar in my pocket had "breathed its last."

The situation became urgent not just because I needed to survive but also to contribute to the housing expenses. At that moment, I understood the meaning of solidarity as the young men excused me from sharing the costs until I found a job and was able to pay off this debt.

Initially, my job search was focused on a sales position in a store, a role I was accustomed to.

However, the difficulty in finding such a job forced me to broaden my options to whatever job was available.

Here, I will convey and interpret what I wrote during those days; those images that I translate into words are the honest expression of what I went through and felt, which my pen captured, especially after returning from job-hunting trips. A sense of lethal despair dominated me, often leading me to believe those were the last moments of my life, the remnants of my existence. I did not know then that those days of misery and deprivation were fueling my soul and resolve, fortifying me over the years with determination and will to change the stereotypes in life.

The memory of those days was always in my mind.

My obsession in this life was to never return to those days and to do the impossible to avoid falling back into the trap of need and deprivation because I believe that with God's help, a person can change their circumstances and create miracles.

In those days, the high school exam results were announced on both banks, and I was anxious to know my own. Finally, I discovered that I had succeeded with a score of 79.6 despite all the difficulties I faced during the exams.

Exile in Amman

Of course, although my joy was immense, I thought of my family and how happy they would be. I remembered the deep sadness from the previous year and how this result would erase the sadness that had marked my father's face.

Also, my life and my hope for the future changed after this result, especially since the world would see me differently after passing high school.

Honestly, at that moment, I wished nothing more than to be among my family and in my village, even in my city, to see this result wash away the failures of the past and to stand on my feet again after I had stumbled and fallen the first time.

(Note: I wrote this at the end of 1979 and the beginning of 1980 when I was 19 years old, without addition or omission.)

In the past, I used to dream like a bird dream; I lived and experienced that serene, angelic life and built castles in the air, thinking they would one day turn into real castles, supported by this great hope, reassurance and optimism.

I thought my life as a student would continue forever and that I would complete my university studies and graduate like the rest of the people I knew.

But the bitter truth is that my battle with life began after I left the homeland after my wings were clipped and my feathers plucked, when my hope of returning was shattered, and the real confrontation began.

It started from the first day I arrived here in Amman, and the journey was nothing but arduous and exhausting.

As I mentioned, in those moments that preceded the suffering and the explosion within me, I began the ongoing, relentless journey in search of a livelihood and the job that would provide it.

Like others believed that no one would die of hunger, I believed it too, in my own way. How could I not, when from the beginning, I was determined to rely on myself and knew I had to carve out my future with my own hands or chisel it into the rock? It made no difference!

Among my options or my belief in this choice was that I would not stay long in Amman; it was to be a transit point for migration and to join my brothers in Kuwait. Kuwait was seen as a land of milk and honey for the Palestinian people, as I had heard such promises after graduating from high school. However, none of this happened, and no replies came to the many letters I sent, which were piling up in the mail.

The few coins I had with me were soon spent, and the big question loomed on my forehead: where would I continue my journey from, where would I start, with what would I start, and what if no answers came?

I began my journey by asking the few people I knew or knew who had come under similar circumstances. Everyone was puzzled, and so was the answer on my lips, which always came with difficulty—either with denial, a shake of the head, trivialization, or regret, all essentially negative responses but delivered in different ways.

I left behind my belts, belongings, and persona that I had wrapped myself in after debts had weighed heavily on me, and I became as though I was begging or asking for charity. Often, my hopes were dashed, and even some acquaintances who were burdened with this task or that task became weighed down.

It was a great concern for me to ask my family for help, as I was someone who refused to accept assistance on the principle of self-reliance.

But even my brothers disappointed me, and I heard neither hide nor hair from them.

At that moment, I decided to put all considerations aside and began my journey by searching and inquiring in every shop, small hotel scattered across the town, institutions, companies, and anything that came my way. I knocked on all the doors. I would go out, buy a newspaper each morning, and head to every potential employer. I walked the streets of Amman all day long, asking around. Often, I felt intense hunger, but I couldn't afford even a falafel sandwich to buy and eat to continue my search among those places. Unfortunately, the answer was always, regretfully, "We do not want."

One of the strange ironies that occurred to me was that I only had a few coins. I couldn't afford to go to and from the city center by bus, buy a newspaper— which was how I searched for work—and live. Given that we lived in the Prince Hassan neighborhood in Jabal Al-Nuzha, I would walk down to the city center, about 8 kilometers away, to buy the newspaper upon arrival and start my search. I couldn't afford a falafel sandwich, which was hard to come by, so I endured on an empty stomach. In the evening, I would take the bus back up, where the young men made dinner, and I would eat with them. That meal would sustain me for the next 24 hours to start the search all over again. Even the little money I had was borrowed.

This situation continued for quite some time until one of the clothing store owners in town told me that he would agree to employ me the next morning, as one of the original employees hadn't shown up and they knew nothing about his whereabouts. He told me to come in the next morning, and this was a glimmer of hope for me that did not end until the end of that day when the absent employee returned. I never found out why he was absent, which led the shop owner to say that he no longer needed me after the original employee returned and gave me two dinars.

Thus, this man abruptly ended my dream and extinguished my hope once again, concluding a work journey that lasted only one day.

When the search exhausted me, one of the residents jokingly suggested who worked in construction at the place we stayed and asked if I wanted to work in concrete with him. Desperate, I said yes, I would work.

He smiled and said he knew I didn't look like a concrete worker, but there was no harm in trying. I was enthusiastic about the idea and went with him after he spoke with the boss, or the 'master' as they called him, and of course, after he asked me to wear old clothes.

I, who had no old clothes for work, arrived at the workshop located in the Al-Muqabaleen area, a place I was seeing for the first time. My friend told me, "Here is where you will work." I asked him, "What will I be doing?" He introduced me to the person who mixed the 'jebala,' as they called it, the manual mixture of cement, sand, gravel, and water used to build houses.

My job was to carry a tray of concrete on my shoulder, like those men who pick up the tray, place it on their shoulder, and climb the ladder to hand it to my friend and another person, the builders at the top of the ladder.

When it was my turn, I tried to lift the concrete tray but couldn't even budge it. The man mixing the concrete looked at me and, with a scoop from the trowel in his hand, took some off; I tried again but to no avail. Then he scooped more off until it was about half full, and still, I couldn't even get it onto my shoulder, especially since the other workers would come, fill theirs easily, and ascend the ladder.

I didn't notice that the foreman was watching me from the roof of the building. He came down the ladder and told me to wait. He approached me and asked to see my hands, and when he saw they were soft, he smiled and said, "This work isn't for you, and you've never done this type of work before." He took five dinars out of his pocket, handed them to me, and added, "Go and find a job that suits you."

Indeed, I left the place after my friend's disappointment, who later joked about the story to our roommates. But at least I gained five dinars, every penny of which I needed, and I resumed my job search once again.

I saw an advertisement for a "farashin" needed at a hotel near the Roman Theater in Amman, and I did not know what the job of a "farash" entailed. But I decided to go in and ask. So, I entered and asked, and after the man stared at me for a long time, he asked, "Do you know what a farash does?"

I told him truthfully that I didn't, but I learned quickly and needed the job.

He said, "My son, a farash, cleans rooms and bathrooms," and he started to explain as if he wasn't convinced by my appearance to change my mind because my external appearance didn't suggest to him that I looked like a farash.

When he saw my persistence, he told me, "Tomorrow at 7 AM, be here with the staff, and we'll give you training for just one day, then you can start working." I told him okay, and indeed, I left feeling elated, even though the salary was somewhat low; the man had told me it was 30 dinars a month. But that didn't matter; what mattered was that I was going to work.

Indeed, I was there at 7 AM when I found that some of the staff had already arrived, and after I had dressed in my oldest clothes, or work clothes,

when that man came, looked, and told me, addressing me, "Go and change your clothes, what do you think you are going to work as, a manager here?" I told him, "These are my clothes that I will work in." He said, "My son, you need to clean the bathrooms," and I explained to him that these were my worst clothes. He said, "On your responsibility," and walked away shaking his head, not convinced by what I said.

I began working and learned everything they told me to do, and my job continued for a month, involving cleaning bathrooms and making beds—everything that the job of a 'farash' entails. Of course, this work was not my ambition in life, but it was a thousand times better than continuing to beg for help.

Two noteworthy things happened to me at this hotel. The first was when a Saudi man came to the hotel. When he checked in and took his key from the reception, he called me over as I was passing by chance. He pointed to a Toyota Cressida with Saudi plates visible from the window and said, "See that car? Here's the key. Go and bring me the bag from the trunk." I did as he asked and brought him the bag, and the man handed me a Jordanian dinar as a tip. It was a great joy for me as it was the first tip I had ever received in my life, and it was worth a full day's work at the hotel.

Another day, while I was working at the hotel, going up and down the stairs, I encountered a beautiful woman in her thirties sitting at the bottom of the stairs. I tried to pass her to continue my way up, returning to my work, but she called out to me, saying, "Hey, boy! Come here," and then she added after I stopped, "Don't you want to know your fortune? What these days are hiding for you?" I asked her, puzzled, "And how can that be?"

At first, I thought she assumed I was one of the hotel guests, not a cleaning staff member. Then she said, "Give me your hand." I complied and handed her my hand. She was holding a thread and began tying it into many large knots. After closing my hand, she placed the knotted thread in it while muttering things I didn't understand. She then told me, "Stretch out your hand." Immediately, she covered it with a black handkerchief and continued chanting. Then she said, "I will lift the black handkerchief from your hand. If the thread is still knotted, go away from me quickly because your life and future will be dark. However, if I find it untangled, it means your life will be easy, you will be among the happiest people, and your tomorrow will be bright." I nodded in agreement. Before she removed the black handkerchief, she started muttering again, then suddenly, her face turned dark, or so it seemed to me. She then said tremblingly, "Put your money here."

When I hesitated and said, "What money?" she replied, "The jinn have tangled the thread, and it won't untangle until you put your money." Seeing that scene and her face turning grim and dark as she repeated, "Put it here, put it here," I put my hand in my pocket. I found five dinars, all that I had, which I had borrowed from one of the young men I lived with. I took them out and placed them in her hand.

Suddenly, her face brightened, her complexion normalized, and she smiled after removing the black handkerchief from my hand. She told me, "Open your hand now." Indeed, I opened it, and, to my great surprise, the thread was untangled, as if she had never knotted it. She then added, "Go on, your path is clear, and your life will be bright," along with other words I didn't understand because my mind was focused on the five dinars she had taken from me. I said to her, "What does this mean?"

I asked her to give me my money back.

She said, "How can I return it when this is my fee for having untangled the knots in your life, and now your affairs are in order?" I entered into a heated argument with her, telling her that I work as a farash in the hotel and am not one of its guests and that she couldn't take the five dinars, which was all I had and also a debt to me, and that these dinars represented five days of cleaning bathrooms.

Eventually, she agreed after I raised my voice and gave me back two dinars. Then, under my persistent pressure, she gave me another dinar but kept two for herself. I quickly went to my supervisor in the hotel and told him what had happened, hoping he could recover the remaining two dinars. However, when we returned to show him where she had been, we couldn't find her at the place; she and the two dinars, my precious capital, had disappeared.

I continued to work at the hotel for one month. One day, as I was going to buy some items for the hotel, I saw an advertisement posted on the front of one of the electronics stores in the building. They were seeking sales staff. I entered and spoke to the person there, who happened to be the company owner's son. He told me that the job was not at this location but at the main branch in Al-Musdar and that his father would meet me there.

I told him I finished work at six in the evening. He said, "Okay, go after you finish your work." Indeed, I went to the address he gave me, where I met his father, who was called Abu Jamal, a well-known man from a prominent family in Nablus. The interview didn't last long; the man liked me and told me to come the next morning and that they would offer me a salary of 45 dinars.

I left, barely containing my joy. First, I would be a salesman instead of a farash, which is something I excel at, and secondly, it was a 50% increase in the salary I was currently earning.

The next morning, I went to my supervisor at the hotel and told him what had happened and that I would be leaving the job. He was not surprised and said, "I knew from the first day that you weren't going to stay with us." He gave me my salary, which I was very happy about, and it was the first time since arriving in Amman that I felt this way.

I headed to my new job, which began with cleaning the exterior of electrical appliances. From the first day, I tried to learn everything.

There was a significant difference; I felt relieved at the end of the day when I returned to the accommodation. The young men had paid the rent for me, and I told them what happened with my new job after I had paid the rent and settled part of my debts with the salary I received from the hotel.

Of course, I settled into my new job, and it wasn't long before I began to learn everything about sales, which was dominated by a man in his fifties named Saleh. He had an authoritative personality, and we had to refer to him for every detail because of his long tenure with the company owner. Essentially, he was the right-hand man of the employer. I later learned that he was unmarried and had no children, which is uncommon in our society for a man of his age to be without a family, and no one knew why.

There was a young Egyptian man named Ibrahim, whose main job was collecting debts and promissory notes from people who purchased appliances on installment and credit. Ibrahim would often go out early in the morning, following a schedule set by Saleh, to collect installments from those who had fallen behind on their payments. Sometimes, he would spend the entire day out and return, having collected only a small amount or sometimes nothing at all. This would drive Saleh mad, and he often complained about Ibrahim to the manager, sometimes describing him in unfavorable terms. According to them, one of the main reasons for Ibrahim's lack of success was because he was Egyptian.

One day, Ibrahim returned angry because he had gone to a house in the Sahab area to someone who seemed to be a respected sheikh among his people. I don't know what Ibrahim did or said, but the man expelled him and even had his sons chase Ibrahim through the alleys.

When Ibrahim returned and told Abu Jamal (the company owner) about the incident, Abu Jamal was very angry. I was listening to the conversation in which Ibrahim told Abu Jamal about what had transpired between him and the man and how he had sent his sons to chase him through the alleys. I asked Abu Jamal for permission and suggested, "Why don't you send me to collect from him? I believe I can do it." I proposed that Ibrahim come with me to show me the house and let me try. Abu Jamal agreed to this.

Indeed, the next day, Ibrahim and I went to the place. He pointed out the house from a distance without getting close to himself. I knocked on the door, and when the man came out, I greeted him with "As-salamu alaykum," he replied, "Wa alaykum as-salam." Before he could ask who I was, I told him, "My name is Younes, and I am here on behalf of Abu Jamal." The man assumed I was his son, as my accent wasn't Egyptian. He welcomed me warmly, saying, "Ahlan wa sahlan, please come in."

I entered, and he poured coffee in the Jordanian style, which is always present in gatherings.

I said to him reproachfully, "Sheikh, we send our employee to you, and you treat him like this?" Of course, I said it while laughing, especially after the fear had dissipated following the first cup of coffee. Then, the Sheikh began to curse the Egyptians and their day and those who brought them to the country.

So, I said to him, "Our Sheikh, here I am. I've come to apologize and to make amends." The man stood up and gave me 50 dinars, saying, "God willing, on this day next month, come, you are welcome, and take the remaining 50."

I bid farewell to the man who escorted me to the door.

Ibrahim was more astonished than Abu Jamal when I handed him the 50 dinars, telling him, "He sends his regards, and on this day next month, I will go and collect the remaining 50."

I was extremely surprised when Abu Jamal, with a commanding tone, said, "Listen, Younes, this is your job from today onward. Leave Ibrahim here in the showroom, and you are now the official collector for the company. I will increase your salary by 10 dinars."

Of course, I was very pleased with this, especially since it ensured my freedom to move around the neighborhoods of Amman in search of people who owed the company.

I forgot to mention here that Abu Jamal curiously asked how I did that. I told him the man asked me if I was his son, but I didn't answer. He said, "It doesn't matter. You are like my son," he said, laughing. The important thing is to collect these debts.

Of course, I went out every day, and within the first week, I brought in what Ibrahim would collect in a month several times. This brought immense joy to Abu Jamal, which led him to promote me to the manager of the Wadi Al-Seer Street branch and raise my salary to 65 dinars.

Here, my circumstances began to change, and even my mood started to improve. I paid off all my debts and began to meet with friends coming from Palestine. We would go out together to Jabal Amman, a prestigious area in Amman then.

One day, the brother of one of my close friends visited me at the showroom where I had become the manager. He was an engineer working in Saudi Arabia, and we had met in Ramallah. His name was Engineer Hossam. He had learned by chance that I was in Amman. After a long conversation, he said to me, "Why do you live at the edge of the world? Come and look for a place here in central Amman to save on transportation costs and commuting time. I will share half the rent with you." He didn't want to live with me because he was staying in his uncle's villa in Jabal Hussein, who owns a group of companies in Jordan, but he wanted it as a backup in case any of his brothers came from Palestine or if he wanted to stay there himself. I thought about his words and found them logical.

Indeed, we looked for a room to live in and found one on Al-Musdar Street with a rent of 30 dinars. I went to my roommates, bid them farewell, and thanked them for their help, making sure I owed them nothing. With my salary at 65 dinars, I could easily afford my share of the rent. Hossam never spent a single night in the room but continued to pay me half the rent.

During that period, my friends changed, and I no longer saw my former roommates often, except sometimes on Fridays when I would meet some of them. Due to my new job and new living situation, I started to meet with friends coming from Ramallah, and I formed a different group, especially since most of these friends came from wealthy families. We began to go out to different areas of

Amman to enjoy our evenings, particularly around the Third Circle in Jabal Amman, with the Central Cafe downtown being our daily meeting point.

That's when I started smoking cigarettes, which I had never done before and had always completely refused, but I began to mimic this crowd of young people who certainly pressured me to smoke like them. Thus, I started my journey by smoking cigarettes—the beginning of a deviation in behavior that I had always utterly rejected, but as I said, either due to bad company or my own weakness.

So, it continued with Hossam, who also had a car, taking me out after work hours. He would wait for me and introduce me to different people.

One night, we visited a friend of his who worked as an official at the Arab Bank. After getting to know me, he asked, "Are you happy in your job?" I told him yes, but that it was not my ultimate ambition. He then asked, "What is your ambition?" I immediately replied, "To work at a bank." "Would you like to work with us at the Arab Bank?" he continued. Before I could answer, he told me, "Come tomorrow to the bank downtown and ask for this person," giving me a name. "I will have spoken to him in the morning, and he will take care of the rest."

I was very excited about this and began to wonder to myself, could it really be that I would work at a bank? It had been a dream of mine, especially since I had been visiting banks for deposits, withdrawals, or any task Abu Jamal sent me. I saw how bank employees were neatly dressed, worked from desks, and enjoyed many benefits. This idea greatly fascinated me, and I dreamed of working like them.

What fueled this dream was the certainty that I would have no place at a university as long as no one could teach me; aware of my family's circumstances and unable to ask them for anything. Even my siblings who lived in Kuwait had abandoned me, and I hadn't heard much from them, so working at the bank became a refuge for me, and I thought I could complete my studies while working.

The next day, I went to the headquarters of the Arab Bank located downtown, a place I passed daily and looked at with respect and admiration. I entered through the main door, asking myself, could it really be possible for me to work here and become one of its employees? Is this the light at the end of the tunnel, and has the world started to smile at me? When I asked the receptionist about the person whose name I had been given, they told me he was on the upper floors. I continued to ask around until I reached the man, who welcomed me after introducing myself. He gave me an employment application, which I filled out, and he set a time for me. He said it was a two-hour exam, passing which was a prerequisite for the bank to consider employing me.

I attended the appointment as scheduled and took the exam along with a group of young people. The exam covered a wide range of topics. They told us to return after a week at the same time to see our results.

When I returned the following week at the appointed time to find out the result, the person who greeted me immediately congratulated me. He said, "Congratulations, you have passed and been accepted. Now, all you need to do is bring a financially capable person who can guarantee two thousand dinars because the bank will commit to training you for two years, during which you must sign a contract that you cannot leave the bank before those two years end."

This news hit me like a bolt from the blue. I had not expected such a request. Being a stranger in this land, how could I arrange a guarantee of two thousand dinars or even find someone to vouch for me with such an amount? I didn't know anyone who had such sums, nor did I have any relatives or acquaintances here, especially since Hossam had received news that his mother was ill and that he needed to return to Ramallah. He left three days before I learned the result and before this request was made. Consequently, I had to find someone from our country to share the accommodation with me. This person worked for a company in Jordan after being in Kuwait and was much older than me, but as I said, Hossam's departure from the scene left a big void for me.

The week given to me by the bank ended, and I was unable to bring either the guarantee or a guarantor. I returned to the man and explained my situation—that I was a stranger from the West Bank and knew no one. The man looked at me and said, "This is a rule at the bank, and I cannot bypass it, but I will help you by giving you an additional week to find a guarantor and then start working." I thought to myself, how could my acquaintances possibly increase in this additional week?

Indeed, the extra week almost passed, and I could not find a guarantor until an idea struck me on the last day! However, I hesitated to make it a reality, but I had no other option.

I went to my manager, Abu Jamal, especially since he always told me, "You are like a son to me." I believed for a moment that this idea was my only option. As soon as I finished my request, he erupted angrily, saying, "You want to leave me and work for someone else, and you want me to provide a guarantor for you?" After a long outburst, repeating that it was his fault for giving me more than I deserved, he said, "Anyway, hand over the key to Saleh, and God make it easy for you. I don't want you anymore, nor do I want you to work for me. Going to look for another job behind my back."

All this while I was stunned, unable to respond to his accusations and his loud voice. The idea that "you are like a son to me" went out the window.

Thus ended my job and my only source of income. Of course, I couldn't return to that man at the bank because I failed to secure a guarantor, and I found myself unemployed.

I went to Bata Shoe Company, where a friend of mine worked and had recommended me for a position as a shoe salesman. When the interview with the

HR manager came, he was pleased with me and agreed to hire me immediately. However, before I got up to leave, he asked to see my high school diploma and transcript. I thought he would be pleased to see my high marks, but he shook his head and said, "This won't work for us because your grades are high, and you will likely join a university soon." I assured him I didn't have the means to attend university, but the man was unconvinced and told me, "Sorry, we cannot employ you."

So, the job-hunting saga began again just when I thought things had stabilized. The search was lengthy.

Finally, I entered a furniture store called Hamouda Furniture, and the owner, after asking me a few questions and hearing about my strengths, said, "Come tomorrow morning and start working. I'll pay you a salary of 55 dinars." I did not hesitate to accept it, even though my previous salary was 65 dinars.

This store had two branches, one next to the Amman Municipality and the other, where I was stationed, on Wadi Al-Seer Street. I worked there with an Egyptian young man and another Egyptian who had quit just the day before without knowing why. Thus, the owner needed someone to replace him, especially since I had gained some experience in selling furniture and electronics from my previous job.

I arrived at work the next morning, cleaned everything with the Egyptian young man and rearranged the store to make it look presentable and attractive to customers. God blessed me, and I managed to sell a bedroom set on my first day, earning a profit well above the minimum the store owner had set for us.

This sale was the first in a whole week before my arrival; the store hadn't sold anything, and the owner was overjoyed when I called him and reported the news. This led to more frequent sales of old items in the store, which I dusted off and moved to the front, allowing me to sell in the first week what the Egyptian typically sold in a month. This greatly improved my standing with the owner and made me confident enough to ask for an advance on my salary, especially since I had been unemployed for a while and my pockets were nearly empty.

I now worked every day except Fridays, and the working hours were long, from nine in the morning until nine at night.

One summer afternoon, while working at that place, I decided to go to Hashem Restaurant to buy a falafel sandwich. After purchasing it, I returned, taking my time eating it. I had also bought a can of Pepsi at that time and decided to enjoy this meal, which hadn't been a common pleasure for me those days. I stood by the street at the traffic light going up Jabal Amman, also known as Tailony Signal (named after the store at that location).

It was one of the few traffic lights in Amman at that time, and as I said, it was a hot summer afternoon, and I was standing in the shade of a building, alone as the street was empty of passersby. A Mercedes 280 S caught my attention as it stopped at the light. Its color and elegance stood out; even the sunroof was open. I looked to see who was driving and saw a familiar face smiling at me.

The face was familiar, so I thought I must know this man!

But who was he?

I scrutinized again, and there he was, waving at me with a smile. As he smiled, I squinted after opening my eyes wide, and it was indeed His Majesty King Hussein. May God have mercy on him.

Confused about what I should do, my hand instinctively rose to wave back while I was in disbelief. He was playfully tousling the hair of a blond child sitting next to him. After snapping out of my astonishment, the traffic light turned green, his car drove off; and I saw no military vehicle accompanying him, just a patrol car at a distance, and I didn't know if it was following him or not.

I was doubting whether it was really him until I saw many people waving at him after following his car to the center of town. I still smile shyly when I remember that moment when he was waving specifically at me when no one else was on the street at that time.

One day, while browsing a newspaper that I made sure to buy daily, my eyes caught an advertisement for a sales position at the European Furniture Exhibition in Abdali, which was well-known at the time due to the widespread advertisements I saw daily in the newspaper. I said to myself, now that I have the necessary experience, why not go and apply for this job? I was sure that the nature of the work and the benefits would be much better than I was currently.

But how could I leave my job? What would I say to the employer, especially remembering what happened with Abu Jamal when I confronted him and he fired me, leaving me without a new job and losing the old one?

I thought to myself that I must invent a plausible reason to be allowed to leave, so I called him and told him that my mother (may God have mercy on her) had come from the West Bank over the bridge to see me and that she was an elderly woman who didn't know anything, so I had to go meet her to take her to my place.

The man agreed, and I set off for Abdali, where the European exhibition was located. To my surprise, there were many young people, even girls, dressed in semi-formal attire waiting in the waiting area, and there were many of them. I told myself it was impossible for me to have a chance among these people, especially since each one had to submit a job application a personal photo, and an interview was scheduled.

When I saw all this, I decided to withdraw because I was certain that I would have no chance in this uneven competition. Indeed, I left, and it was two in the afternoon. I didn't even fill out the job application. I crossed the street, waiting for a bus or a service to take me back to my workplace. The vehicles passed by without stopping because they were full (filled with passengers), and I couldn't afford a taxi. I waited until four in the afternoon until the idea struck me to return to the European exhibition. I told myself that at least the rush might have subsided, and I should fill out the application and hand it in, just in case.

I went back, and there were only a few young people left, not more than a handful when we heard the secretary say that anyone who hadn't filled out an application should do so now because the manager was present and would meet with those who were there now. We went forward and handed her our job applications, and my number at that time was the fifth. Each person took between ten and fifteen minutes, so I said to myself, I don't think I have a chance at this job.

When it was my turn for the interview, I entered the room to meet a man in his forties, well-dressed and speaking calmly and slowly. He stood up, greeted me, and said, "Have a seat, Younes," after looking at my name on the application. He carefully examined the application for a while and then began asking me some questions about sales, and I asked him others outside of sales and about various aspects of life. He was smiling all the time, although his demeanor was very serious. Then he surprised me by asking, "Younes, have you tried working in something other than furniture sales?"

I was puzzled by his question and thought perhaps I hadn't succeeded with the right answers as he expected. So, I told him honestly that I had applied and passed the entrance exam for the Arab Bank. Still, I was unable to provide the required two thousand dinar guarantee for my employment because I came from the West Bank and didn't know anyone who could vouch for me with such an amount.

He asked me, "What did they bring to you in the exam?"

I told him, remembering all the questions by heart, "They brought us this and that."

Then he asked, "What did you answer?"

I replied, "I answered this and that."

Then he asked, "What else?"

So, I continued to give him the questions and answers.

The man suddenly smiled and said, "Your place is in a bank, not a furniture showroom. You must come to the Jordan Kuwait Bank in Abdali next Saturday, which isn't far from here. Do you know it?"

I said, "Yes."

He said, "Come and ask for Yusuf Said, and you will be taken care of."

He said this and stood up, extending his hand in a respectful handshake I hadn't experienced in such interviews before.

But I was caught between dream and reality as if I were in a pleasant dream and did not want to wake up. What had happened? Could it be possible that I would work at a bank instead of all this struggle? I returned to the showroom where I worked, talking to myself in disbelief, wondering who this man was, his connection to the bank, and why he spoke with such confidence.

As soon as I entered the showroom, I found the shop owner there, very angry with me because of my delay. I apologized to him, mentioning the bridge issue, and continued the rest of my shift until the shop closed, still thinking about what had happened in disbelief.

That week, I planned what to say to him the next Saturday when I would leave for the bank appointment that the man had told me about.

Finally, Saturday came after a long wait, and I decided to continue with the story about my mother, an excuse he couldn't refuse, especially as I had become one of his favorite people due to the excellent sales I was generating for the shop.

I told him, "I'm going to take my mother to Zarqa to see some of her relatives there."

Indeed, he agreed.

Indeed, I headed to Abdali and went to the bank after changing my clothes, switching out of the jeans I wore daily. I entered through the main door, asking for Yusuf Said. Each time I asked, they told me to go upstairs, and I continued until they directed me to his office.

I found the door marked "Human Resources" closed, so I knocked and opened it. Inside, there was a middle-aged blonde woman sitting at a desk wearing reading glasses that were slipping down her nose, busy writing something I couldn't see. I said, "Hello." She replied, "Hello," without looking up, and I hesitated, unsure what to say next.

I asked her, "Excuse me, I want a job application." She continued writing, saying, "We don't have any vacancies." I remained standing and told her, "I didn't ask about vacancies; I just want a job application." She continued her work without looking at me and said, "You didn't hear me; no vacancies mean no applications."

I remained standing, but for some reason, I felt bold and said, "Do you want me to pay for the application? I'll pay, but I need a job application." Her tone rose, and she looked up, her glasses nearly falling off, and sternly asked, "Which part did you not hear and understand? There are no jobs and no job applications."

She gave me a disdainful look, and before she could continue her fiery speech, I asked, "Okay, where can I find Mr. Yusuf Said?" Her tone softened somewhat as she asked, "And what do you want from him?" Though it was hard for me, I responded defiantly, "It's difficult for you. Just tell me where his office is; it's nearby, and I want to see him."

She stood up from her desk and asked, "What's your name?" I told her my name and entered the large office behind her.

Suddenly, the large door opened and out came the same man who had met me days earlier at the European furniture showroom. I was very surprised to see him. He greeted me warmly, extending his hand, saying, "Hello, Younes," then turned to the woman who had given me a hard time and who turned out to be his secretary. "Hanan, give us a job application and make us two coffees," he instructed.

Then he asked me, "How do you like your coffee, Younes?"

Still in the shock, I replied, "Medium."

He led me into his luxurious office, and I felt at ease like I had known him for a long time. I told him about my encounter with the lady named Hanan. He reprimanded me, "Why did you ask about a job application when I told you to ask for Yusuf Said?" He then explained, "We tell her to say that to people because we get many visitors, but you are a special case."

I could never have imagined for a moment that he would be the same person to meet me in both offices. When Hanan brought the job application and handed it to me, he gave me the pen he was holding. Before I started filling out the form, I gave her a knowing look, remembering how she had treated me moments before at the door and how she was acting now.

I started filling out the application and sipped Hanan's coffee. After finishing, he said, "Come next Saturday to meet the assistant general manager after you stop by my office first, and I will send you to him."

By the way, it turned out that Mr. Yusuf Said is the HR manager at the bank, who is also a very well-known and influential figure there. No job at the bank is secured without his initial approval.

I returned, hardly believing what had happened and how, thankfully, God was about to open a door I thought would never open.

I reached the store where I worked and didn't hear any of the usual scolding words from the shop owner, which typically centered around my being late.

All week, I pondered what to say to the shop owner next Saturday so I could attend the final interview at the bank with the assistant general manager.

Of course, the fabricated story about my late mother was the trump card I had to play. This time, I told him that my mother was returning to Palestine and that I needed to go with her to the bridge. Naturally, this news irritated him, and then he said, "Thank God she's going back so you can stop saying you need to leave."

Indeed, the following Saturday, I went to the bank and first met with Yusuf Said, who told me what the assistant general manager would ask and how I should respond. It was like a scripted scenario; I went, and the man asked me exactly as Yusuf Said had described, and I responded with the answers he had given me. Then he told me to go back to Abu al-Saeed, and when I returned to him, he told me to come the next Monday to start working and assigned me to the shareholders' department, mentioning that I would be moved to other departments in the near future.

I returned to the store and the shop owner, who was extremely surprised when I told him that tomorrow would be my last day because I would return to Palestine on Monday due to an urgent matter.

I didn't tell him that I would be working elsewhere, and I don't know why lying in this case saved me from being unemployed. It's still fresh in my memory when I confronted my previous manager with the truth and honesty, only to be fired. So, this time, I let my imagination shape my next steps. Even the man told me, when you return from Palestine, return to your workplace. I replied, "Insha'Allah (God willing)."

Thus, my time there ended, and a new chapter at the Jordan Kuwait Bank began, forever changing my personality and being.

It remains to be said that someone like Yusuf Said is what you might call an angel of mercy, the cause, or a righteous man, as our mothers pray for us to encounter someone whom God facilitates in our path and who undoubtedly changes the course of life. I don't know why I would stand in respect whenever we met by chance in the bank corridors later.

As for Hanan, that secretary, we became friends later on, and I would always remind her of her haughtiness in that incident, and she would laugh a lot.

I began working at the bank, and in my initial days in the shareholders' department, as Yusuf Said had mentioned, I started training with the other employees in the department. It became necessary to radically change my appearance because, like the rest of the employees, I was required to wear a formal shirt and tie—a matter I was unfamiliar with. So, I went to the Friday market and bought five ties for one dinar, and I started changing them to match the shirt. Often, I would leave them in my desk drawer and put one on when I arrived in the morning like the rest of the employees.

I started arriving early in the morning to avoid being late, even before the other employees. Thus, gradually, my situation stabilized, and I integrated wonderfully with them, starting to get to know them little by little, even though the job they initially assigned me was routine.

I learned what shares in the bank and companies meant and what it meant to trade them—buying and selling. After a while, I began accompanying the person responsible for trading stocks in the financial market to the trading floor. This gave me a kind of insight and experience to become a strong trader in the stock market later on.

This continued for a while after my mental state greatly improved, and I began to pay off the debts that had accumulated, especially to the person I was living with. I also started going to work regularly and returning home after the end of the shift, which was quite early compared to the jobs I had before, where I often worked very late.

This gave me free time, which I spent meeting friends from Palestine. We would meet at Central Café, which overlooked downtown. We played cards or talked about our memories in Palestine. Sometimes we would go to Jabal Amman, specifically the Third Circle, to Ma'touq Restaurant, which was very famous at the time. One of our friends, who came from wealthy families in Ramallah or from abroad, particularly Kuwait—a place teeming with Palestinians coming and going—would take care of the bill.

With our modest salaries, we couldn't afford the expenses of such places. Those days and moments gave me a taste of happiness that somewhat compensated for the past days of hardship and misery I had experienced.

Things continued this way while we still lived in Tal'at al-Misdar, and during this time, I was earning a monthly salary of seventy dinars from the bank. Despite this modest amount, I managed to carve out a decent life for myself. As I mentioned, I changed the type of clothes I wore, dressing conservatively due to my daily work environment, and I wore jeans only on the weekend break on Fridays.

This development also extended to my way of thinking and my relationships with the employees after I got to know most of them. It helped that the bank's cafeteria was very close to our department, so my relationships with them began to branch out. Additionally, I joined the bank workers' union and participated in all its activities, which expanded my social connections with these people.

My star began to rise gradually, especially among the women who I noticed would whisper, glance, and try to interact and get closer to me. Still, I seriously felt that none of these relationships would have a future.

I also realized that working in the stock department was just repetitive and somewhat monotonous, so I approached my manager in the department to request a transfer to either the deposits section or the foreign exchange department. After persistent requests and submitting the transfer application more than three times, I was finally moved to the deposits for a few months and then to the foreign exchange department.

Settling in my room in Amman

Love and the Snows of March

The Day of Love and the Snows of March 1980

One day in March, we woke to a snowy morning, unusually heavy, which shut down the town—cars stalled on the roads, and even pedestrians on the streets were very few. This slowed our morning rush to work, and we stayed home.

After a few hours, the young friends from the neighboring building called us to come out and play in the snow.

I was reluctant to leave, to the extent that I didn't even bother to change out of the pajamas that I was wearing. I went out with them, and we climbed to the roof of the building. All the buildings were occupied by young men and women exchanging snowballs.

Naturally, I excelled at this, having practiced throwing stones at the army back in Palestine, my throws reaching far.

Suddenly, as we exchanged snowballs amid shouting and laughter, I saw a girl with long black hair shyly emerge from among the other girls. She put her hand in the pocket of her jeans, also wearing a white sweater as white as the snow she played with.

The other girls tried to pull her into the game to throw snowballs at us, but I saw her turn her face away, paying no heed to them and not touching the snow.

And in that moment, I targeted her with a snowball from afar, intending to draw her into the fray. The snowball hit her shoulder, and she gave me a stern look, moved aside, and tried to enter her house to avoid the snowball fight. I threw a second snowball at her, but it missed.

She decided then to stay away, especially since the other young men with me had tried to throw snowballs at her, too, but I was trying to stop them.

I thought to myself, who is this girl who hasn't paid us any attention, acting all high and mighty and ignoring us?

I swore I'd find out more about her, and that's what I told the young men standing with me, saying that I must get to know her.

One of the young men standing with us said, "Surely she's Christian, thinking highly of herself, and you won't be able to win her over. It's well-known that Christian brothers mostly inhabit the areas of Musdar and Ashrafiyah in Amman."

But this talk didn't satisfy me, so I told them, "But I have a feeling I'll be able to!"

The gathering of young men and women dispersed as we entered our homes, but the matter of that girl remained an obsession that troubled me—I had to know more about her, and I was known for conquering challenges.

My friend and I at the bank were known to be among the first to get acquainted with new girls coming to the bank, and not just that, but even with girls who passed by on the streets.

How could I fail with this girl?

Sami, that friend with whom I had worked at the car showroom in Ramallah, after he inquired about me and found me, came to me and said, "I want to live with you," and another friend we had met in the neighboring building also came and said, "I too want to live with you."

An idea occurred to me to go to the owner of the building we lived in and the building opposite where that girl lived. I had a good relationship with this man; he also owned a furniture store on Musdar Street, and I often sat down to have a cup of tea with him, whether I was coming or going from town, especially when I had no money in my pocket and had to walk back and forth.

Anyway, I went to the man, and as soon as I presented the idea to him and told him I wanted an apartment in the opposite building, a cunning idea flashed in the man's head. He told me, "Listen, I have an apartment on the top floor of that building. I'll give it to you for ten dinars less, you and your friends, on the condition that you work to drive away the families who have been living there for a while and paying cheap rent. The second condition is that the lease must be in your name, and you are responsible to me. I don't want to know about the others with you." I said okay, and we shook hands on that, agreeing to pay 70 dinars rent for the apartment, split among five people after we brought in a fifth person. The apartment had three bedrooms.

I took advantage of the conditions the man had set for my benefit. I gathered my friends and told them that the man had agreed to give us the apartment and that the lease would be in my name. I didn't tell them about his idea to drive out the tenants because I didn't intend to do that. I told them that I had one condition I would not compromise on before we moved into this large house. They all asked what it was. I said I would first choose the room I wanted to be alone in.

They all agreed to this, and I chose the room opposite the house where the girl lived, and they each shared the other rooms in pairs.

I worked on arranging my room in my own way, from the furniture to the curtains, until it was completely different from my roommates'.

The obsession to know more about that girl persisted, and since everyone was telling me something different, I decided to take another approach. I thought to myself, who knows more than the shop owner in the neighborhood?

So, I decided to befriend him. By sheer coincidence, this man was also from Ramallah, and his wife's brother was one of my closest friends, who had studied with me at Our Lady of the Annunciation School for the Roman Catholics.

Luck was on my side at every step.

After establishing common ground with the shop owner, who is called Abu Mitri, I began to inquire about my friend Maurice, whom I learned from had emigrated to the United States after high school, as is the norm for many from the city of Ramallah.

Abu Mitri was generous with information, the first piece being that the girl was also from the Ramallah area and lived alone with her parents with all her siblings in America. He mentioned that her father was a devout, conservative man who owned the entire building and described their situation as very comfortable. He even doubted that they would agree to a marriage proposal from someone like me, and of course for me, taking such a step was not in my plans at the moment.

However, what I heard from Abu Mitri only strengthened my resolve to get to know her. My roommates knew about my obsession with this matter and how I would start with her after she noticed my interest. She would appear on the rooftop and disappear whenever she saw me looking at her, which only increased my determination to know her.

How could I start with her without the people around us and the neighbors noticing? The neighbors' nosiness, who were always watching us, especially since everyone knew that we, a group of young men, were living here, made it challenging as the houses were close together and crowded.

The challenge was to find a way to contact her secretly to maintain the privacy of this relationship. It occurred to me to write her a letter to introduce myself. I liked the idea, but how would I deliver the letter to her? Would she even receive it, and what if she didn't want to get to know me?

I would sit on my favorite chair by the corner from where she could be seen, listening to Fairuz, writing and remembering that I had torn up many letters I had written. Soon, the idea would fade from my mind. With the memory of the near and distant past, I recalled that love letters never bode well. They had turned my life upside down when I was just starting. I told myself that I did not want that experience to repeat.

I gathered with my close friends and sought their advice on achieving my goal. Each one suggested a method; one said to write her a letter and give it to a little girl to deliver it to her. I dismissed that idea because that happened to me seven years ago back home, and I didn't want to repeat it.

The meeting with friends ended without a decision, but ultimately, I decided to go ahead with the letter, tying it to a stone and throwing it onto her house's roof when she appeared, but without my name. If she picked it up, I would proceed with this method. If she didn't pick it up, or if her father, Hajj Abu, did, it could become a problem, but at least no name was attached.

I had devised a way to catch her attention and even make her smile often. I began writing messages on cardboard signs and placing them for her to read. I wrote things like "I want to talk to you," "I admire you," "Talk to me," or just my name. She responded well; I even imagined her coming to see what I had written for her that day. This gave me confidence that we were progressing and that she would ultimately respond to me.

I remember that, as usual, I would wake up early and stand on the balcony watching her as she descended the stairs and also when she went down that long street on her way to school at 7:30 AM. She would occasionally look back and smile before meeting a friend at the end of the street, who would accompany her to school. All this before I got dressed and headed to work at 8:00 AM.

Indeed, I decided that I must send the letter. One day, while we were looking at each other after she appeared from her corner, I wrote on the cardboard that I would throw her a letter. She smiled, and I threw the letter tied to a stone. My joy was immense when she picked it up, took it, and hurried inside their house.

In this letter, I introduced myself, who I am and what I do. Although I knew it, I asked her for her full name, but I wanted her to write it down for me, along with her phone number. I waited a few days, but nothing happened, so I felt compelled to write again with a message that was stronger than the first.

I included a box of Sahm gum (chewing gum) that someone had brought from the West Bank. This time, I told her she either had to respond or I would withdraw quietly and not bother her again (this was just to scare her). Thus, my plan succeeded, and we contacted; she called me at the bank. The call wasn't long, but I got her phone number, and we started exchanging phone calls. One of the strangest and first questions was what I wanted, and I told her I wanted to get to know her better and meet.

I got to know her schedule, but her mother often answered the phone. I would hastily hand the phone to one of my female colleagues in the department and ask her to request to speak to her from her mother.

The women in the department found enjoyment in this, given the way it happened, which led to some jealousy from a divorced lady in our department who looked at me admiringly. What intrigued me the most about the situation was that my girl had an angelic, childlike, soft voice, unlike all the other girls around.

This lady would tell me that this girl was just a little child and ask if I was sure she was mature enough. I would proudly respond that this girl was the one I loved and no one else.

Finally, we decided to meet. It was a brief encounter downtown, near the Cairo Amman Bank. She came with her friend; by a striking coincidence, we were both wearing white shirts. I wanted us to go somewhere to sit, but her intense fear and hesitation prevented her, and as she walked away without looking at my face, she said, "I can't, I can't."

I was really surprised by this. The long-awaited date ended even before it began and lasted less than five minutes. She and her friend disappeared into the crowd while I watched them, still stunned by the brevity of the meeting and because it was the first time I saw her up close and our hands touched.

As soon as I got home, I wrote her a long letter expressing my strong disappointment, which she would later memorize by heart.

After that, we met several more times due to my insistence. As did phone calls, letters also became a way for us to express our feelings during those days. I often spoke to her from street phones, which were common back then. During this time, I also looked for additional work and started working in an advertising company, and I stopped going to the Central Café, where I used to meet with friends.

I also got involved in the union for bank employees, which I had joined. I quickly expanded my circle of acquaintances after meeting many young people in the union. I became involved in all the activities at the union. I began to attract the attention of all the employees, both at my bank because I was active in inviting bank employees to join the union, and at other banks whose employees frequented the union. This was almost considered taboo because bank management did not like their employees to join unions.

When the elections for the social committee, which oversees all the union's activities, whether it be trips organized by the union or any social activity or even coordination with social committees in other banks and insurance companies, took place, I was elected as the chairman. This committee included thirteen women, myself, and another guy, which gave me a significant popular base.

As for my additional work with the advertising company, I started achieving excellent results and got to know the owners of companies and shops. I was running between them to the point where my presence became essential for the company because I achieved better results in my part-time work than those who worked there full-time. I started earning more additional income than my salary at the bank, which positively reflected on my overall life. My financial situation improved significantly; I no longer owed anyone money and began to dress well and stylishly, as was my habit. This created a unique popularity for me among young women, whether at the bank or the union. But despite all this, my heart was set on one girl who did not belong to the world of these people.

It wasn't only the young women who noticed me but also the leaders of the political factions competing for seats on the union's administrative board and for support among the general body. These factions represented Fatah, the Popular Front for the Liberation of Palestine, the Democratic Front, and the Communist Party. Each of these tried to attract me to join their parties.

But as per my principle in life which does not change, I remained steadfast in not joining any party or group so as not to restrict my thoughts and methods to one direction. I stayed on this path, even when one of the union leaders, who was part of a front that adopted communism as a way of life at that time, came to my house and stayed until late, trying to convince me and even tempting me with an offer to send me to the Soviet Union to continue my education at their expense and under their scholarship. However, I firmly refused because I reject the communist ideology entirely, especially the aspect of atheism and many other principles that socialism relies on.

Thus, I remained steadfast and was known as "the independent," earning respect from everyone because I was not affiliated with anyone.

I had all the elements complete, and I lived those days as some of the best days of my life, especially after I moved to the foreign department at the bank and worked in the guarantees section.

Additionally, my side job and also my repeated meetings with my beloved, whom I introduced to all my friends at the union and the bank as my fiancée, let the world know that I was committed. I also started officially smoking cigarettes during those days, specifically smuggled Marlboro Reds, which weren't allowed to be bought from groceries. We used to buy them from a blind man who sat on the steps next to the famous Jordan Restaurant downtown. That place also witnessed many meetings with my beloved. She had successfully completed high school and entered the Arab College in Shmeisani.

I often went to pick her up from college, and we would go together to upscale restaurants in Amman and take taxis together, where I would drop her off at her house, making sure to get out a few distances before her. Financially, I could do this after my financial situation had greatly improved.

But these happy days did not last. One day, she came to me and dropped a bombshell that stunned me: she told me that her father and her family in America wanted her to go there, to travel to America to continue her studies.

After hearing this sudden news, questions crowded my mind, and they started spilling out of my mouth: "Well, what about our relationship? What happens to our future?" She replied that her family was pressuring her, and we parted that night under an unusual strain between us.

I stayed up that night and wrote her a letter that I believe was among the finest I wrote during those days, and I write it here just as I wrote it that night:

My beloved "Noon",

I want to pose a big question to you, which may seem small to you, but in my humble opinion, these are very big inquiries, seemingly minor in your view. Yesterday, when we spoke for a few minutes—I do not know how many—in our brief meeting, you outlined something to me that quickly seeped into my heart as if lightning had struck land covered with brittle tinder, which you know very well what its echo was.

You will travel to a far and very distant land to study there or to live, as you say, among your family members...

And what next?

The journey of these long months of sincerity, even with others, and of sacrifice with ourselves, and of living with dreams steeped in transparency that lived with me every minute, whether I was awake or asleep, whether I was near you or far from you...

I know that I was deeply in love, and still am, up to my ears, but this was not within my power to control. I chose you, your heart, willingly with my heart, mind, feeling, and will. The space before me was vast, yet I do not regret this choice, nor do I regret a single moment spent with you, whether it was by your side physically or just in my feelings. In fact, those moments are truly the happiest I've ever lived, minutes when time seemed to stop spinning to point its major hands at our hearts and to seal them with red wax as the truest hearts on earth.

Your excuse, my beloved, which I will continue to call you until my tongue dries up and stops moving, hoping it continues to echo the letters of your name with every word it utters, is that you say you will remain faithful. Perhaps this guess is correct, one in a thousand, but nine hundred and ninety-nine say no.

Distance, Noon, gradually dries up love and loyalty until the day comes when you deny ever knowing someone by this name, with these features, with that face.

A time will come when fate plays its dirty game to ultimately destroy even the most beautiful palace, even if it was built from dreams and illusions we built together.

There will come a day after these years during which you said you would be absent when you do not recognize me if you happen to see me by chance among the people passing on the street.

You might say this happens to others, but it could never happen to me.

But rest assured that this has happened to many like us, or perhaps for many reasons, we find that the long, thick rope that stretches between the distant spaces connecting our hearts suddenly snaps without warning.

And then, what do you imagine will happen to me? What will happen to the heart that has waited so long? What happens to those who have read your image on my forehead and in the features of my face? What can I do about those tongues that sometimes extend in sympathy but often in schadenfreude? Where do I flee from them and from the incessant questions, they hurl at me as if I were a criminal being chased by the law?

What do I tell them, and what do I answer? Do I say it was against her will, knowing I would be lying? Do I say that circumstances forced her, knowing I would also be lying?

If I fled from all the people, those who know you were everything to me—you were my past and my future, my tears and my smile, my joy and my sorrow, and even my life and death—where can I flee from myself, which would accuse my heart of madness?

Because I know that this step will ultimately be an illusion and a deception, living on a mirage far, far away with no truth in it,

Should I cry at that hour, or should I laugh hysterically knowing that neither will be of any use, that the sun will set at sunset and rise again the next morning, and that the moon will rise on its scheduled days?

Should I live on memories, and what good would that do if I remained drowned in them forever? What will happen? Will I be happy on the day I met you, or the day I spoke with you, or the day we met, or will I cry?

And what next? If time and fate are harsh, Noor, why should we be harsh on each other when perhaps, with a bit of sacrifice, endurance, and challenge, we could ease the pain and stray a bit from the path of thorns and also approach the path of roses a little?

May God forgive you, my beloved, and I hope that all I have written is just a disturbing dream from which we awake to continue our steps toward a brighter tomorrow.

With all my love and loyalty, on 1/4/81.

Of course, I wrote this letter and stayed up all night working on it, and its impact was profound. She cried upon reading it and managed to resist her family's pressure, rejecting the idea of traveling. Thus, our relationship continued, and we kept stealing the most beautiful moments of our lives despite the obstacles and rumors that followed us.

Events accelerated. During that time, I enrolled at the Arab University of Beirut, which was the available option for me at the time, whether in terms of my financial situation or work conditions. This decision was also encouraged by many of my colleagues at the bank who had preceded me in joining the Arab University of Beirut. I believed that if circumstances allowed me to attend classes at a university, this should at least be the one, especially since its degree was recognized and graduating from it would greatly improve my situation at the bank. However, our joy did not last long after the bank issued a decision not to grant employee students leave at the same time and specified first-year students to prevent this from happening in the future. This meant that the registration, the cost of books, the fees for the first year, and all the time I spent preparing for exams, which I was ready to travel to Beirut to attend, were all wasted.

Thus, that decision demolished the bridge that would have led me to complete my education.

After that, I had no choice but to intensify my work in the advertising company, where I became a star, achieving a high income for both myself and the company, more than those who worked full-time. This was also coupled with my volunteer work in the union and my frequent meetings with my beloved, which began to take on new forms until we became very well-known in the neighborhood.

The situation was further complicated when one of the friends who lived with me in the accommodation went and proposed to a girl from the building owned by my beloved's family. This created a kind of pressure, especially since he started visiting there freely on a daily basis and deliberately made his and his fiancée's presence known, which caused us some provocation and jealousy. I was urged by our neighborhood and friends to take action because our love was the most famous.

However, I was not ready to take any uncalculated steps. Firstly, both of us were young in age; secondly, financially, despite having cleared my debts; and thirdly, there was no one from my family in the picture, all of which made me psychologically unprepared.

What made matters worse was that the bank then issued government instructions regarding our status with the military service, which lasted for two years. I had to make a choice.

I began to see traveling as an escape, and then the first opportunity came from the Housing Bank of Oman in Muscat. Their representatives met me, among many others, accepted me, and signed a contract with me that offered a salary four times that of my salary at the Jordan Kuwait Bank. I accepted immediately.

They told me to wait a month for the visa, but after a month, they replied that they were unable to obtain a visa for me due to security reasons, given that I was of Palestinian origin.

This incident did not pass peacefully.

From this incident, it became clear to me that Palestinians are not treated like everyone else and that many countries around the world have reservations about allowing Palestinians to enter. Despite knowing this, this was the first time I was placed under scrutiny, and this ordeal would add to the many challenges in my life. How could this be when I was tying my fate to that of my beloved, who I was beginning to think about starting a new life stage with? She was pampered, receiving everything easily, and her entire family had acquired American citizenship—the most important nationality in the world. How could I possibly involve her in the Palestinian plight of displacement, and would she be able to endure it? It was essential to test how serious her commitment to me was.

Not much time had passed before my friend Khalid, and I drove to the college where she studied. It was supposed that he would drop us off, and we would sit somewhere to have a drink, as we had gotten used to. However, I decided at that moment that this meeting would be the real test of our relationship to see whether we could continue or not.

Of course, I had told my friend what I planned and what I intended to do, and he advised me at that time not to do it. But I was determined to vigorously shake up the relationship because if it was strong, it would withstand the wind; otherwise, it was better to part from this moment before we became more attached when later, the wound could become too deep to heal. After she got in the car, I surprised her by asking her several serious questions. I started by asking her what she would do if I had to leave the country, what her family's stance would be, whether she was ready to marry me if I left Jordan and couldn't return, and if she was prepared to be a wanderer with me since I would not serve in the army, no matter the cost.

Her answers were disturbed; she stuttered, not knowing how to respond, as she hadn't expected to be bombarded with such questions, and she couldn't find what to say and burst into tears.

It was necessary to shake her up like that so she could wake up and understand that I was no longer just the romantic dreamer who held her hand as we moved around. There were other aspects to my personality. She needed to understand that life isn't always comfortable, especially as the spoiled child of her family. Would she be able to endure my potential displacement if Jordan implemented these laws, which were often influenced by the political climate and their proximity to the Palestinian issue?

As I said, the situation overwhelmed that young girl who was not accustomed to or expecting the stern tone in my voice. That tone showed her the full truth without any romantic embellishments, and she did not know how to respond, which led my friend to stop the car when I started yelling at her and asking me to stop.

At that moment, I firmly believed she needed to decide whether she would continue an unstable life with me, subject to my circumstances, which were likely to involve moving around this vast world or choose her comfortable life connected with her family in America.

We then took her home, and I asked her to give me an answer the next day. Yes, I was very harsh with her, and as I said, all this was intentional. My friend later severely criticized me for this harshness, but I explained to him that this was the true test of our relationship and that I needed to illuminate the path ahead and warn her of the many difficulties we would face if she decided to marry me unless the political situation changed.

After two or three days, I called her wanting to know where she stood. In those moments, she confirmed her commitment to me despite everything and said she would sacrifice for me. Later, in a letter she wrote, she affirmed that she had tied her fate to mine.

Everything changed then; I knew in those moments that her love for me was genuine. It then became imperative for me to reciprocate her sacrifice with the kind of beautiful response every girl expects from a romantic relationship.

I began to consider the correct path to take to ensure things would go smoothly without causing any harmful backlash for everyone. Careful and thoughtful planning was necessary, and so it was done.

After the issue with the Housing Bank of Oman was closed, relief came through the National Arab Bank in Saudi Arabia. My faith and certainty that relief comes from God and that if one door closes, trust in Him will open a thousand more has always guided my life—plan and trust!

The offer from the National Arab Bank in Saudi Arabia was much better than the one from the Omani bank. The contract was financially enticing and it would also resolve the issue of my hesitation regarding military service. I didn't hesitate for a moment to accept it.

I did not succumb to the financial temptation offered by the general manager at that time through my direct manager, who one day came to inspect the work and the employees. At that time, I was working in the Guarantees department, and he stopped by me by chance and asked my name. I told him, and he asked which department I worked in. I informed him, and then he asked how long I had been in this department. I told him it was my third month, and he asked if I could answer questions about guarantees. I confidently replied yes, as I knew the department by heart, especially since the department head was on maternity leave and I was managing the department's work.

The general manager started asking me questions, and I responded comprehensively, impressing him to the extent that he looked at me and smiled, clearly impressed.

My direct manager commented on that, saying, unfortunately, to Abu Khalid (who was the name of the general manager), "Younes is one of the young people who will be leaving to work with the Arab Bank in Saudi Arabia."

Abu Khalid jokingly said, "I will not allow this."

I saw an opportunity and said to the general manager, "May I bring to your attention some complaints that perhaps do not reach you?" He replied, "I'm all ears, go ahead."

This all took place within sight and hearing of all the managers and employees. Indeed, I conveyed to him all the complaints and grievances the employees had been suffering from in clear and bold language without hesitation. This led to the employees applauding me while the managers looked at me with disdain. However, I was unconcerned. More importantly, the general manager listened to every word I said, which increased his admiration for me.

He turned to my direct manager and said, "A person like Younes should not leave the bank. Study his situation and prevent him from traveling at any cost." All of this happened in front of everyone. He shook my hand firmly, saying, "We will meet again soon, God willing."

Indeed, afterward, my direct manager came to me and said that the general manager was very interested in me and offered me a 50 percent salary increase and formally recommended me to become the department head, with everything put in writing. However, my decision had already been made to go with the Arab Bank to Saudi Arabia because I was looking forward to a future life that included my beloved.

Here, too, while I was in the Guarantees department, an incident occurred that is worth telling. This department is one of the main departments and a primary source of income for the bank. It is responsible for issuing guarantees from company owners and merchants, especially those dealing with tenders, both governmental and otherwise. This made me interact with major clients or their representatives, and as I said, I became the driving force in the department.

One day, company owners or their representatives came to request a guarantee for a partial provisioning project for the Jordanian army. The guarantee exceeded half a million Jordanian dinars. They were seeking guarantees to participate and compete through us, and the winner of the project would be the one offering the lowest price that met the conditions agreed upon by the suppliers. I was busy preparing these guarantees according to the bank's system and approved by the army. The company representatives were waiting outside in the client lounge.

I was moving quickly, going between departments to finalize these guarantees when one of the employees called out to me saying that there was a phone call for me and someone wanted to speak with me. I went to answer the phone, and on the other line, someone said, "This is Adel," a well-known businessman in Jordan and one of the bank's major clients. He asked if I was Younes, to which I replied yes, quite surprised. After welcoming him, he asked how I was. I asked how I could assist him or if he wanted to speak to his representative, who was waiting with the other clients. He said he did not want to talk to them but to me and then asked if I was married.

I told him no, but I was planning to get engaged soon. He then said, "What do you say to someone who pays for your engagement and wedding expenses?" I was very surprised and asked him how that would be possible. He said all I had to do was tell him the lowest bid offered by the other suppliers, and he would pay me one thousand five hundred dinars or even, say, two thousand dinars.

I was utterly astonished by this bold request as I heard him repeat that this matter would remain between us and no one else would know. All I had to do was tell him the lowest number, and he would secure the money for me today, enough to get me married, not just engaged.

Thoughts raced through my mind about what this man was proposing. Two thousand dinars—that meant twenty months of my salary at that time, which did not even amount to a hundred dinars a month. This meant all my problems would be solved.

But at the same time, this meant that the man was buying me, and I would become a cheap commodity to be bought and sold. I was not and would never be like that in my life. I was raised by a nobleman who lived his entire life with honesty, integrity, and uprightness—all this while I was only partially hearing what the man on the other end of the line was saying.

I found myself responding, saying, "Mr. Adel, I think you are speaking to the wrong person. If you want to speak to my manager, I can transfer you to him, but I am not able to help you." I insisted on this, and then I finally said, "Mr. Adel, I am very busy and need to complete the rest of the guarantees. If you don't want me to transfer you to the manager, I will have to end the call. Goodbye." I heard him say, "You will regret this!"

But as soon as I hung up, I went straight to my manager and explained what had happened and what he had said. My manager, who was a paragon of virtue and integrity, cursed him and told me he was proud of me for resisting the temptation. He then added, "As you know, this person is one of the bank's most important clients, and we can't do anything about him. Now go back and continue your work as if nothing happened."

At the time, I was thinking about the steps and the plan that needed to be implemented to formally propose to the love of my life to her family. It was essential to ensure that I was ready both psychologically and financially at this sensitive stage of my life.

Especially since I will undoubtedly face severe difficulties in convincing Hajj Abu Rasmi, her father, to accept me; he is known in the neighborhood not only for being financially wealthy and owning the building where many people live, which faces us but also for his integrity and devoutness. He would not allow anyone to come close to his only pampered daughter, who is the main concern of him and her mother. How would they agree to a young man who lives alone without his family, about whom they know nothing?

This was the big question swirling in my mind: How to navigate all this?

The joy of my beloved was immense when I told her that I would formally propose to her. Isn't that every girl's dream in her relationship with a young man?

I told her I did not want to travel to Saudi Arabia before officially marrying her. I have nothing now, but we will rely on God, and I will work there, and God willing, we will succeed, and you will be patient with me until God makes it easier for us.

She, too, expressed her willingness to live with me on just bread and olives, as the popular saying goes. I told her we would make a plan: she would work from inside her home, keeping me informed about what was happening there, while I would work on executing the plan.

The first thing I thought about was that if I went directly to Hajj Abu Rasmi, he would surely reject my request, especially since I would be alone without my family.

I thought long and hard and said to myself that I would go to a man of his age who has a good relationship with him and let him take charge of the matter.

My first choice for this was someone who met all these criteria, none other than Hajj Abu Aahed, a seasoned trader in the sugar market, originally from the village of Attara, which lies just a few kilometers opposite our village.

I had a special relationship with this man, as he knew my father, may God have mercy on him, and knew my brothers, as well as many people from our village. He was a trusted figure known for his integrity and honesty, where people would place their trust.

He was the one I chose to approach to ask for my beloved's hand in marriage from her father. Especially since one day, I saw him coming out of the shop owned by Abu Aahed in the downtown sugar market. I asked Abu Aahed if he knew the man, and he confirmed that he was one of his closest friends and spoke very highly of him.

It also happened that Abu Aahed's daughter came to the bank for training by coincidence, and I trained her as if she were one of my sisters. She regularly told her father about this, which increased my standing with him.

One day, I decided to visit Hajj Abu Aahed, who welcomed me warmly and offered me a cup of coffee. At that moment, I felt I needed to bring up the subject, but I had to be careful not to be misunderstood and make him think I was referring to his daughter, who, as I mentioned, I knew well because she was training with us at the bank.

I decided to start with him as follows:

"Hajj, do you know Hajj Abu Rasmi well?"

He replied enthusiastically, "Yes, he is my friend and often comes to visit me" (and I had seen him coming out of his place once, as I mentioned earlier, and had asked him about him).

So I said to him, "Well if I asked you for a favor, could you grant it to me even if it's a bit difficult? I mean well, and you are known for doing good deeds." The man cheerfully responded, "Of course, tell me what you need."

I continued, "I am a neighbor to Hajj Abu Rasmi, and I want to ask for his young daughter's hand in marriage."

He looked at me surprised, then said, "Does Abu Rasmi have daughters? I know all his sons and daughters are in America."

I assured him that I had seen the girl, and when I asked about her, she was definitely Abu Rasmi's daughter.

He said, "I am fully prepared; you are as dear to me as my own children, and these are good people. Let me inquire about the matter and call him to arrange a visit to his home."

He began searching for Hajj Abu Rasmi's home phone number, and to his surprise, I quickly provided it for him. He looked at me puzzled, wondering how I knew it by heart. I quickly told him, "So you won't have trouble looking for it. I found it for you."

Indeed, just a few days later, when I met him again, he told me, "I have arranged with Hajj Abu Rasmi to visit him next Wednesday after the 'Isha prayer."

I asked Abu Aahed if he wanted me to bring people to accompany him, but he said, "No, I will go alone and see how things go, and God willing, all will be well."

On the agreed Wednesday, I waited on the balcony for the arrival of the classic Mercedes that Abu Aahed owned, just after the 'Isha prayer, as he had told me. When I spotted him approaching, I hurried down to where he was looking for a parking spot in front of Hajj Abu Rasmi's building. After greeting him, I showed him where I lived, and I believe that then he understood how I had seen the Hajj's daughter.

Hajj told me, "God willing, I will come to you after finishing at Abu Rasmi's, who has said he will come for a cup of coffee at your place."

Now he is with them, and there hangs my fate with my beloved, suspended between the two Hajjs (Abu Rasmi and Abu Aahed). Time passed slowly as I waited for the man to return with the result, counting moments over and over again. I paced back and forth on the roof and the balcony, my cigarette never extinguished during this time, wondering to myself whether he would agree or not and whether things might get confused for him. And why not? Abu Aahed also has young sons, and when he broaches the subject, he might think he wants her for his sons, not for me.

I kept thinking to myself, how am I acting on my own like this without consulting any family member? What will I say to them while they are living in

Palestine? Have I become man enough to take this step on my own at the age of 21?

Thoughts crowded my mind as I waited. What if Hajj Abu Rasmi refused? How could I blame him when I, a bank employee, earn a salary that doesn't exceed 100 dinars? And suppose they agreed, what would I do then?

And where would I find the expenses for the engagement?

It would cost a lot, and I only had a few dinars, some bank shares that I had bought while working in the stocks department, and a small number of dinars in my bank account at that time. But I said to myself, none of this matters. I don't know how I found the strength, determination, will, and trust in God. I said if they agree, God will facilitate matters. All this, and destiny is the master of judgments, playing the primary role in our lives.

While I was immersed in these thoughts, the young men living with me would come by: sometimes, they would encourage me, and at other times, they would joke about it. One of them, the eldest among us and from the same village, blamed me for not telling him to take on that role.

But I was in one valley, and they were in another. It was only a few minutes until the lights on the stairs turned on, and I saw Hajj Abu Aahed descending. I didn't wait for him to come down; instead, I hurried to meet him and invited him to come up, but he said the stairs were difficult, and I didn't even wait for him to finish.

I asked him, "What happened?"

He told me, "It required some clarification for Hajj Abu Rasmi about who you are, what you do, and about your future. As you know, these topics are what the conversation revolves around." Then he asked me about my family, and I told him they would come if there was an agreement. He promised well, saying he would ask her brothers in America about me.

He promised to get back to me within a week, God willing, and that he would visit them again after a week; God willing, all will be well.

That was where Hajj Abu Aahed's conversation ended, and I listened intently; then he got into his car, said goodbye, and left.

But these uncomfortable and new answers caused many questions to roam in my mind. However, I was certain that I would learn all the details of what happened from my beloved, who would surely relay to me the inside picture as it occurred.

Certainly, it was a surprise for Hajj Abu Rasmi to accept the idea when he called her and told her that Hajj Abu Aahed had come to request her hand for someone he knows well, who works at the Arab Bank and whose name is Youssef. Of course, he got my name wrong as well as my place of work. She almost corrected him to say Younes and the Jordan Kuwait Bank, my father, but she chose to respond shyly with her concealed smile and said, "Whatever you see fit, father, I have no objections." This answer raised question marks in his mind, especially since she had previously been opposed to the idea of marriage and the idea of moving to her brothers and sisters after being engaged to her sister's husband's brother.

However, he continued, muttering many words, among them that it was a strange, wondrous generation, and God protect us from this generation.

Of course, my joy was immense when I learned that Hajj Abu Aahed would take me with him on his next visit to introduce me to my new uncles. This was the first time after he convinced him and after Hajj Abu Rasmi, who trusts him greatly, asked him the most embarrassing question:

"If this young man, with his limited means, had proposed to his daughter, would he have agreed?"

Abu Aahed replied without hesitation, "Yes."

Then he confided in me secretly, as he later told me, that when I first spoke to him, he initially thought I meant his daughter, but I had been careful to clarify that point and explained that it was Abu Rasmi's daughter I meant. When Abu Rasmi heard this, he agreed to let me go with him on the next visit.

The visit was as good as it could be; I met my beloved face-to-face at her home in front of her mother and father. It was an indescribable feeling.

At that moment, I had to send word to my family to come, which I later learned hit them hard. How could I act this way without them knowing anything about the bride or her family, and considering that I was still young? They thought for a moment that one of the girls from Amman had bewitched me (as my mother, God rest her soul, told me later).

Nevertheless, my parents packed their bags and headed for the bridge. In those days, there was a ban on men leaving through the bridge, a punitive measure imposed by the occupation authorities on the people of Palestine if something happened in the occupied territories. This made them wait a long time on the bridge, and finally, they allowed my mother to pass but sent my father back where he came from.

My mother and another lady from our relatives who accompanied her came. Of course, my mother was very happy to see me, and so was I, especially since it had been more than three years since I had seen her since I left Palestine.

My mother asked me what was happening, and I explained the details to her, reassuring her about who these people were and how I had met them. All this while my mother knew very well how independent my decisions were.

We agreed that my mother and that lady would go to see the bride and meet her family. After my mother returned from there, I was very curious to hear how she found the bride. My mother said in her simple rural dialect, "God bless her; she is stunning, and her hair is beautiful, but she is a bit thin, and her cheeks are like stuffed zucchinis."

I laughed a lot at the comparison my mother used, and this is one of the things that make people laugh when I recount what my mother, may God rest her soul, said when she went to "review" the bride, as it is called in our colloquial dialect, meaning to see her.

After that, we quickly agreed to go for the marriage registration and prepare for the engagement because I did not have much time and was preparing to travel to Saudi Arabia in those days.

We went to the Sharia court, and my brother Mar'i had also arrived from Kuwait on his way to Palestine. When we began the marriage registration procedures, we hadn't yet agreed on the dowry or even discussed it.

When we stood before the judge, he asked about the requested dowry. My father-in-law, Hajj Abu Rasmi, was about to respond when I began by saying, " Father-in-law," but he said, "One Jordanian dinar." Then the judge asked about the deferred dowry, and my father-in-law said, "One thousand dinars." Then my brother said, "Make it two thousand dinars." I stood up and told the judge, "No, sir, make it three thousand dinars."

My father-in-law, the judge, and everyone present turned to me in great astonishment. I believe I made quite an impression in those moments.

From that moment, my father-in-law regarded me with respect and would even recount the story to everyone afterward, praising us and saying that we were of good stock and wouldn't compromise on our honor.

After writing our marriage contract and officially becoming engaged, nothing could stand in my way. I took my fiancée, my beloved, from the courthouse after asking everyone for permission and said that we would leave together, not with them. My family and father-in-law returned home for lunch.

I held my beloved's hand and wanted to fill the world with shouts that this was my beloved and fiancée. I felt like the world could no longer contain me.

I remember that day, the 13th of May. It rained heavily despite the generally warm spring weather, and all the rain fell within half an hour. It was highly unusual for it to rain in May, but I told my fiancée that the world was celebrating us, and this rain was God's blessing from the sky to the earth. We couldn't believe ourselves as we wandered the streets of Amman, where we used to be afraid of being seen even talking to each other, but now we told the whole world, "Look at us, people."

The news spread quickly. When we walked back home, we made the most of every minute, holding each other's hands while crossing the street in our neighborhood. To our great surprise, we saw all the residents come out to their balconies, waving at us and offering their blessings, sometimes smiling at us. In other words, we represented them with a love story that triumphed and translated their wishes into reality.

We remained like this, filled with joy until we reached my father-in-law 's house.

Now, things were getting serious.

I had to figure things out and muster everything I could to cover the costs of the engagement party, which we had agreed to hold on the rooftop of my father-in-law, Hajj Abu Rasmi's building, with my family in attendance.

First, I went to my friends, and they gave me everything they could, which was a loan of 400 dinars. Then, I worked on liquidating my assets, which were, as I mentioned, bank shares, and gathered the cash in my account, bringing the total to 250 dinars. That meant I now had 650 dinars altogether.

The most important step was my agreement with my beloved that her demands would remain reasonable because she knew the reality of the situation, and I was transparent with her about my steps.

This money had to be enough for our market trip to buy the engagement dress and jewelry, as well as other necessary purchases for the party.

One amusing incident was when we went to a bridal shop. The shopkeeper showcased various styles and prices of dresses, ranging from 15 dinars to 95 dinars. My father-in-law and mother immediately agreed on a dress worth 30 dinars, but when the bride tried it on, she didn't like it. Instead, she set her sights on the most expensive dress. She tried it on and loved it, and I liked it too. I told the man, "This is the one we want," for a price of 95 dinars.

At that point, my father-in-law and mother were furious, considering it wasteful. They argued that she would only wear it once. Somehow, I managed to convince them calmly, saying, "This is what the bride loved, and I love it too."

This was my first open defiance of the family's wishes, and they soon realized that we would do what we wanted rather than what they wanted. However, it was done in a way that did not incite their anger. Surely afterward, they muttered, "A generation that won't listen."

One of the amusing things I did to invite my colleagues from the bank was to ask one of my colleagues, who worked with me at the advertising company, to design an invitation card on a large cardboard panel. I then asked the bank messenger to pass it around to all the employees, who were many, so they could sign it to acknowledge the invitation. The board became a mural, with each person writing their blessing and comments in their own style.

Of course, everyone knew the date and venue of the engagement.

Our engagement was indeed a historic event for us, and I believe that the entire neighborhood came, either with or without an invitation. Almost all my colleagues from the bank, union, and company came, so much so that the rooftop couldn't accommodate the crowd despite its size.

They all came to see the lovers crowned, or as we were called, Qays and Layla. Everyone looked at us as if we were movie stars. It was truly a night to remember.

The period between our engagement on May 13 and my departure for Saudi Arabia on July 2 was honestly among the happiest moments in my life and my beloved's life. I say moments because the days passed quickly, like fleeting moments.

That's life: the beautiful moments pass quickly like the wind, while the sorrowful ones are stagnant like mountains, slow and immovable.

We obtained our license our marriage contract, to hold each other's hands and walk proudly in front of the world without fear because we were engaged. We made the most of that time, going out and returning, staying out late, and even visiting friends together. We seized every opportunity to be together. For the first time in my life, I celebrated my birthday at my father-in-law 's house. They brought cake and gifts, and some friends attended, making my 22nd birthday a special day.

Visiting my father-in-law 's house daily became a major part of my day. My mother-in-law refused to let anyone eat a meal without my presence. She would even stand on the rooftop opposite my room and call out to me. It was a remarkable twist that this stranger had now become one of them.

My fiancée and I would stay up late on the rooftop of the building, sometimes walking under the moonlight, watching its shape, or counting the stars as if we wanted time to stand still or didn't want the dawn to come. I would often slip back to my room while she quietly sneaked into hers, pretending to be asleep after hearing the call to the dawn prayer. At that point, we would hear my father-in-law starting to wake up for prayer.

Our Wedding Day in 1983

Chapter 5 - Saudi Arabia

We did not wake from this long dream until the travel bell rang, and I began preparing for it. My resignation from the bank also took effect after I obtained a visa to Saudi Arabia and booked my travel date for 2/7. That was when the countdown began for our joy and beautiful dream, wondering how we would part and live with each of us in a different country.

But our hope for the future strengthens us to start planning how our small house will look, where it will be, our children in the future, God willing, their names, and how this family will be under one roof.

I started preparing for the fourth migration of my life and quickly began to get rid of things I was accustomed to, whether it was my living room or my small furniture and some necessities I used to consider essential. However, with this migration, I do not know how long I will stay, how long it will last, or if I will return again.

All this ended with my purchase of the travel ticket, at which point my beloved realized that what was happening before her was real and that I would travel. She may have secretly wished that something would happen to cancel this trip because we had truly gotten used to each other. I had become everything to her, as she was everything to me; we were one soul. How could one imagine separating a soul from itself?

But the reality was that we didn't have many options, and the travel day, 2/7, arrived.

We got into the taxi heading to Marka Airport, the only airport connecting Jordan with the rest of the world, after a friend and his wife came along with us. I sat next to my fiancée, who couldn't stop crying continuously. I showed composure and tried my best to comfort her, talking to her about the future to lighten the burden of those heavy moments, even though I held her hand between mine, and she leaned her head on my shoulder, which was soaked with her streaming tears.

The situation was even more painful when she almost collapsed as she bid me farewell at the last checkpoint they were allowed to reach. She kept looking at me with intense sadness, tears streaming from her eyes profusely. Despite the firmness I tried to display on my face, I couldn't hold myself together. I kissed every part of her in farewell—her face, lips, and forehead. Despite all this, I let go of her hand and tried to hide a tear that rolled down my cheek that I couldn't prevent.

I kept waving my hand to her until I disappeared into the crowd and could no longer see her. Yes, this was a new experience for me, and here I was, about to board a plane for the first time in my life. It would take me to Dhahran Airport in the Eastern Province of Saudi Arabia after the bank had determined my destination.

I left a part of my soul and heart there. As the plane moved on the runway, I looked out the window, hoping to catch a glimpse of something. A girl sitting next to me had seen part of what happened at the airport. She quickly asked me if she was my wife. I told her she was my fiancée and the love of my heart. Then the girl said she would visit her sister, whose husband worked as a manager for the Olayan company, one of the largest companies in Saudi Arabia. I asked her how long she would stay, and she said three weeks. Immediately, an idea sparked in my head, and I asked her if she could take a gift to my fiancée in Amman when she returned. She gladly agreed and gave me her phone numbers, and so it was arranged.

My friend and his wife didn't let my fiancée go home alone in that state. They invited her to go with them, where they had a meal together and calmed her down before taking her to their house.

The plane flew for only about two and a half hours, which is the direct distance between Amman and Dhahran Airport. The pilot announced that we should fasten our seatbelts in preparation for landing.

This was my first time in Saudi Arabia and my fourth migration. When the plane doors opened, we thought Hell had opened its doors as extremely hot air mixed with high humidity hit our faces. I wondered what this was and why the weather was like that. Could it have been the plane's engines? No way this is the actual climate! One of the passengers on the bus heading into the airport smirkingly used this moment to foretell what's to come with a sarcastic "welcome to Saudi Arabia."

I started sweating profusely, new to all this, so I took off my suit jacket. After completing the procedures, I bid farewell to the girl who had stayed with me during this time since she experienced visiting her sister. I exited the reception area, where people were waiting for arrivals, and I saw someone holding a cardboard sign with my name on it. I signaled to him, and several other people on the same flight were coming to the bank. When we followed that man, who later turned out to be an employee, out of the airport, he went to get the car while I loosened my tie and unbuttoned my shirt, trying to relieve the suffocation I felt.

The employee, who introduced himself and mentioned that it was his tenth year at the bank, took us to the bank's accommodations, where a group of young men from Amman were also staying, and we began to get to know them.

Thus began a new phase in my life that lasted more than five years—the duration of my stay in Saudi Arabia.

Life in Saudi Arabia

Beginnings are often not easy, but with clarity of vision due to age and the accumulation of experience, those beginnings become possible and feasible for starting life anew.

The stifling weather, the extreme heat, and the high humidity are only known to those who have lived in Saudi Arabia during the summer months. These conditions were entirely new to me and typically peaked in July. However, our consolation was that the central air conditioning in the bank's housing alleviated the intensity of this inferno.

The next day, the new guys and I went to the bank with one of the employees. I noticed that the bank had created a designated area for housing unmarried young men (bachelors) and that there were also special buildings nearby for those who were married, coming from various countries and occupying different positions in the bank.

The first day was spent getting to know these people, and I found that some of them had been living and working there for decades. I observed that most of the senior positions in the bank were held by employees of Palestinian origin. This phenomenon can be explained by the fact that the Arab National Bank was an essential part of the Arab Bank, which the late Shoman founded in Jerusalem in the 1930s. Later, it was Saudi-ized, with Saudi Arabia acquiring 60 percent of its capital, while 40 percent remained with the Arab Bank. The management continued to be in their hands, so most of the bank's managing employees were from Jordan, most of them of Palestinian origin.

And so we mingled with these employees and immersed ourselves in the new work, which, over time, we began to master, adhering to the bank's internal regulations. We even started to adapt to the hot and humid external weather.

As time went on, we noticed the deep-rooted selfishness and caution that prevailed in interactions between bank employees, especially from the older employees towards the new ones. This atmosphere was not present among the employees of the Jordan Kuwait Bank in Amman, to the point that one day, I became very frustrated. I stood up and addressed the employees, particularly the older ones, saying, "Don't be afraid. We did not come here to take your jobs. Everyone has their position, and we came to work just like you."

My words were well received by the new employees on whose behalf I spoke, and it caught the attention of the older employees, making them realize that someone had a strong voice and wasn't afraid to speak up. After that, the perception of me changed among all the employees.

I deeply missed my beloved, who was far away in Amman. It is worth noting that the intense longing for family and the place they came from led many employees to decide to return to their original homes because they couldn't adapt here.

I didn't forget the promise of the girl who sat next to me on the plane and told me she would travel back to Amman in two days. I counted the hours and went to the finest perfume shops in Khobar, where I bought a famous French perfume named First, a black shirt, and a red skirt, which I chose and wrapped in a wonderful gift for my beloved in Amman.

As for the money, I borrowed it from a colleague who received his monthly salary before me, as I hadn't received mine yet. I went to the workplace of her sister's husband and left it there, so they delivered it to her as I had arranged, with the help of a colleague who knew the area well. I later learned she was extremely happy when she received it in Amman.

The days and months passed heavily at the beginning of this exile, even though I had formed a group of friends whose thoughts aligned with mine. Most of us lived together in what was known as the bachelor housing. We got to know each other and our social circumstances, some being married, some engaged, and others in romantic relationships. We killed time by talking about our ambitions and hopes for the future, often strolling through markets together to pass the time.

One day, one of them suggested that since we had all come here to save some money and move forward in our lives, why not rent a house outside the bank's housing? We were five young men and could save a whole month's salary by doing so because the bank either provided us housing or gave us a housing allowance, which was more beneficial for us.

We decided to do that and lived in a suburb of Khobar called "Thuqbah," which means "water spring" in the local language. We only felt embarrassed about pronouncing the area's name when others asked where we lived, as it didn't sound appealing in our local dialect. However, it was normal for the Saudis, and we quickly adapted to the new housing in the heart of the commercial area.

We were a curious mix of Jordanians and Palestinians, Muslims and Christians. I was a Muslim Palestinian (from Ramallah), Issam was a Christian Palestinian (from Tulkarm), Zaki was a Christian Palestinian (from Jaffa), Adel was a Christian Jordanian (from Karak), and Jamal was a Muslim Jordanian (from Madaba).

In our new home, we divided our tasks and responsibilities so everyone knew their duties. I was assigned or rather chose, the external shopping duties because I excelled in purchasing and negotiating.

We shared the rooms: Issam and I stayed in the small room, always clean and tidy, with no smoking allowed, even though we both smoked. The large room, however, was characterized by extreme chaos, and smoking was an essential part of its atmosphere, as all three of them smoked there, in addition to us.

What alleviated my constant longing for my beloved were the letters we exchanged, which became well-known. The bank's "mu'aqqib" (the employee responsible for handling transactions outside the bank) and the Saudi employee who managed government transactions would call my name from the door before entering the bank, saying, "Younes, your relief has arrived."

Our need to acquire a car increased after relying on public transportation, but before getting a car, we needed to obtain driving licenses. We trained a little as a friend from outside the housing came and gave us lessons in his car until we mastered the basics of driving. Then we went to the Dammam area and took the driving test. Issam and I passed on the first attempt, while the others did not.

Thus, I obtained my first driver's license. It didn't take long before Issam bought a Volkswagen, which we called "the Beetle" in our local language, and it became our daily means of transportation to work.

My financial situation improved significantly, and I was able to repay all the money I had borrowed from friends for the engagement arrangements in Amman. I even started saving from my good salary. We used to go together and meet friends in entertainment places, most notably the famous Half Moon Beach in Khobar, especially on Fridays when it was crowded with people.

I was always looking forward to buying a car, to help me travel to Amman the following summer, a year after my arrival, to marry my beloved. By then, I would have saved money and bought a car that would take us everywhere.

Not long after, I saw one of the bank's Lebanese clients by chance when he came to the bank and mentioned that his Trans Am, an American sports car, was for sale. It was a convertible with a powerful engine that made a thrilling roar. I didn't hesitate much and didn't consider my lack of experience or that it might be too early for me to drive such a car. After consulting my close friends, who all encouraged me as if they wanted to see one of us own it and believed that I was the only one with the courage to do something extraordinary, I decided to buy it.

We went to a mechanic friend we had met, who inspected the car and told me it was in good condition. I agreed with the Lebanese owner to pay him 8,000 riyals for the car. I had 5,000 riyals on hand and arranged to pay the remaining amount at the end of the month.

Yes, I was ecstatic with the car, feeling its immense power and feeling like the king of the road as I drove it through the streets. Everyone wanted me to let them drive it, even if just for a little while. It was not an ordinary car; it was exceptional in every way, and most importantly, it was the first car I ever owned.

Afterward, my trips became more frequent, and I never hesitated to boast about driving this car on every occasion. My fiancée was also thrilled when I described it to her, and we dreamed of driving it together through the streets of Amman the following summer.

This dream didn't last long. Less than a month after buying the car, and after I had paid off the remaining balance, we agreed with some friends to meet at Half Moon Beach on our Friday holiday. After filling the car with fuel, which was very cheap in Saudi Arabia, I set off in the morning. According to the plan, everyone was supposed to come in their cars.

The coastal road in Khobar, which we called the highway, was a flat, wide road surrounded by thick sand on one side and the sea on the other. Cars usually drive very fast on it, especially in Saudi Arabia, which is known for high-speed driving on roads. This road was perfect for testing my new car. After mechanically removing the convertible roof and turning up the music, I set off to fulfill that childhood dream of driving my car at high speed.

I was lost in thought and began singing along to the voice of Abdel Halim coming from the car's tape recorder as the car sped along the highway. Suddenly, I felt something wrong with the car. At that moment, I didn't know the nature of the problem, but I noticed the car was traveling at 120 km/h and veering to one side. Glancing in the rearview mirror, I saw one of the tires had detached and was heading toward the desert.

I saw the car veer sharply toward the desert in those critical moments. With an instinctive movement, I adjusted the steering wheel in the opposite direction but couldn't control the car, which swerved onto the median strip in the middle of the road.

For a moment, I thought that if I ended up on the opposite side of the road, I would collide with oncoming traffic at high speeds, and I didn't think I would survive. I turned the steering wheel with all my might once more.

Then, I lost consciousness and didn't realize what happened until a few minutes later. When I looked around, I saw the car had hit an electric pole in the middle of the median, breaking it in half. The pole fell to the ground beside the car, but fortunately, it didn't touch the vehicle.

As I regained consciousness from the shock, I found people gathered around me. I tried to open the door to get out, but it was damaged and wouldn't open. I jumped out through the window or the sunroof, then noticed fuel leaking from the gas tank onto the ground. I told the people to move away, fearing that a spark from the pole might cause the car to explode.

Thankfully, nothing like that happened. At that moment, one of my friends, who had arrived earlier and wondered why I was late, came to check on me and found me amidst all this.

Between confusion and shock, we decided to go to the bank manager's house to inform him of what happened before going to the police station. It was a Friday, a public holiday, and despite our long wait, the police didn't arrive at the scene.

After the manager scolded me for buying such a car, he went to the bank to arrange a bail for me. We went with him to the police station, where they took my information and accepted the bail, with the condition that I return the next day to follow up.

The next day, the tow truck removed the damaged car from the accident site, along with the short-lived dream and the disappointment that coursed through every cell in my body. Upon inspection, it was found that the car's axle, which connects the rear wheels, was broken and welded. This was why the Lebanese owner sold the car, and we couldn't detect this issue when we bought it, not even the mechanic who inspected it.

The disappointment didn't end with the 8,000 riyals I paid for the car. It was compounded by the cost of the broken electric pole, which was 12,000 riyals. My bank colleagues generously covered this cost for me.

This harsh lesson was a significant setback, bringing me back to square one regarding morale and finances. This pivotal accident made me rethink many things, starting with believing that lasting happiness is forbidden for someone like me. I survived death by a miracle, thanks to God's grace.

If a spark from the fallen electric pole had ignited the fuel leaking from the car, which was damaged on the driver's side, the car would have exploded, especially since I had lost consciousness for a few seconds before waking up and getting out through the window.

As I said, this accident didn't only reset me financially but also emotionally as I read the reproachful looks in the eyes of the employees who had donated to help me, some of whom might have done so reluctantly to save me from paying for the pole the municipality forced us to cover.

After returning to work, things proceeded slowly and monotonously. I couldn't resist the idea of getting a new car, so I offered to buy a colleague's old car, paying in simple monthly installments. This car needed many repairs, which my Palestinian mechanic friend, who had emigrated from Lebanon and owned a garage, promised to fix for me at a pace I could afford. I decided to use it until my situation improved, especially since its price was very tempting.

I left the car with my mechanic friend, who began the repairs. This situation encouraged my friend Issam, who shared a room with me, to ask if we could take his old Beetle to the same garage for repairs, as it needed extensive work.

We drove through Khobar's streets to the garage. Issam was driving another housemate's car while I drove his Beetle. The plan was to leave Issam's car at the garage and return to the other car.

As I remember looking in the rearview mirror, Issam followed me in the other car. After that, I didn't remember anything until I woke up in the hospital four days later.

I woke up as if from a long dream. It felt like I was coming back from death, a feeling only those who have experienced it or have been unconscious for four days can understand. When I awoke from a deep sleep, lying on a white hospital bed, I was in a state between consciousness and unconsciousness. I noticed a plastic bracelet around my wrist with my name on it. Yes, it was my name. I wondered why I was there.

I tried to get up but found my other hand tied to a metal pole with a glucose bag hanging from it. Looking out the window, I realized I was on the hospital's fifth floor.

Again, I wondered what had brought me to the hospital. I didn't come out of this confusion until some nurses entered, telling me to stay in bed. Then, I felt my chest was bandaged with white gauze. I tried to ask them what had happened, but they just said, "Accident."

Still in shock, a group of young Saudi men entered the room, greeting me and saying, "Thank God for your safety, Brother Younes. You're awake." I asked them, "Excuse me, why am I here? Who are you?"

They said, "Don't you remember the accident? We rescued you." I asked, "What accident?" pointing to the Half Moon Beach accident. They said, "What are you talking about?"

The accident with the small car, when your friend was with you, and the yellow bus driven by the Pakistani hit you...

But don't worry, your rights won't be lost because the Pakistani is in jail.

I kept trying to remember what they said about that accident and what happened. To this day, more than thirty years later, I still can't remember.

Then Issam came with a group of colleagues after the bank closed to visit me. Issam told me what happened: We were following each other on our way to the garage, and you were driving in front of me on one of the streets when a large yellow bus driven by a Pakistani person didn't stop at a stop sign and kept driving, crashing forcefully into the car you were driving. The impact was so strong that it carried the car a long distance, crushing it over your head. The bus wasn't affected because it was armored. We tried hard to get you out, and then some Saudi youths came and helped me pull you out from the other side.

Two-thirds of the car on the driver's side was destroyed. After ensuring you were alive, we brought you in their car to the hospital, where you were admitted to the intensive care unit because you were unconscious and had seven broken ribs. But in the end, God was merciful, and here you are now.

Issam was telling me what happened, and I felt like I was living in a movie, one of its protagonists, without knowing it.

I stayed in the hospital for a week, cut off from my fiancée, who hadn't heard any news from me. I had asked that no one tell her anything if she called, but she became frantic, calling the bank. Every time, someone told her something different until one of my friends told her I had a minor accident, was in the hospital, and would be discharged the next day.

She didn't calm down until I spoke to her on the day I was discharged, reassuring her that I was still alive.

I should mention that the Pakistani driver stayed in jail the entire time I was in the hospital. After I was discharged, his family came to the bank. The bank manager called me and asked what I intended to do. I asked for his guidance, and he said, "It's a shame; he's an expatriate like you. Forgive him and leave it to God. It's enough that God saved you from this terrible accident." So I did.

The hospital gave me an additional week of rest to allow my wounds to heal. During this time, I stayed at home and feared cars, driving, and roads.

One day during my leave, my friends Hussam and Mohammad (a Syrian) visited me to convince me to break free from the prison I had put myself in. They said I needed to go out and overcome the fear that had taken hold of me.

Finally, I agreed to go to the nearby beach, with Mohammad driving my car, which I had bought after it was repaired. This was our first outing.

We set off, and when we reached the beach, we parked the car right on the shore. We sat and talked, having brought some snacks like nuts. Hussam and Mohammad joked with me, asking when I would start driving again, and I told them I didn't think it would be anytime soon.

Mohammad insisted that I at least sit behind the wheel. I agreed, and we continued talking. It wasn't even five minutes before something extraordinary happened.

A Saudi driver, driving a small truck loaded with sheep and goats, was on the main road. For some reason, he veered off the main road, entered the service road, headed towards the beach, and drove straight towards us. He crashed his small truck into the driver's seat where I was sitting in my car.

All this happened in seconds. I lost consciousness for a few moments after the deafening sound. We were all in shock, especially me and my friends. The main road, the side road, and the entire sandy beach were completely empty, with no cars or people around.

The car's windshield shattered into our faces, and we felt the front of the car and the door smash. The sheep flew out of the man's truck as we looked at each other, unable to believe what was happening.

When the police arrived, the officer was puzzled by our story. He asked the Saudi driver how it happened and how he left both roads and the beach to crash into our car. The man couldn't explain, only saying that his truck was headed towards my car, and he couldn't stop it.

At that moment, I thought something was wrong with me. These bizarre accidents must have another explanation. The police, of course, ordered the Saudi driver to pay for the repairs to my car later.

That night, on a friend's advice, I called my father-in-law, Haj Abu Rasmi (may he rest in peace), in Jordan. I asked him to buy and slaughter two sheep and distribute the meat to the poor as a sacrifice for me. And that's what he did.

After that, my situation improved significantly.

Our friend Mohammad from Syria wanted to return home permanently to settle in Syria. He offered to take over his lease and buy all the furniture and contents of the house. We agreed I would pay half the price in cash and the rest in monthly installments.

This was months later after my life had returned to normal.

So, I moved from the bachelor's house to my own house, which had an attached outside room where our friend Hussam lived, while Mohammad lived there. The situation remained the same.

Summer began, and we started preparing to drive to Amman so I could get married. However, I could only get a week off from the bank.

Those accidents and buying the house had financially drained me. But my commitment to my fiancée was my top priority: to be gone for a year and return to get married.

I took out a loan from the bank, and we agreed to cooperate on many things to complete this marriage and come together under one roof.

More than thirty years have passed since that day, which I considered part of this scattered big dream whose pieces could not be gathered. That dream stayed with me as I watched the days slowly pass until our departure from Khobar, Saudi Arabia, to Amman.

I and a group of friends who lived together in the housing had decided to travel together to Amman. We were all bachelors except for one who had a wife and children. I was the youngest, having just turned 23 a few days before.

Our joy was indescribable as we got into the car. We could hardly believe ourselves as the car drove on the highways, and we shared stories about what each of us planned to do during this short vacation, which barely totaled two weeks after the bank agreed to grant me an additional week's leave.

But I knew exactly what I was going to do: I was going to marry the love of my heart. Despite the few coins in my pocket, most of which was borrowed from the bank, despite the many accidents I had experienced, and despite paying off all the debts incurred after the engagement and before coming to Saudi Arabia, which were a priority on my financial agenda, and despite buying the house.

All this was driven by our determination to come together under one roof and piece together this big scattered dream to form the foundation upon which we would build this small family.

After a journey lasting more than 18 hours, covering a difficult road of over 1400 kilometers surrounded by a desolate desert and crowded borders, we finally reached Amman.

Yes, we arrived, and my heartbeats increased as we headed towards Al-Ashrafieh. As the car drove at sunset on the same street, we used to walk together, and where we used to live, I couldn't help but notice how tall the hills of Amman seemed.

The distinctive smells of Amman's neighborhoods, the scent of preparing dinner and frying falafel, greeted me once again after a year of absence. What about the love of my heart, whom I had been away from for a year? How would I see her now, and had she changed? These questions crowded my mind, racing with my heartbeat as I climbed the many steps leading to my father-in-law Haj Abu Rasmi's house.

This man, whom I loved and always regarded as a father figure, may he rest in peace. I was practically jumping up the steps, even with the suitcase and items I had carried from the car.

Finally, I rang the bell, waiting until the door opened and my father-in-law and mother-in-law came out.

And finally, I caught a glimpse of the face I had missed every minute. I completely forgot myself and rushed to hug and kiss my fiancée before greeting these kind people. Suddenly, I realized the situation, and that moment left a mark on my relationship with them, especially with my late mother-in-law.

I could hardly believe I was sitting among them, feeling such longing after a year of absence, especially after the dinner my mother-in-law had prepared for us. I stared at this scene and these people.

And here she was, my beloved, sitting beside me, not just a voice on the phone as it had been for so long. After waking up to the reality that I was truly in

Amman, we began the preparations with the help of some relatives and friends for our wedding day, one of the most important days of our lives.

We booked a hall in Jabal Al-Hussein, then reserved a suite at the San Rock Hotel, the most famous hotel in Amman then, to make our first night together something we would remember for a lifetime. Despite the many challenges, I sometimes skipped over some details, but my goal was clear and specific: to be with my beloved on our wedding day.

Sometimes, skipping over details made family and friends criticize me, but honestly, I didn't pay attention to any of that. I told them these were traditions; the important thing was to achieve the goal we had worked on together for so long.

I can't describe my feelings as we finally left my father-in-law 's house in the Mercedes, "the Loop," as we called it, which a friend had decorated with flowers. We sat together in the back seat, driving through the streets of Amman, but this time as newlyweds, until we reached the hall where all our friends and family were waiting for us. That night, which we had long dreamed of, was coming true. We stood on the stage (the place designated for the bride and groom), and our friends, family, and loved ones came to greet and congratulate us.

Afterward, we got into the car to spend the night at the San Rock Hotel, where we would spend our first days as a married couple.

My feelings at that moment made me forget everything else, even the family and friends we left behind at the wedding. I wanted everyone to forget us for the coming days. All I remembered was that we were married, and those who celebrated with us were now singing and cheering for us, wanting us to be united under one roof.

And now, the ceiling of this suite in this hotel would witness our night, marking the peak of all this effort and the journey through countless challenges.

We wanted time to stop that night. We wanted the clock's ticking to cease, for the world to forget us, and for us to step out of its timeline. We wanted this dream to remain suspended in the sky, not to wake up from it even the next morning. We wanted nothing to disturb our peace in the coming days, not even the customs that dictate the lives of newlyweds in our society. We didn't want to see anyone, and we didn't want anyone to see us. We wanted to rebel against these traditions.

But time and the ticking clock raced on relentlessly, ignoring our desires. We had to wake from our beautiful dream, mistakenly believing it would never end. I had to prepare to return to Saudi Arabia, leaving my beloved, my now-wife, alone.

Despite overcoming some challenges in extending my military service booklet, I managed to travel with the guys after spending a few days as a husband and wife. Now, I could bring her to Saudi Arabia, to the marital home I had prepared for her. Why not? I could take her to the ends of the earth, and no one would blame me. This hope drove me back.

We set off, returning to our city of Khobar in Saudi Arabia, crossing deserts and rough roads. But now, all my friends' faces were sad. We were leaving loved ones behind as if Amman had taken our happiness before allowing us to return. We didn't talk much; we were lost in thoughts of what we had left behind. This somber mood stayed with us until we reached our city.

Then, we immersed ourselves in work again, returning to letters and phone calls. It wasn't long before the assistant bank manager, who had been appointed as the manager of the new branch the bank had established on King Abdul Aziz Street, surprised me by saying, "Younes, I have chosen you to join me in the new branch because I have always admired your work."

His words warmed my heart, and he added, "I have chosen you to be the bank's treasurer in the new branch." Surprised, I replied, "What? I don't know anything about this position. I've worked in all departments, but I've never handled cash. I don't think I'm suitable for this job."

I asked, "Isn't this position reserved for Saudis and requires sponsorship and experience?"

The man smiled and said, "Don't worry about all that. I'll handle the sponsorship and management with the administration. As for experience, you are smart and will pick it up quickly. Just train in this branch for a week, and I'm confident you'll learn everything. I also requested a 35% salary increase for you as an allowance."

Of course, I was thrilled with this trust and the salary increase, especially after returning from Amman, having spent every penny I had. I thanked the man who showed me such respect and appreciation by making me the first person he chose for the new branch staff. A few days later, we transferred to the new King Abdul Aziz Street branch.

Working in this branch marked a new beginning for me.

I had started the process of obtaining a visit visa for my wife, who was coming to Saudi Arabia for the first time. I had applied for a residence permit for her, which usually takes time. I preferred to bring her for an initial visit of one month, especially since her relationship with her mother had taken a new turn. Perhaps it was a mother's selfishness, especially regarding her only child, who is her whole world.

My wife focused on talking about me and preparing for the trip. She began packing her bags for the trip to join me, which made her mother very sad. Her only daughter, her entire world, was not only leaving but was also preoccupied with someone else who had taken all her thoughts and time.

I was also overjoyed as I went to meet her at Dhahran Airport. I had prepared the house and the car for her. We couldn't believe it as we drove through the streets of Khobar on our way home from the airport, accompanied by some colleagues and their wives who had also come to greet us.

We held hands throughout the journey, singing songs by Warda Al-Jazairia as if the world couldn't contain our happiness.

The joy was immense when my wife took her first steps into our marital home, which I had prepared well. I placed flowers everywhere and scented every corner. I even stocked the fridge with all kinds of food.

Interestingly, we stayed in the house for over 17 days during my leave. If it weren't for my need to go to work, I would have stayed at home. Even when I went to work, I couldn't believe that my beloved would be the one to open the door for me.

I informed our friends that we were on our honeymoon and wouldn't receive any visitors despite their insistence on coming to congratulate us. The first month of her visit passed, and we continued living the dream until it was time to bid my beloved goodbye as she returned to Amman after her first month's visit.

Before she left, I immediately started the process for her next visit, so she spent a month in Amman and a month in Khobar.

Working at the Arab National Bank in Khobar, Saudi Arabia

Lara & Leana

This was no ordinary visit to the famous Egyptian doctor. When my wife complained of dizziness, nausea, and the urge to vomit three months into our marriage, we decided to consult a gynecologist to ensure that what she was experiencing was not something serious.

The surprise came when the doctor emerged from the examination room with a broad smile and said to me in the Egyptian dialect, "Congratulations, sir, your wife is pregnant!!!" What?

The surprise was wonderful in every way. I hugged my wife and started kissing her after she came out of the examination room, having heard what the doctor said. I told her, "Congratulations, my love, for this news."

We found ourselves heading to the Corniche in Khobar at that moment, where the weather and sky were perfect. We walked along the beach, with the gentle waves breaking at our feet, as I held her hand, unable to believe the wonderful news. I asked myself, isn't the next step in marriage for the wife to become pregnant? This is the natural check-up that couples eagerly await; to pass, it means we are normal people capable of having children and there is harmony in this relationship. These are all blessings from God, granted to whom He wills.

I cannot describe the feelings that overwhelmed us at that moment. It was a mixture of manliness, joy, and tears, blending into the single outcome that we would be parents.

This feeling was enough to give us wings to fly. Even as we ate something we found being sold on the beach, we still stared at the beautiful sea that harmonized with our emotions and this beautiful clear night.

We started guessing the baby's gender, wondering if it would be Firas,

Lara, or perhaps both. We did not realize how late it had become and that we needed to return to our small home.

I then hugged my wife and said, "Let's go home," and we slept that night dreaming like birds after spending a night that was truly one of the most beautiful nights.

And how could it not be? This is the translation of the dream we built. Isn't this the beginning of the family we have longed for since a long time ago?

The days of pregnancy did not pass easily. The sudden change in my wife's movements and behaviors was surprising and unexpected. I did not know at the time that the cause of all this was the pregnancy, to the point where I was becoming frustrated with some of the new habits and behaviors my wife had adopted. For example, she insists on going to a falafel restaurant we used to pass by daily.

I wondered what had happened and why she didn't want to eat anything unless we passed by this place so I could buy her a falafel sandwich. Her irritability continued, which was not a characteristic of my wife, as did her insistence on the falafel. It wasn't until one of the experienced employees explained to me that this was part of the nature of pregnancy and that a woman goes through a sensitive and critical phase with changes in her physical and psychological makeup that I understood what was going on. This understanding helped me to accept it as a reality that began to ease as the months of pregnancy progressed.

We agreed, three months before the due date, that my wife would travel to Amman to stay with her mother and to give birth at her family's home so her mother could take care of her and the upcoming baby. She was the only one who could care for her and the baby, especially since I would be helpless in this strange city, unable to do anything for her.

Saudi Arabia

That phone call I received from Kuwait from my older brother and many relatives who lived there was not just an ordinary call. They informed me of my father's death.

The news hit me like a thunderbolt. I couldn't hold back my tears when they told me the news, and I didn't even realize I had hung up on them. It was evening in the city of Khobar, Saudi Arabia, on the shores of the Arabian Gulf. I was alone at home and didn't notice myself until a wave of sobbing and crying overtook me for an unknown period.

I don't know why I felt such intense orphanhood at that moment. I was sad because he died without me seeing him or bidding him farewell, and without being able to tell him, "Forgive me, father, for the trouble I caused you when I was young," and without him seeing that I had begun to blossom in this life or seeing his grandchild or the grandchild on the way, as my wife was expecting.

It had been five years since I last saw that unique, faithful man in this world. I remembered those moments when he tried to strengthen me when I thought the Jews had come to arrest me, and he would say, "Trust in God, my son. Nothing will happen to us except what God has written for us."

He died a faithful, righteous death that does not happen often. I later learned that he died on Eid day during the Asr prayer. He went with the group he always prayed with and led them in prayer. That day, a friend who had been ill but had recovered came, and my father invited him to lead the prayer as a thanks to God for his recovery. They lined up behind this man for the Asr prayer. When everyone finished the prayer, my father remained in prostration and did not lift his head.

The man beside him, a relative of ours, tapped him on the shoulder and said, "Hajj, Hajj!" After that, my father leaned to his side, and his soul ascended to its Creator in the purest place where a servant is in direct contact with his

Creator.

That evening, I had an appointment with a friend to go out together. When I didn't call or show up, he called me and recognized from the tone of my voice that I was not holding myself together. He came immediately and informed the other friends, who began to arrive to console me and support me in that ordeal.

I lost touch with my wife for a while and couldn't contact her or even answer her calls when she tried to reach me. They would tell her I was out of the bank as I had instructed the switchboard operator.

I don't know why I was afraid that my wife would detect my deep sorrow in my voice. She is perceptive and can sense my feelings from the first word and my voice tremors. I couldn't pretend around her, especially in her final days of pregnancy. She didn't need the bad news affecting her and the baby.

About two weeks passed, and my wife was nearly going mad, wondering why she hadn't received a proper answer other than "I'm fine" and what I was hiding from her. I couldn't avoid it much longer, so I answered the phone at home one night. She was very angry about my absence.

I stayed silent and didn't defend myself. But I couldn't hold back my tears, breaking down as if she suddenly reminded me of what had happened. She was stunned on the other end of the line.

Then she asked what had happened, and I told her. I noticed her gradual breakdown in her voice, and this was what I had feared. I felt a pang of guilt as she told me she needed to see the doctor immediately. That was the last thing I heard from her.

My father-in-law took her directly to Al-Khalidi Hospital in Amman, where we were blessed with our first daughter, Lara. Yes, Lara came into the world, thank God, thank God.

I didn't feel reassured until I heard my wife's voice first, congratulating her on her safety. I asked to hear my daughter Lara's voice after she brought the phone close to her, and Lara started crying.

Alongside my baby daughter's cries, I heard my father-in-law's laughter as he received congratulations and distributed sweets to everyone around him. It felt like a new sun had risen on our little family.

I gathered my strength and awaited the bank's approval for leave, no matter how short, so I could travel to Amman and see my newborn daughter, Lara. Yes, I was ready at that moment to give up many things just to see my daughter, like matters related to military service and my situation in the West Bank, which hadn't yet been resolved. But I was confident that every issue could be solved, especially in Jordan.

After the bank approved my leave, I gathered my strength and arranged to travel with a friend. Now, my longing was not only for my wife but also for my new daughter. Even as we drove along the desert road, the images floated before me.

I became a father for the first time after becoming a husband. After the long journey with my friend, each of us driving his car, and the hardships at the border crossing, we finally reached Amman safely.

No words describe the feeling of holding and seeing my daughter for the first time. I left everything behind and looked neither right nor left except at the newborn, smiling at me like an angel, as if she recognized me before hugging my wife and congratulating her on her safety.

We had a wonderful vacation in every sense, especially since my mother had come from Palestine and stayed with us throughout the holiday. I remember one of the things we did together that brought joy to my mother's heart was spending a whole day in Jerash. Also, we took a tourist bus trip to Aqaba with some friends during that vacation.

As soon as the bus departed, they started singing and dancing as usual, which made me very scared of the loud noise and commotion's effect on my little daughter. I stood the whole way, trying to cover her ears, fearing that her hearing might be affected or harmed. Seeing how upset I was, one of the older passengers asked me if this was my first child. When I said yes, he replied, "That's why you're so worried about her. Don't worry; you won't be so scared when you have three or four."

We arrived in Aqaba and had a good vacation, spending several nights in a hotel with our three-month-old daughter. Preparations for the return trip began, and I struggled with renewing my military service booklet (mandatory military service), a process that took so long that I missed my appointment to return to the bank. I had to call my manager to explain the situation, and he told me to take care of my matters before traveling.

I resorted to a ruse to renew the service booklet and get the permit. We set the travel date after arranging it with another friend, as the friend who came with me had already returned with his wife by plane.

We set off, my wife, our little daughter, and I in my car, with our friend driving his car. We traversed the vast desert after completing border formalities. We traveled a considerable distance within Saudi borders in the dark, desolate desert, where no sign of life or light existed.

Suddenly, we heard a loud explosion that shook the car and us. We were terrified that something had happened. I had to pull over, especially since it was pitch dark, fearing I might stop in a sandy area and get stuck. The gusts of wind from passing trucks nearly blew us and the Toyota sports car I was driving off the road, especially since the road was narrow with no divider between the opposing lanes.

After getting out of the car, I checked what had happened and found that one of the rear tires had burst into pieces, not just gone flat. I had to change the tire, but how could I do that in such darkness? When my wife asked what had happened, I told her, and she became very frightened. I reassured her and said I would try to fix it despite being unable to see anything and my lack of experience in such matters.

I started feeling my way to loosen the tire when my wife screamed in fear, imagining someone was about to attack me from behind, claiming to hear noises in the desert coming towards us. I was alarmed but looked around and saw no one. I asked her to look after Lara and not look outside, assuring her that there was nothing to worry about.

With a mix of tension and great effort, I managed to change the tire, and we continued our journey until we reached a village where, by chance, we found a man closing his car service station. I pleaded with him to sell me a tire, and he, seeing my family with me, sold me a new one at an exploitative price. After installing the new tire, my friend noticed I wasn't behind him and stopped.

I told him there was no point in traveling together if we didn't help each other. We should stay close; it would have been much easier if he had stopped when I had my problem and lit the area with his car.

We continued our journey, and I followed my friend closely. I didn't drive fast because I was worried about my baby. We hadn't gone far when we heard another explosion. I immediately pulled over and found that the other tire had burst, just like the first. I was very surprised, especially since my car was a modern Toyota Celica, a head-turner in Amman.

It was 2 AM, but this time it was easier because my friend hadn't gone far. He returned and helped me change the tire, and we continued until we found a small town at dawn. We parked the car and slept a little until sunrise. After a long, arduous trip, We found a place to buy an extra tire and continued our journey until we reached Al Khobar. However, having our little daughter, Lara, made the journey's hardship more bearable.

After settling in Al Khobar with our new baby, Lara, our world filled with joy, and our social life became more active. We started visiting many friends, most of whom also had new families. My job situation at the bank improved, and my outlook changed after returning.

I took on extra work with an advertising company in Dammam, the largest city in the Eastern Province of Saudi Arabia, leveraging my experience. The company was managed by an Egyptian director with whom I developed a good relationship. I used my extensive bank connections to generate significant income for the company. I achieved higher sales than the full-time employees, so much so that the manager offered me a full-time position and used me as an example to motivate his employees to improve productivity.

What helped me as well was that my wife was naturally sociable. She had developed her own network of acquaintances, which helped her pass the time during my long hours of absence. We had friends outside of my bank colleagues, especially in the city of Aramco, which we often visited because it did not adhere to the strict Saudi regulations due to its diverse mix of races and ethnicities. She also kept herself busy learning to cook, something she knew nothing about initially, but through persistence and desire, she began to master it. This allowed us to invite friends over for meals, reciprocating the many invitations we received as a small family.

Lara also grew up a little, saying her first words and taking her first steps. We had to change the house's layout as she wanted to touch and explore everything. One amusing incident was when Lara's only joy was to circle a marble table in the middle of the living room. She would forget herself and try to stand on her legs without leaning on the table, losing her balance and falling backward on her head. Even with the carpet, she would cry out from the fall. When she stopped crying, she would try again, and so on, until I thought of putting something behind her small head to protect her from falling.

I spent all my time at home playing with her. I couldn't stand coming home to find her asleep, so I would wake her up, and she would smile when she saw me. Her smile lit up our days and nights.

When she grew a little older and started walking well, I couldn't believe it, so I took her everywhere I went. One amusing memory that sticks with me is when we went shopping at the Dhahran Mall, which our clients and friends owned. I would put her in the shopping cart, and the worker who gave me the cart would give her a small shopping bag. She would put everything her little hands could reach, like chocolates and sweets, into the bag. Often, when I started checking out at the cashier, I would find many things we didn't need that she had added because she couldn't reach them. As for her bag, my friend who owned the store would often let her keep it without charging us.

When we got home, she would sit on the floor and start opening everything, refusing to let us take anything from her, and she would eat them, which caused her teeth to be damaged at an early age. I never said no to her for anything.

We started seriously thinking about moving to a bigger house, especially now with Lara joining our small family. She needed her room, and we learned that my wife might be pregnant again. The opportunity arose when a group of colleagues and I decided to move to an apartment building next to each other in an area called Al Rakah, located between Dammam and Khobar, just ten minutes away from the bank on the main street linking the two cities.

After the move and ensuring that my small family was surrounded by friends and colleagues' families, I had more time to dedicate to my additional work at the advertising company. I also met a person who managed a survey and research company, and I started working with them. I got to know another friend with whom I began investing some money, as he imported goods from China and Japan and sold them in the Saudi market. With my help in increasing his capital, we managed to grow this business well.

All of this only increased our social activity. I divided my time among all these commitments, benefiting from these social relationships to boost my work activity, especially the additional work. My position at the bank also improved, and I became one of the most prominent employees. Everyone knew my name, especially since I was at the bank's front line, directly interacting with clients. I had to represent my institution well, which helped me form friendships with many clients. This position also fed one of my strengths: my love for people and my natural sociability. Anyone who has worked in sales for a long time knows how to engage with people and provide them with excellent service, leaving them satisfied, smiling, and waving goodbye as they say, "See you later."

The trust my superiors had in me, and my good relationships with my colleagues were among the most important qualities I relied on. I could sense this from the praise I received from the bank's clients, which they conveyed to my manager and superiors directly.

Among the many stories that remain etched in my memory from my time in the customer-facing position at the bank, the first story is about a man dressed in old, tattered, and dirty clothes who was standing in line. It was the end of the month, and during those days, we were disbursing salaries for Saudi Arabian Airlines and Royal Medical Services, a time when the bank was usually crowded. When it was the man's turn, I thought he was a beggar, especially after looking at his appearance, particularly his worn-out white cap. I asked him how I could help, assuming for a moment that he was seeking assistance. I told him, in essence, that if he wanted help, he should go to my colleague, pointing to a colleague who wasn't busy and who usually asked employees to contribute to helping people. Unlike the long line that stretched to the bank's outer door, I couldn't request financial assistance for this man.

The man was surprised by what I said. He responded in a Saudi dialect, "What are you saying? I want to ask about the interest rates." I was taken aback by his question and asked him what he needed with the interest rates. He said, "I want to open an account with you. Before I open one, I want to ask about the interest rates."

I asked him how much money he had. To be honest, I didn't give him enough attention. He replied, "I have eight." I asked, "Eight, what?" He said, "Eight thousand." I directed him to the employee who could open a savings account.

He then said, "What are you saying? Eight million! And I won't open an account until I know the interest rates. Don't think you can fool me. I came from the Saudi American Bank, and they offered me seven and five-sixteenths." He said this in his Saudi Bedouin dialect and showed me a certified check from the Saudi American Bank for eight million Saudi Riyals.

I was astonished. How could this person, who I initially thought was a beggar, carry such much money? His precise knowledge of these exact interest rate figures puzzled me even more. I told him, "You know what? The only one who can help you is the manager. He can give you the correct rate." I sent an assistant with him to take him to the manager.

Meanwhile, I called the manager and informed him of the situation. The manager welcomed him warmly, gave him a competitive rate, and opened his account. When he left the bank, he came and thanked me, praising the bank.

Another story involved a man similar to the first, with dirty and worn-out clothes, who carried a bag in his hand. He told me he wanted to open an account, so I directed him to the employee responsible for opening accounts. After completing the procedures, my colleague asked him how much he wanted to deposit into the account.

The man kindly said, "Honestly, I don't know. They're in the bag, and I don't know if it's sixty or sixty-five thousand." My colleague told him, "You need to let us know so we can write the amount on the deposit slip, and our colleague will verify the amount." The man replied, "I honestly don't know." So, my colleague wrote sixty-five thousand on the deposit slip, brought the slip and the bag to me, and explained what had happened.

When I opened the bag, I was astonished. I saw all denominations of Saudi currency mixed together, along with sheep and camel hair, and the bag emitted a very foul odor. I didn't hesitate to call my manager and explain the situation. He sent the bank attendants and the guard to clean and sort the money while I counted it. After counting, the total was 137,500, not 65,000 as the man had said.

I called the man and told him, "Sheikh, this amount isn't correct." The man replied, "Are you saying it's short?" I said, "Your friend wasn't sure." He replied, "No, it's not short. There's a lot more." I told him the amount we found, and he started laughing and mocking me, insisting that he doesn't take forbidden money. "My money is around sixty thousand," he said. I tried to convince him otherwise, but to no avail. I had to call the manager and explain what had happened. The manager told me to make a deposit slip for the full amount and put it in his account since he wouldn't know. I did exactly that and gave him the deposit slip. He then asked me if I had put any forbidden money in his account, and I assured him that I had not.

The bank had a client, a sheik from a prominent family, whom we called Sheikh Eid. Sheikh Eid owned a chain of bookstores in all major Saudi cities. He was a very amiable and humorous person, often telling me many jokes, most of which I couldn't understand because they were in the Bedouin dialect. He also refused to call me by my name, always referring to me as "the good Palestinian" or something similar.

Sheikh Eid called from the road on his new, large, white mobile phone from his luxurious Mercedes. He told me he wanted 40,000 riyals in cash and that he would come to the bank after working hours because he was traveling to Jeddah afterward. I told him, "At your service, Sheikh Eid."

When he arrived, he, as usual, shared some jokes, signed the withdrawal slip, and gave him four bundles, each containing ten thousand riyals, along with an envelope to put them in. He asked what I wanted from Jeddah, and I told him, "Your safety, Sheikh."

He took the money, said goodbye, and left. I got busy closing at the end of the day, and when I finished, I noticed a bundle of ten thousand riyals still on the counter. Sheikh Eid had forgotten it. I took it and tried to call him on his phone, but he seemed to have already boarded the plane. I called my manager, who suggested I put the bundle in an envelope, label it "Sheikh Eid," and keep it in my drawer since we couldn't put it in the bank's vault, given that the administration sometimes conducted surprise inspections.

A few days passed, and Sheikh Eid returned from Jeddah. As usual, he came to me, saying he had brought new jokes, but he didn't mention the bundle of money he had forgotten.

I told him, "Sheikh Eid, didn't you notice anything about the money you took from me?"

He replied, surprised, "No, I didn't notice anything. I took it from you, didn't count it, and gave it to my friend in Jeddah, who took it in the same bag you gave me and put it in his safe without opening or counting it."

I told him that he only took 30,000, not 40,000, and had left a bundle on the counter. I took it out of the drawer and handed it to him. He then called his friend in Jeddah, who confirmed that he had put the bag in the safe without counting it. When he opened it, he found that it indeed contained 30,000.

Sheikh Eid told him, "Rest assured, the 10,000 is with this good Palestinian, and I will transfer it to you at the earliest opportunity."

After settling into our new home, Lara now occupied her own room, which we decorated and furnished beautifully. The situation in Amman regarding my military service was unclear, so I decided not to go there that summer. I always faced problems whenever I went there and needed many connections to get a permit to travel across the borders. That year, we brought my mother-in-law over from Amman for a visit.

During those days, I focused on my additional work, especially feeling that things were getting tighter for us after the Saudi government announced the Saudization of jobs in institutions. I sometimes worked more than 18 hours a day, especially in the absence of family, juggling my three jobs as expenses increased.

We decided to expand our small family and were deeply saddened when my wife miscarried our second child after Lara. But our strong faith in God's plan and destiny kept us moving forward. Not long after, God compensated us when the doctor announced that my wife was pregnant again, which alleviated the emotional and physical pain we endured after the miscarriage.

During that time, we had canceled the idea of going to Amman due to the unclear political situation regarding Palestinian representation. At the same time, my wife's family in America, who had been living there since the 1950s and 1960s, insisted that we visit them so they could meet us after hearing so much about us but not knowing us as a family.

I wasn't keen on the idea of going to a new land with a new language and people I didn't know. Moreover, I had my job, home, and a good situation for my family. However, in the end, her brother convinced me to visit this very new continent, especially since I had about 40 days of vacation from the bank. It didn't take much discussion with my wife, who was excited to see her siblings, whom she hadn't seen since she was eight years old.

Additionally, we had another reason: our upcoming baby would be American if my wife gave birth there. We didn't intend to settle there, as I and a friend planned to establish a Swiss jewelry and watch center in Amman. My friend was an agent for several Swiss watch companies in the Eastern Province of Saudi Arabia. He went to Amman and chose a location in Shmeisani, a prestigious area in Amman at the time. All that was left was for me to leave Saudi Arabia and settle in Amman to manage the project while he stayed in Saudi Arabia.

I said to him, "Let me go with my family first to visit America and get to know this continent that everyone talks about, and then we'll take steps to settle in Jordan."

We went to the American Consulate in Dhahran, and it didn't take long before they granted visas for me and my family for five years after we completed the necessary paperwork.

Things became more complicated after we got the visa, and before preparing for the trip, King Hussein announced the severance of administrative and legal ties between the West Bank and Jordan. This confused many people, including us. We didn't know whether we had become Jordanian or Palestinian, which authority we were supposed to follow, and what our future held.

We began preparing for the trip, and traveling to America was unlike any other trip due to the long hours spent in the air. This was our first time, and we chose to fly with Kuwait Airways, which was at its peak in those days. We had a shortstop in Kuwait and continued our journey to New York.

We spent many hours in the air, waking up and sleeping, including Lara, who was exhausted and not yet two years old. We continued flying after New York until we reached Greenville, South Carolina, where my wife's family members lived. They were all waiting for us at the airport.

We met them, and they recognized us from the photos. My initial impression in those days was immense amazement at what I saw around me. Everything was green—the land, the trees, water everywhere, and even the people smiled at you whether they knew you or not. Unlike what we had left in Saudi Arabia, the weather was wonderful, with no high temperatures or extreme humidity.

We had a wonderful vacation by all standards. We didn't just stay in South Carolina; we also visited North Carolina and went to Florida to attend Jalal and Lina's wedding. Jalal later became one of my dearest friends. The wedding was a fantastic opportunity to introduce us to the rest of the family and those living in Florida.

It was also a new experience for me as they gave me a car to drive from Greenville in Carolina to Tampa in Florida, a ten-hour drive or about 1,000 kilometers. I only had a Saudi driver's license and was following them. At one point, the American police stopped the three cars ahead of me but didn't signal for me to stop despite the speed at which we traveled. It would have been a big problem if they had stopped me since I was driving without an American driver's license. But in the end, we arrived safely.

It was an opportunity to present ourselves as a family. Despite my wife's late-stage pregnancy, which was physically and emotionally exhausting for her, we had a great time and left a positive impression on everyone we met.

We had agreed with the family that my wife would stay in America to give birth there while it was time for me to return to Saudi Arabia. I boarded the plane, which is usually a small one, from Greenville to New York. This flight typically flies at a low altitude, allowing me to take in the vast, enchanting landscape of forests, green fields, and numerous rivers until we reach New York. From there, we transferred to Kuwait Airways.

I was worried about how I would communicate with these people with my broken English, which I barely knew, but things went smoothly. We switched to the Arabic airline, which took us back to Kuwait Airport across the Atlantic Ocean. We had to stay in transit at Kuwait Airport and continue our journey the next day to Dhahran Airport.

My siblings lived in Kuwait, so I called them and told them I was at Kuwait Airport and wanted to see them. They couldn't believe it and gathered themselves. My older brother, younger sister, and her husband came to see me.

After explaining that I hadn't seen my siblings in five years, I managed to convince the Kuwaiti officer to allow us to meet in his office. He kindly brought us tea and let us stay for about two hours. Afterward, my siblings left, and I returned to the hotel inside the airport and slept there that night. The next day, around noon, we boarded the plane that took us to Dhahran Airport. The distance between the two cities was short compared to the long hours from America.

As the plane approached Dhahran Airport, the pilot announced our arrival. As we descended gradually, I looked out the plane window and saw the barren land—the vast, sullen yellow desert sands stretching for miles around the airport. It felt like I could see the heat rising from the ground. All this made me think of the green landscapes and the abundant water from rivers and lakes around the airports in America.

The intense humidity hit us as soon as the plane doors opened, in stark contrast to the gentle breeze that greeted us when the plane doors opened in American airports. We started the entry procedures, and the frowns on the faces of the Dhahran Airport staff were evident. When I got home, welcomed by my friends, who picked me up at the airport. They asked me how I found America. I simply said, "I decided to move there."

That night, I sat and compared the differences between the people in America, with their many stories of social justice that I heard from my group, and our life in Saudi Arabia, where we were treated less than foreigners. In Saudi Arabia, foreigners were Europeans and Americans.

After deep reflection that night, I decided to immigrate to America despite my job, additional work, friends, house, and car. Even the project we had planned in Amman was postponed indefinitely.

I decided that I should live in the land of freedom and eventually obtain its citizenship to end my state of unknown affiliation. I was neither Jordanian nor Palestinian. It was a once-in-a-lifetime opportunity that I had to seize.

I decided to leave and embark on a new chapter of exile. Why should I stay here? There, I can build my future with my own hands and be my own master. I don't want to be an employee working for someone else, especially since Saudization is currently happening in Saudi Arabia, and they can easily replace us. So, I called my wife to assure her of my safe arrival and told her about my decision, which made her very happy.

I returned to my job at the bank, but I was determined that the new migration season would begin, this time to America. I was resolute in saving every penny I could after the trip to America had financially drained me, especially since my wife was still waiting and would continue to wait there for over two more months due to her pregnancy.

During those days, I immersed myself in my primary job and extra work to compensate for the financial drain. At the same time, I had to be honest with my manager about my desire to migrate to America. I had a good relationship with him, but when I presented the idea, he completely rejected it. He was astonished and asked why I wanted to go to America when I had a good position at the bank and was doing well, even involved in activities outside the bank. What would I gain from there? People come from America to work in Saudi Arabia.

I said, "There is freedom and respect for human dignity, civilization, beautiful weather and nature, everyone gets their rights, and they will grant me citizenship. I won't feel like a stranger as I do now; it's a completely different world. Also, I want to stop being an employee and become my boss to enjoy my time and life, working the hours I want."

He replied, "You can do that here."

I said, "How can I when I have so many bosses, including you, who hold me accountable for everything? I don't want anyone to hold me accountable; I want to break free into this vast world and travel without anyone counting my breaths, how long I stayed, and how much I spent. I'm looking towards the future. What happens if I stay? What will I become in a job that threatens Saudization, telling you to leave the country in a few days?"

He said, "You'll become a branch manager like me."

I quickly responded, "I don't want to be like you, with all due respect."

My manager was provoked by my words and looked at me in surprise as I continued, "You have a boss in the end, meaning you are not independent in your decisions. I want to be independent."

The discussion continued until my manager reached a solution. He said, "Listen, don't resign. Instead, take a two or three months leave, go there, and see what happens. If you don't like it, come back to your job as if nothing happened. I will manage your situation with the administration."

I reluctantly agreed and thanked my manager for his understanding, but in truth, my mind was set on something entirely different.

Days passed, and I was informed that my wife had been admitted to the hospital. All her family members (her brothers, sisters, and their children) were around her. It wasn't long before one of her brothers called and said, "Thank God she's safe. You have a baby girl." My quick response was, "Thank God, and thank God she's safe. The important thing is that she and the baby are well."

He confirmed this, saying, "The baby is fine, and, masha'Allah, her head is heavier than her body." I was delighted with the baby and asked to speak to my wife to check on her. As soon as I spoke to her and said, "Thank God you're safe," I asked to hear the new baby's voice. We agreed to name her Leana if she was a girl and Firas a boy. My wife put the phone next to the baby, Leana, and I heard her cry for the first time.

Of course, everyone in the hospital, including her family, called to congratulate me and tell me that she would be the most beautiful girl. I don't know why, but it seemed they were trying to console me because the baby was a girl. But not for a moment did I feel disappointed; on the contrary, I was very happy that both mother and daughter were safe and that Leana had come into the world.

These moments of anticipation were filled with great joy when the family, now consisting of four members, reunited at Dhahran Airport. My wife and our two little daughters were there. A month after Leana's birth, after completing the formal procedures and registering her as born in South Carolina, she obtained American citizenship. That's the greatness of America. Here, a child is born and lives their entire life without being granted any citizenship or rights. On the contrary, they might even lose their residency and be deported within 24 hours.

My wife's father accompanied her and our two daughters from America, passing through several airports until they reached Amman, where they stayed for a week before returning to Khobar with me.

As I said, the joy was immense when I saw my little daughter for the first time. My heart beat faster for her, and she was more beautiful than described by my wife's family.

I drove my little family to our home, not far from the airport. Leana's features began to become clear, and she started to grow, showing typical baby behaviors. We noticed that Lara, the elder and sensible one, began to show signs of jealousy toward the new arrival, who was getting all the attention and care that used to be exclusively hers. Everyone wanted to play with the chubby-cheeked, big-headed baby.

We began preparing for our final days in Saudi Arabia after setting a departure date in June to move to America. We started documenting and filming our last days and trips in Saudi Arabia on videotape. We wanted those tapes to capture all the memories and moments of joy, celebrating becoming a family of four.

One experience for Lara before she turned three was suggested by a friend who owned a private school and kindergarten. He proposed that we bring her to interact with children her age. Her inexperienced mother thought she would spend the whole day at school and needed a big breakfast, as her mother used to do. Lara's small stomach couldn't handle it, and as soon as she started playing with the other kids, she felt unwell and began to vomit. The school administration called me, and I rushed from the bank to pick her up. I still remember her innocent face and her cheeks flushed with redness, especially as she was wearing a small red and blue outfit. She refused to enter the school and said, "I want to wait for Daddy here."

As soon as she saw me, she ran to me, hugged me, and I took her to the bathroom to wash her face. I carried her and told her, "Now you'll be an employee with me at the bank. You've grown up and don't need school." When we entered the bank, the staff welcomed her, everyone wanting to pamper her in their way.

Lara spent the rest of the day with us at the bank.

The final preparations for the move included selling our furniture and unnecessary items after announcing the things we intended to sell to our friends. We also gathered the items we planned to ship, arranging with a shipping company to transport our belongings door-to-door, including personal items, albums, and videotapes, which were part of us and couldn't be carried in our luggage.

All our friends came to bid us farewell. I handed the house key to a friend living nearby who knew to hand over everything in the house to the buyers and keep the remaining unsold items.

As I mentioned in my conversation with my manager, I was convinced that I would not return to Saudi Arabia, even though he had offered me the generous option to go, try it out, and come back if I didn't like it. I believed in what the Arab leader Tariq bin Ziyad did when he attacked and conquered Spain, burning the ships behind him, telling his soldiers it was either victory or martyrdom, with no turning back.

So, I wrote my resignation and handed it to a friend, instructing him to place it on my manager's desk and convey my greetings and apologies once he heard my plane had taken off from Dhahran Airport. I had to face this new life and exile with its challenges and hardships without looking back.

And so began our new, voluntary exile. We flew to Amsterdam, then to New York, and finally to Greenville, South Carolina, where everyone awaited us. But this time, we were a family of four.

Chapter 6 - America

This migration is vastly different from all my previous ones. For the first time, I am migrating with my small family of four, crossing oceans to a distant land, a new world with vast differences from the regions I had previously migrated to. This continent is different in its customs, traditions, system, and language, and here I am, a stranger in every sense of the word.

Firstly and most importantly, I don't understand the language, nor can I speak it. How will I integrate into this new society, especially since I have no job, residence permit, car, or driver's license? Will I be able to drive on these streets that I do not know and am unfamiliar with the system?

All of this is different from what I was accustomed to in the past, but alas, I am the one who wants to do this and came here. This migration was by my own will, my choice, and my complete desire to change my life and the monotonous life of an employee that I was living.

Didn't I believe that beginnings are never easy? I am the one who accepts challenges as I did in the past, so I will surely accept them this time. Didn't I burn all the ships behind me, leaving no way back?

After spending the first days at one of my wife's brother's houses, we tried hard to find a house to settle in until we found one near her sister's house or my brother-in-law's house. We rented the house with what is called the "option to buy" after a year, which is the duration of the contract, after paying two thousand dollars as a deposit for this contract, and the owner of this house had migrated to California.

We started preparing to move into our new house after buying some furniture and furnishing it as best as possible. Of course, I was able to do that now after the situation changed, and I brought with me the amount of money I saved from my work in Saudi Arabia after declaring it at the airport as advised.

I also started training to get a driver's license, which I obtained, opened a bank account, and deposited my money in it after obtaining my social security number. I also bought an American car, a Caprice, which was very popular in Saudi Arabia. This was the first family car I bought after previously buying only sports cars.

After laying the foundations for family stability, it was necessary to look for a project, and my brother-in-law, who expressed his desire to be my partner in any project I started, joined me in the search.

I have always believed that the franchise system worldwide is successful and proven. For the sum of money you pay to a globally renowned company, you become part of its success, benefiting from its experience and name.

I was inclined to try this first due to my lack of market experience and the limited options before us. But my brother-in-law, from a different generation, believed that we did not need a famous name to succeed and could succeed on our own.

Of course, our debates often became heated, with each presenting the merits of his ideas. My brother-in-law, a former teacher who had served in Jizan city in southern Saudi Arabia, which was a village at that time, migrated like me because his in-laws had been in this city long before him. He did almost everything, from working in factories to being a seller, carrying his merchandise like the early Arab migrants called (Al-Bakja) until he opened a shop, which he didn't maintain for long before closing it.

As for me, I consider myself open to new ideas and the new world. I saw how global brands lead the global economy and was a keen reader of Fortune magazine, the world's leading economic magazine, which I subscribed to in my early years in Saudi Arabia. Despite its publication only in English, I diligently strove to read it.

As I mentioned before, it was my wish as a young boy to read a magazine, book, or even a newspaper in English, and I worked towards achieving this goal. However, my progress in conversational skills was slower. When we started looking for a project to work on, I began to muster the courage to engage in my brother-in-law's conversations with the parties we were negotiating with for the project. These included postal service shops, video rental stores, which were very popular at the time, and gift shops. But as I said, my brother-in-law's insistence on building a shop from scratch made me hesitate to accept those ideas.

I recall an incident that happened when we were still guests at my wife's brother's house. I took my daughter Lara and her cousin Rola, who was the same age as Lara (both were three years old at the time), to a nearby shop. Little Rola started talking to everyone in the place in perfect English, having been born there. Lara and I just watched. I don't know why, but at that moment, I felt intense jealousy that a child her age could speak so fluently in the American accent while I, an adult, could not. Even after all these years, despite my knowledge of English, I still cannot speak it with an American accent. For Lara, it came naturally due to her age. As for Rola, she is now a pediatric dentist.

Our diligent search continued for more than a month, and we discussed many ideas. My brother-in-law's experience and language skills gave him the upper hand, even though my confidence in joining conversations with people had grown during that month. We would wander the city streets, looking for a shop for sale or an appropriate vacant shop to rent for our business.

One day, we crossed a major road that connected many parts of our new city. The road was called "Wade Hampton Boulevard," a huge sign caught my attention. It read, "Here will come Walmart stores." It was just land, and no construction had started yet. For those who don't know, Walmart is the largest retail store in the world, with over two million employees, more than 15,000 branches, and annual assets exceeding half a trillion dollars.

When I saw the big sign, an ingenious idea sparked in my mind. Before I told my brother-in-law, I knew he would agree and would be thrilled to hear it. I stopped the car next to the sign, got out without saying anything, pointed to the land, and said, "This is where our first store will be." My brother-in-law was puzzled by my actions and asked me to explain. I told him, "We will open a men's fashion store here. It's something I love doing, it won't cost you anything, and you have experience in it since you had your own shop. You also want to be my partner and leave the partnership with your brother and brother-in-law, with whom you had a very successful store on the other side of the city. You bring your share of the merchandise, or if they give you your share in cash, I will cover the establishment costs, and we'll buy new merchandise as well. This location will be ideal next to Walmart."

But my brother-in-law was very afraid of being a neighbor to Walmart, which sells everything, including men's clothes, at very cheap prices. I told him not everyone wants to wear clothes from Walmart, and the foot traffic that Walmart brings would be a huge advantage. I remember he told me that day, "It's like you want to feed yourself to the big whale."

However, I insisted that he contact the company owning the project. They asked him to send a letter requesting the amount of space needed and the type of business he wanted to set up. They would inform us by mail whether they accepted or rejected our proposal. After a period of waiting, we received approval from the company. They specified the size of the shop, the lease duration, the price per square meter, and all other necessary conditions. We agreed, made some modifications they approved of, and they sent us the contract. After establishing a company with the required licenses, we signed the contract and sent it back to them.

All this was done by mail without seeing anyone and without anyone seeing us, all in secrecy without announcing it to anyone. Things went very smoothly once construction began at the site.

However, things did not go as planned when my brother-in-law went to confront his brother and brother-in-law about his desire to leave their partnership and join me in a new venture on the other side of the city. As soon as he told them, they became very upset and angry, even though they had been hinting all along that they did not want him as a partner. They thought we would be competing with them, so I explained that we would be far away from them and that we believed everyone in life takes their own share.

This did not convince them, so they wanted to retaliate against my brother-in-law in their own way. They immediately implemented an unfair division of the inventory, designed to make me reconsider the partnership. This left my brother-in-law with clothes divided in such a way that for every three pieces, they gave him one, regardless of color and size. In the clothing trade, this is called "broken sizes," which we usually buy at a quarter of the regular price.

When they finished, they threw his share of the pieces on the ground. My brother-in-law looked at me, seeking my reaction. I told him not to worry that I would accept his share in the partnership, and I would rent a truck to transport these clothes and store them in a warehouse until our shop was ready. So, I rented a truck, and we loaded all the clothes and took them to a warehouse we had rented until our shop was completed, and we moved them in.

Of course, my brother-in-law never forgot this moment, and he spoke about it to people until the last day of his life after being let down by his close ones in a moment of intense anger.

At that time, we had to choose a name for the shop, and we settled on the name I suggested, which translated to Arabic as "The Elegant Man." I got the idea after reading about it in GQ, the world's foremost men's fashion magazine.

During this time, I received the rest of our belongings and my remaining fees in the bank, which they sent as a certified check. They also sent me a gold-plated bank emblem in the shape of a heart.

We began the preparations and set up for the shop ourselves—my brother-in-law, his children, and I—despite not knowing anything about such work. Despite my insistence that we hire professionals to set up the interior décor to make the shop presentable, since it was a fashion store, albeit a men's store, which is usually simpler than women's stores, my brother-in-law had his theories and firm beliefs. Firstly, he was very religious in his own way, and it was very difficult for me to sway or change his beliefs, including his theory of extreme simplicity. For example, he believed we should do everything ourselves to save money and avoid drawing attention to ourselves. Most importantly, he believed that any money saved was better than supporting other causes, such as Israel.

I came from a completely different school of thought. For example, I believe in the proverb, "Give your bread to the baker, even if he eats it all." I firmly believe that advertising and promotion are among the most important factors in establishing and growing a business. Having worked long in this field, I also believe that our struggle with Israel is over our land and on the battlefield, as per our religion and Prophet's teachings.

Even though I was never religious, I was driven by principles, the most important of which was integrity and not taking what was not rightfully mine.

Of course, the shop's interior work was not done by us; we had to hire professionals for certain tasks, such as fitting rooms, electrical work, and the exterior sign. We brought in the clothes from the warehouse that my brother-in-law received from his former partners, and they did not take up much space. We had to resort to the nearest wholesale exhibition, which luckily was in Charlotte,

North Carolina, about 100 miles away. I went there with a friend who also owned several shops in different parts of the city. Another exhibition followed in Atlanta, Georgia, about 150 miles away.

I went twice, with my brother-in-law staying at the shop, giving me instructions on what to buy. I succeeded in getting the things we needed for the opening.

Finally, we opened the shop to the public, who received us with clear reluctance, partly because we didn't have a comprehensive collection. Most of our clothes were the "broken sizes" we were forced to take, and the new merchandise was limited. Moreover, people didn't know us or the shop's identity, whether it was fashion or classic clothing. Customers entered hesitantly, and I thought to myself, yes, beginnings are always hard.

We continued like this for a while, but I gained the confidence and courage needed to talk to customers and suppliers. It took me a long time to convince my brother-in-law to invest a little in advertising. He asked what kind of advertising we should do, and I suggested targeting the youth. He agreed, and I proposed advertising on the FM radio station most listened to by young people. We negotiated a package with the station to broadcast our shop's name and a 30-second promotional message 25 times over two days during the weekend when shopping traffic is high.

The result was remarkable. On that Saturday, we made as much in sales as we had in the entire previous period before the opening. My brother-in-law saw the difference and was convinced.

The Double-Edged Sword of Opportunity

As things progressed and we began to advertise regularly, we noticed a steady improvement in sales. However, as I mentioned earlier, we encountered a problem rooted in my brother-in-law's belief that we should seize every opportunity to extract money from companies. He even went so far as to preach this during a Friday sermon, as he was the imam at the small mosque in the city, which led to the congregation's dissatisfaction and a request for him to step down from leading prayers.

Complaints from suppliers started to mount, alleging that someone from our store was calling them to claim that shipments were incomplete, even when they were not. As the suppliers got to know me during my frequent visits to the wholesale exhibitions in both cities, they often expressed their frustration directly to me, which puzzled me.

Each time, I would sit down with my brother-in-law, who had made these calls and complained about the missing goods. I would reprimand him, saying it was wrong and that I did not want to feed my children with ill-gotten gains. He would promise each time not to resort to such actions again.

However, he would quickly revert to his old ways, and I continued to hear harsh words from the suppliers. Eventually, I confronted him seriously, telling him that what he was doing was wrong and unacceptable and that we couldn't continue together if this persisted. Within a week, one of the suppliers called me, asking to speak with me. When I took the phone, the man was very angry, stating that the shipment had been weighed before leaving and could not possibly be incomplete.

I apologized to the man, telling him there must have been a mistake on our end. My brother-in-law overheard the entire conversation. I was very angry and realized that my brother-in-law would not stop his behavior, and I needed to make a tough decision. I told him, "Unfortunately, we have to part ways. We cannot continue like this, and the shop isn't sufficient for both of our families."

"You continue with what you're doing, and I can't agree with it. So, either you buy or sell."

He tried to persuade me otherwise. I told him, "You have been one of the most helpful people to me; you're my friend and brother-in-law, and our wives are sisters. I don't want to lose you. What happened between us will stay between us, and we'll remain friends. But our approaches to work are completely different."

"You have the choice to buy or sell." When he realized my determination, he said, "Sure, I'll sell. I've had enough of this business anyway."

I replied, "Let's proceed, then." We shook hands on it, and I agreed to buy his share of the shop. The next day, we evaluated the shop, and I gave him all the cash I had in my bank account and issued checks for the remaining small amount, each worth a thousand dollars, to be paid at the end of each month.

And so, we parted ways. Despite my father-in-law, Haj Abu Rasmi, coming to ask me not to separate because I was still new to all this and, as he put it, my bones were still soft, and my language skills were weak, I told him, "Father-in-law, I love you very much, but please excuse me this time." I did not tell him my real reasons but rather what I had agreed upon with my brother-in-law.

This way, respect was maintained among everyone. I maintained a very special friendship with my brother-in-law; may he rest in peace, even after he left me. He never withheld advice whenever I sought it until he passed away a few years ago.

I needed to work with a different method, will, and determination.

The Double-Edged Sword of Opportunity

The first thing I did was bring in a professional friend who worked on home repairs. I had him remodel the display on the wall to showcase the clothes differently and professionally. I completely revamped the entire store and brought all the items and clothes my brother-in-law had acquired from his former partners, placing them prominently at the front after applying a significant discount. This allowed me to generate cash flow initially and helped me get back on my feet. I then used a large portion of this to buy new and modern merchandise.

Soon, my shop's name was well-known and on everyone's lips, and sales reached record levels. I had to hire someone to help me, so I employed a young man and a young woman.

My relationships with suppliers improved steadily, and I built a good credit record for my shop. I turned it from a sole proprietorship into a corporation, allowing me to request whatever I needed before other stores. I expanded my sourcing circle by attending major exhibitions in New York, Chicago, and Las Vegas. The companies would ship me the goods, and I would pay for them two or three months later. Often, I would sell all the merchandise before the payment was due, sending a check by mail ten days before the due date, which raised my company's credit limit to record levels.

I also intensified advertising on various radio stations until my name was on the lips of fashion enthusiasts in our city. Young people would come to the shop saying that my store's name was well-known among them and that they took pride in wearing clothes from "The Elegant Man."

Generous promotions announced regularly strengthened my relationships with customers, turning many into friends. I introduced a VIP customer list, recording their names, addresses, and phone numbers in a special notebook and later on my personal computer. Fashion-conscious customers would be contacted when new shipments arrived, and I would set aside their sizes separately, labeling them with their names. These customers felt important and trusted me implicitly, often paying the price I asked without question.

For other customers, I would send them a birthday card three days before their birthday, inviting them to stop by the shop for a gift. Usually, they would come in, and I would have a gift wrapped and labeled with their name, tailored to their personality and preferences. In nearly all cases, the customer would not just take the gift and leave but buy many other items, drawing these buyers into the shop. This list included church leaders, businessmen, lawyers, and others.

I also managed to break a traditional barrier followed in stores in the city and even across America. Typically, when a customer walked in, the salesperson would ask, "How can I help you?" to which the customer would automatically reply, "I'm just looking." I instructed my employees not to use this cliché to avoid hearing the same response. Instead, when a customer entered, we would break the ice by asking how they were or talking about the weather or the recent sports game if they seemed interested in sports, as many Americans do.

As for me, I had a different kind of intuition. I could look at a person and know their exact size. I would start by saying, "I think the shirt you're wearing is size such and such," and they would nod in agreement. If they seemed uninterested, I would mention the jacket or suit size, and they would agree, asking how I knew. I would tell them, "I know your pants size and even your shoe size." They would be amazed and ask if I practiced magic. Of course, it was through experience and training that I could tell. They would see me as a professional and trust me completely. I would suggest colors that suited their complexion and put together a complete package for them, which they would purchase, often returning because of the compliments they received and the lack of personal service in big stores where customers had to help themselves.

Certainly, with all this, my language skills improved significantly, and my confidence and ability to navigate and integrate into the community increased. I got involved in charitable activities, donated to local charities and the police, and kept up with fashion by subscribing to and reading fashion magazines published in America. I also watched night-time shows like the Arsenio Hall

Show, which was a fashion and style icon influencing public taste. People often asked me if I saw what Arsenio was wearing the previous night, and I would reply, "I ordered it, and it's on its way," which I often did.

All this fame led to a men's fashion magazine from Charlotte interviewing me and featuring my photo and shop on their cover page. This provided me with additional publicity, allowing me to establish my presence among the important stores in the city and throughout the southern states.

The Double-Edged Sword of Opportunity

My progress at work was also tied to our small house, which we lived in next to my brother-in-law's house. This proximity allowed my wife to spend most of her time with her sister and for my young daughters to bond with their cousins of similar ages. Even as they grew older, they remained close friends. This provided me with comfort and reassurance about my family and allowed me to focus more on work despite the long commute I had to make daily.

But things don't always go as planned, and events always change the course of life. A young Black man had been watching me for some time without my knowledge.

He waited for the day of the Super Bowl, a famous day in America when the top American football teams compete in the finals after making it through the playoffs. It's a historic annual event where people gather around the TV to watch the game, usually in groups.

On a cold night in mid-February, we had planned to visit friends and watch the game at their place. It was a Sunday holiday, and the streets were nearly empty. The young man took advantage of our absence, and the deserted streets broke into our house by smashing the large window overlooking the garden and entered. He went straight to the office where I kept my work bag. He took it, which contained all the weekend's work, my checkbook, and credit cards. He didn't stop there; he also took all the gold rings and necklaces I used to wear and, most importantly, my valuable watches. Among them was a Rolex and a Raymond Weil, a gift from a friend who was a dealer for that brand in the Eastern Province of Saudi Arabia. I bought a matching set for me and my wife on our first wedding anniversary, along with more than four less expensive watches.

The thief couldn't complete his task, thankfully, as he heard our car pulling into the garage. Our habit was not to stay out late because of the children. He exited through our bedroom and escaped through the balcony into the garden. If he had searched our bedroom, he would have taken all my wife's gold, which she kept in the drawers.

When we entered the house, it was very cold. At first, I thought we had left a door open. Upon investigating, we realized someone had broken in and shattered the back glass door. I immediately called the police.

I also called my brother-in-law, who arrived before the local police. This was our first experience with such a situation, and my wife was very frightened. Even after the police spent most of the night taking fingerprints and listing the stolen items, we didn't sleep until a man came to replace the broken window and clean up.

The losses from this incident exceeded $20,000, between cash, gold, and valuable watches. It was a painful blow that I tried to hide to minimize its impact on my family. By morning, the news had spread among the local Arab community, who called to check on us. The financial loss was not the only thing we suffered; we also lost our peace of mind and the psychological comfort of knowing that someone had invaded our home, especially affecting my wife and my young daughter, Lara, who was old enough to understand what had happened.

The wound didn't heal quickly, even after a police officer called to tell me they had caught the thief and returned some small items like the bag, credit cards (which I had already canceled), and some checks. They asked if I wanted to see him but refused my request.

Three and a half years after the incident, a Black man I had never seen before entered my shop, dressed impeccably. I approached him, trying to start a conversation. He smiled a hidden smile, avoiding direct eye contact. I asked if he was looking for something specific.

He said no but mentioned he wanted to talk to me. I was puzzled and asked, "Talk to me? Do we know each other?" He replied, "Yes, but not in the way you'd like to remember."

Curious and cautious, I asked how we knew each other. He insisted I promise not to get angry or act rashly. I agreed, saying it depended on what he had done.

He began, "First, I came to apologize. I am the one who robbed your house more than three years ago. I was caught and sentenced to five years in prison but was released after three and a half for good behavior. I have reformed and am a good man now. I can't return what you lost, but I believe God will compensate you. I hope you can forgive me."

Listening to him, my blood boiled, but I tried to control my anger. His regret was evident. I asked his name. He said, "Randy."

I told him, "Listen, Randy, your actions caused me over a $20,000 financial loss. You also inflicted a deep psychological wound on my family, forcing us to move and incurring more expenses. As much as I would like to, I won't shoot you with this gun in my hand," and I showed him the gun I had picked up from my side. "Had I seen you that night, I might have. Since you've come to confess, I won't get angry or act rashly as promised. But I can't forgive you for the fear and pain you caused my family. I leave your fate to God."

I then asked him what he did with my valuable watches, especially the

Rolex. He smiled and said he sold them for $20 to $30 each. When he saw someone particularly interested in one, he asked for $50 and got it. He admitted he didn't know their value.

I told him, "God damn you! Had you sold them to me, I'd have paid you $100."

We had already decided to leave the house, which we considered cursed, knowing the financial loss would be significant since the landlord refused to refund any part of the $2,000 we had paid. The long commute and familiarity with the city made me realize we were living in the wrong part of town. My wife and I decided to move to a more upscale part of the city, believing that one's residence determines one's place in society.

Despite all family opposition, I moved forward with the plan. No one else dared live in the wealthy area where we planned to move. My wife's family had always lived simply, almost naively. They had immigrated to this new continent in the 1950s and 1960s, and time seemed to have stopped for them. They hadn't progressed until the next generation, who were well-educated and spread across America, came along.

Unlike them, I decided to take the initiative and not revolve around their circle but to be distinctive and different. We moved to our new house after hiring a specialized company to move and arrange all our furniture as we wanted.

Our psychological and financial situation improved significantly once we settled into the new house. With sales flourishing, I decided it was time to reward myself and my family with a new car, as the old one was breaking down often.

I had always dreamed of the Trans Am, a fast and sporty car that was totaled in an accident in Al-Khobar, Saudi Arabia. I kept it a secret and didn't tell anyone, planning to surprise my wife and daughters.

I headed straight to the dealership on Motor Mile (the area with car dealerships in the city) and asked for a salesman who was a regular customer at my shop. When he saw me, he welcomed me warmly and showed me the current year's model, which was stunning. He whispered that if I waited another week, the new model would arrive with a completely new design, and I'd be the first to own it in the state.

I agreed immediately, asking him to reserve the red one with my specifications. A week later, he called to say the cars had arrived. I went directly to the dealership; he had prepared it by washing it and placing it on the platform. The moment I saw it, I knew it was what I wanted.

He told me I needed to sign and take the car without paying anything upfront. I asked about the interest rate, and he said he had given me a preferential rate. I immediately contacted my bank manager, with whom I had a very active account and a good relationship. She offered me a better deal, asking me to fax her the invoice so she could prepare the check.

When I arrived at the bank, the check was ready. I signed and took it to the dealership, where the salesman handed me the keys. I drove the car, feeling like I was flying, parked it in front of our house, and called my wife and daughters to come outside and see our new car.

It was a fantastic surprise. The Trans Am, in the Firebird class, resembled a Ferrari at that moment, known from the popular TV series "Magnum." Many thought it was a Ferrari. This car turned traditional family concepts upside down, with whispers and open comments about how the new guy had the nicest car, even though he had been here for only a short time. They wondered how I, the newcomer, had surpassed those who had been there for decades.

Opening of Elegant Man in Greenville, SC

Firas & Nadeem

Surprises continued in our small house as well. One evening, I came home to find my wife unwell. She told me she had spent the day in the bathroom, vomiting. I asked her if she might have been pregnant. She said she didn't know, so we decided to see a doctor the next day. We could hardly believe it when the doctor confirmed the pregnancy that morning.

We were overjoyed, as this meant a fifth member would join our family. The happiness echoed throughout the house and among our small family members. The girls started touching their mother's belly, saying, "There is a baby here." As the months of pregnancy passed, speculations increased. Some said it was a girl; others said a boy. We said, "Thank God," because if it was a girl, she would be a sister to our daughters. If it was a boy, he would be the awaited Firas. People started debating what to call me—some said "Abu Lara," others "Abu Firas" because Firas was on the way.

Yes, he is Firas, not just a name. It was the idea I had built in my mind since I was a child. When I was a kid and a teenager, my friends called me "Abu Al-Ans," which never made sense to me. As I matured, I decided I should be a father to something meaningful, not just "Al-Ans." Often, I was serious, even in my childhood. I loved the name Firas, filled with Arab identity and pride, especially as it is one of the names of the lion. I also admired the poetry of Abu Firas Al-Hamdani, that great poet whose verses I often recited.

I told myself that if God blessed me with a son, I would name him Firas, and I would, God willing, be "Abu Firas." This dream had to become a reality, God willing. My wife's belly continued to grow, and the pregnancy became more apparent day by day, along with the speculations, analyses, and probabilities. Finally, the time came for the baby to be born. It was spring, on April 5th, when my wife's pain intensified. I carried her to the car and drove to the hospital, where they decided it was time.

My wife was admitted to the hospital, and the necessary procedures were carried out. At that moment, we were in the room with her. However, we were surprised when the doctor, after examining her, said that the baby needed to be delivered via cesarean section because it had turned around.

The doctor was unusually insistent. My wife hesitated to accept the surgery, and he kept asking if she didn't want to know the gender of the baby inside her. We had agreed not to find out the baby's gender before birth. Whatever came would be a gift from God, and that was enough. Usually, doctors don't focus on the baby's gender; they just do their job. But this doctor was unusually persistent, insisting that the surgery be done as quickly as possible, especially since the baby was very active and had turned its head upward instead of downward. He refused to say anything about the baby's gender because my wife didn't want to know and didn't want her delivery to be unnatural.

I quickly thought of something at that moment. I went down to the hospital flower shop and bought a very large bouquet and a big balloon. I returned to my wife with a card on which I had written, "It is the awaited Firas, my love. Please agree to the surgery!"

I placed it beside her head after kissing her. As soon as she read what I had written, she gave me a radiant smile and signed the consent for the surgery. Only then did the doctor announce that it was a boy and that he was in good health?

The preparations for the surgery were made, and I asked the doctor if I could attend the operation, be the first person Firas saw, hold him, and videotape the birth. The doctor nodded in agreement, so they dressed me in the special clothes, and I entered the operating room.

I held my wife's hand in one hand and the video camera in the other. It was the first time I attended a birth, and I saw Firas come into this world, crying his first cry of life. I cannot describe my feelings then, but I know well that I cried tears of joy. My wife was screaming in pain, even though she was semi-anesthetized. Then, her face was covered with a bright smile of peace after she saw him and after Firas entered this life.

The doctor handed me the scissors to cut the umbilical cord. One of the assistants took the camera from me, and I held Firas, placing him between his mother and me, saying, "Thank God, thank God."

I embraced her and said, "Here is the moment we have been waiting for so long." I looked closely at my son's face, which I found very beautiful. His eyes shone with intelligence, and his hair was thick and long. The doctor even said he would grow up to be a handsome young man, and the nurse said he would be the center of attention for the girls, pointing out his eyelashes.

Thus, Firas came into the world. His mother, I, and all our family and friends who were gathered outside the delivery room with flowers, congratulating and celebrating Firas's arrival, were overjoyed.

Seeing all these people coming to congratulate us, I decided to celebrate Firas's arrival and invite everyone after forty days. We would slaughter sheep in his honor. I rented a large hall for this purpose and asked a friend who runs a restaurant in the city to handle the sheep and the cooking. We had a party for all the Arabs in the city without exception. They danced and sang until late.

People talked for a long time about that party, some saying, "If this is for Firas's arrival, what will his wedding be like?"

But the world didn't know what those moments meant to me. They didn't know that Firas meant the whole world to me. Isn't it enough that the world started calling me "Abu Firas" from the moment of his birth?

The features of Firas started to become clearer little by little, and signs of intelligence began to show in all his features and movements, especially his eyes, which constantly moved around, searching for everything happening around him. His sisters wouldn't leave him alone, especially Lara, who had become aware and played with him and sat beside him. Little Leana, who had been the pampered one, was now displaced from her throne with the arrival of the new member, Firas. She began to feel jealous of the attention everyone was giving to Firas instead of her, as they used to. Lara, who had been jealous of Leana, found this an opportunity for revenge and focused her attention on Firas.

Firas was only three months old when we had the opportunity to buy our first house in the prestigious Pelham Road area. It was a deal that worked out in our favor in every way after I managed to arrange the down payment for the house. Thus, we moved to live in our first big, sprawling house, giving each family member their room and me my office. The house had a wonderful large garden planted with all kinds of fruit trees. This house's first resident was an Iraqi agricultural engineer, which made the garden exceptional.

Of course, our move to the house also meant that our daughters would transfer to a nearby school, which was famous and ranked first in the state. Moving to our new house and enrolling our daughters in the school marked a qualitative shift for us and started a new phase in our lives. After furnishing our house completely, that phase witnessed the best days of our lives. Our family of five became active, going to nearby children's entertainment places on weekends. I also started taking vacations with my family to neighboring states and to the beach.

The sports car was no longer suitable, as we needed a large family car for our big, small family. I went to a friend who owned a car dealership and bought a family car. My wife started driving it, putting baby Firas's seat in it, and it became our means of transportation when we were together as a family on our trips, visits, and travels. As for my pampered Firebird, I used it for commuting to work and for my personal errands.

During that time, my stock portfolio, which I had started in my early days in America, was also growing and prospering. My passion, monitoring, and knowledge of stocks made me trade in buying and selling stocks in the stock markets, whether in the New York Stock Exchange or the Nasdaq, which specializes in technology stocks. I specialized in the details of these markets during the beginning of the technology revolution and the establishment of dot-net companies, as they were called. This made me earn a lot and increase my portfolio daily. An American broker I dealt with helped me, and we quickly became very close friends. We even played tennis together, a game I played well.

One of the amusing stories that happened, where I made the fastest $5,000 in my life in less than two hours, was when the famous Yahoo company offered its shares. I tried hard with my broker to buy any IPO shares before they were offered to the market, but I couldn't. I told David, my broker, to inform me as soon as the stock started trading. Usually, the offering price was $17, and then it started to rise. David called me at the moment the stock was offered, saying it was very high, having jumped to $31 as soon as it hit the trading floor. I told him not to buy it now as it was high but to watch it for me. If it dropped to $25, buy me 1,000 shares. By noon, usually 12 PM, brokers go to lunch, and the price drops due to low demand. At 12 PM, David called me, and I was watching the stock. He said it was $26, and I told him to buy it. He bought 1,000 shares for $26,000. By 2 PM, it went back up to $31, and I called him to sell. He sold them for $31,000, and I made $5,000 in less than two hours. If I had waited until 4 PM, the closing time, I could have sold them for $56,000 and made $30,000. However, my satisfaction and fear of the price dropping led me to sell early.

The girls and Firas were growing and thriving before our eyes, and thank God, they were all extremely intelligent. Firas, being the youngest, naturally drew the most attention. He was speaking and walking everywhere before he even turned one year old.

One day, we met an elderly man of Syrian origin who lived in Canada. He was visiting my wife's brother's house. The man called Firas over while he was playing and started asking him some questions. Firas answered with high confidence as if he were not a child.

The man's face lit up, and he told everyone present, "Remember my words well. This child will have a great future when he grows up and becomes a man. Pray for me, as I won't be alive by then, but witness my words."

At that time, we believed we had truly become a complete family—five members, all healthy, thank God, and the children, as I mentioned, were extremely intelligent.

It wasn't long before my wife came to me after a long, hard day at work and said she suspected she was pregnant. I was surprised by the news and asked her how that could be, given that she was cautious. She said she didn't know.

My anger exploded towards my wife as if she were to blame. But within minutes, I thought to myself, "What am I doing? This is God's will, and God has destined this for us. I should not be ungrateful for this blessing."

I sat with myself, blaming myself heavily, and sought forgiveness from God for my hasty judgment and anger over something I should have been thanking God for. I then thanked God repeatedly. I also went to my wife, kissed her head, and apologized for my quick judgment and anger over something I should have been grateful for. After all, some people can't even have children. I also thanked my wife, who always found pregnancy difficult and endured a lot. Who was I to object to God's will?

Yes, the fourth child was on the way.

My wife's pregnancy began to show, and her life turned into a struggle. Her size increased unusually, and her movement and sleep, especially in the later stages, became difficult. I had to buy her a large, round chair for the living room, and sometimes, I would find her asleep on this chair. I would cover her and leave her to sleep because she found it difficult to sit or sleep on regular chairs and the bed. This was something I hadn't seen in her previous pregnancies.

The days passed quickly, as usual. One winter morning in December, my wife woke me up at four-thirty in the morning and said, "I think it's time now. Let's go to the hospital!"

Indeed, we got into the car, and I drove to the main hospital in the city where the other children had been born. At the entrance, I told them that my wife was in labor, and within seconds, they admitted her to the hospital. Doctors and nurses started coming and going from her room, giving her medication and pain relief to ensure a natural birth. Then she slept.

The doctor called me over after I had been standing by her side and said, "We've given her medication so she can rest and sleep for a while, allowing everything to take its natural course. If you have anything to take care of, go ahead; she won't wake up before noon, and sitting here won't help."

I said, "Okay," and decided to go open my shop, especially since it was already past ten-thirty and I was late. The employees were waiting, and it was the Christmas season, a very busy time for us. I got into my Firebird and sped towards the shop.

My mind was clouded—my wife was in the hospital, my children were at home (after I had called them, especially since Lara was now grown up and responsible enough to look after her siblings), and my employees and customers were waiting outside the closed shop.

All these thoughts were racing in my head, and I didn't realize I was speeding until a police car caught up with me and signaled for me to stop with its lights flashing. I pulled over to the right.

The officer approached after I rolled down the window, and the following conversation took place:

Officer: "Good morning. Do you know why I stopped you?"

Me: "Good morning. I think I was speeding a little."

Officer: "Actually, not a little. You were going 20 miles over the speed limit."

Me: "I'm sorry. I wasn't paying attention. I am coming back from the hospital and my wife is in labor and my mind is scattered."

Officer: "If your wife is having a baby, why are you in the car and not with her?"

He seemed skeptical - probably because my fast, red car itself was a suspect and attracted police attention at the time.

He asked for my license and registration.

I handed him what he asked for, and he took them back to the police car, where another officer was sitting. I remained in my car, as is customary in America. After a few minutes, the officer returned with a hefty ticket and began explaining it, but I didn't hear his words. My anger flared because the fine was over $180, and what really mattered were the 4 points on my license.

The officer returned to his car after placing the ticket on my windshield. My intense agitation made me leave the car and approach him, where he sat calmly next to the other officer. I was very angry, and I didn't realize I was hurling a barrage of curses at him, saying, "I told you I'm coming from the hospital, my wife is having a baby, and what do you care? You're just issuing this harsh ticket."

I spoke a lot, interspersed with American-style curses that I had become proficient in, and the man looked at me calmly while I was at the peak of my anger. Then he asked, "Are you done?"

I said, "No," and continued cursing while he said nothing. Suddenly, I realized how foolish I was acting. I felt ashamed and thought, "What am I doing? This officer can arrest me and put me in jail."

He then said, "Are you finished? Go back to your car, please."

Indeed, I returned to my car, but instead of calming down, I started the engine forcefully, making a loud noise due to its powerful engine. I looked in the mirror and saw the same police car behind me, not far away. I slowed down when I approached the shop and parked on the yellow line in front of it, which was reserved for fire trucks and was also a big violation.

I got out of the car and opened the shop, finding my employees and customers waiting for me. I looked and saw the police car parked across from my shop. After I finished opening the shop, I looked at them, and the officer called out to me. He said, "First, move your car off the yellow line reserved for fire trucks. Second, I stopped you because you could have caused an accident with your speed. Third, this is your court date," and he pointed to the date on the ticket. "Don't pay it; come to court, and I'll talk to the judge to reduce the fine and points."

I said, "I want to apologize for the curses and my behavior."

He said, "No problem," and he and his partner left.

Once I opened the shop for the employees, I left them; my mind was occupied with my wife, who was going to deliver the baby that day as the doctors had said. I headed back to the hospital and called my wife's family on the way. When I arrived at the hospital, some of them had already arrived. I went to the doctor who would oversee my wife's delivery and asked if I could attend the birth.

He said, "Go get ready," and the nurse gave me the special attire, which I put on and entered my wife's room. She was in intense labor.

The delivery process began, and this time, it was natural. Nadeem came into the world with a cry of life, and my wife and I had agreed to name him that if it was a boy. It was one of the greatest moments of my life, and I couldn't contain my tears in front of everyone present.

I was holding a video camera, recording those moments. After the doctor delivered, cleaned, and wrapped Nadeem, he handed him to me, and someone took the camera from me. I remember nothing but that face that appeared in this world.

Yes, Nadeem, with a round face like the moon, was healthy and weighed more than usual. The hospital staff nicknamed him "the big boy" from that moment on.

In those moments, I forgot everything and only remembered how foolish I was to be angry when I found out my wife was pregnant with him. Here I was, holding this vibrant gift of life from God, feeling overwhelming guilt and unable to hold back my tears.

Yes, the sixth member of our family had arrived. I approached my wife, kissed her forehead, congratulated her on her safety, handed her Nadeem, and said, "Now Firas has a brother, just as Lara has a sister."

Thank God, our family was complete.

A thousand thanks to you, Lord, for this blessing. I went out to the family waiting outside and announced the good news of Nadeem's birth and his large weight.

The joy among family and friends who flocked to the hospital was immense. Bouquets of flowers and balloons came from all directions, along with numerous congratulatory phone calls for the new arrival. Only a few days later, we took the newborn, along with the flowers and many gifts, and headed with our small yet large family—large in love and joy—back to our home, which was filled with love and smiles shared by all its members.

I must say that that year, thank God, was full of blessings and good fortune. I even achieved the highest sales of my career that season and year, a record I had never reached before. This was all from God Almighty, who teaches life lessons and reminds us not to fear the future. God created tomorrow and provided its sustenance, just as He created humans and provided for them. Since then, I have never feared the future and always trusted in God.

Let's return to the policeman who told me to come on the court date. Indeed, I went to the court, and when our turn came before the judge, who recognized me, I entered, not knowing what would happen. The judge said, "You are Mr. Frija," mispronouncing my surname as usual since no American ever got it right. I answered, "Yes." He asked what had happened, and I was about to speak when the policeman requested to speak. The judge allowed him, and he said, "Mr. Frija was distracted because his wife was having a baby, and he was heading to the hospital. He didn't notice the speed limit sign. When I stopped him, he was very cooperative, so I ask you, Your Honor, to reduce his fine."

The judge was surprised by the policeman's request, considering he was the one who fined me. He asked, "Is this what happened, Mr. Frija?" I replied, "Exactly, Your Honor." He then said, "Okay, go pay $30 for court fees," and removed the fines and points. He added, "Take care of the new baby."

Despite my poor behavior toward him, I was very happy about the officer's kindness. I had used every curse word I knew, and he responded with such understanding. I waited outside for the officer to finish his cases and told him, "You don't know how sorry I am for every word I said to you. I extend my hand to become friends and ask for your forgiveness." He said, "Don't worry; I understand your situation. I went through the same experience months ago and was in your position." We became friends, and if he passed by, he would stop in for coffee, always refusing to take anything from the shop without paying for it.

This was one of the bright moments I experienced in the United States, a significant lesson I often spoke about. It was an ordinary Friday for me when I was surprised by the entrance of my friend Dr. Islam into the shop. It was his first visit to my shop.

Of course, I was surprised by the visit but welcomed him. We sat, chatted, and drank coffee. We had a family friendship as our wives were friends, and we visited each other's homes occasionally. Dr. Islam, an Egyptian, was the son of the famous actor Sidqi, who was renowned in the 1950s and 1960s. As he told me, he didn't want to follow in his father's footsteps. Instead, he became a devout and well-known doctor in his field, as was his wife, a pharmacist. Both worked in a large clinic (almost a hospital) that I passed by every day on my way to work.

After we finished our coffee, he asked me directly, "Younes, why don't you come to Friday prayers?" I hesitated, or rather, I couldn't find a reason to give him. He said, "Go and perform ablution, and let's go to the mosque for Friday prayers together."

I tried to excuse myself, citing customers and that I didn't know how to pray, among other reasons. He calmly and simply responded to each one, saying that someone would help me and that if I was gone for an hour, nothing would happen. He assured me that God would compensate me much more than the lost hour. He said I could stand next to him, learn from him, and do as he did. He said this while looking into my eyes.

He added, "Look, God has given you everything: health, wealth, beauty, family, and everything you want. Don't you feel like thanking Him a little with

Friday prayers?" At that point, I felt deeply ashamed and went with him in his car after performing ablution. It was my first time praying in the city mosque.

The people who knew me were surprised to see me there. I performed the prayer next to Dr. Islam and felt at peace afterward. Many people came to greet me and congratulate me on attending the mosque. Dr. Islam continued to come and pick me up an hour before Friday prayers. He insisted on coming with me, not letting me use my car. We would go early and spend the time reading the Quran, especially Surah Al-Kahf. During those days, my former partner and brother-in-law led the prayers and delivered the sermon. He had tried many times to bring me to Friday prayers before Dr. Islam succeeded. He was very happy when I attended with Dr. Islam.

Since then, I have been committed to attending Friday prayers early reading as much of the Quran as possible. I have never missed a Friday prayer since then. Even if I am in another part of the world, I look for a mosque and go early to pray in the first row. This commitment also led to my regular observance of the five daily prayers rediscovering my faith and beliefs. This was all thanks to God for making it easy for me to meet this person, whom I consider a great blessing. May God reward him wherever he may be in this world.

Certainly, my commitment to my faith protected and fortified me from making any mistakes, especially since I traveled frequently to the fashion capitals and participated in exhibitions in major cities like New York—the city that never sleeps. I was captivated by its markets, towering buildings, and numerous lights. We stayed in the most luxurious hotels, especially the Marriott Marquis, which overlooks Times Square in the heart of the city. We also visited its landmarks, such as the Empire State Building, the Twin Towers, and the Broadway theater district. Twice a year, we would go to the largest exhibition center in America, the Javits Center, and by a twist of fate, my eldest son Firas is now the director there.

America

We also visited Chicago, the Windy City, though we didn't like it much due to its reputation as the city with the highest crime rate in America. The most important exhibition was in Las Vegas—the crazy city, or the Sin City, as Americans call it. There, you could find anything you could think of or not think of as long as you had the money and the intention to do what you wanted. I watched with great pain many young Arabs who came from other states getting immersed in gambling, which those hotels and casinos offered along with the temptations they provided—luxurious suites, women, food, and drinks. Sadly, I saw many of them continue gambling until they lost tens of thousands of dollars and sometimes had to borrow money for their return ticket to their home state.

Seeing them end up in such states of downfall and collapse, I felt sorry for them. However, my friend and I enjoyed the city's bright side without losing a single dollar in gambling or forbidden activities. I considered all these activities as prohibited and did not engage in them in any way, shape, or form. Despite visiting many places around the world, whether in America, Europe, or even the Middle East, such activities were something I always avoided.

Even though we were young and had money, we chose not to participate in the debauchery, drinking, and women that characterized the city. We received many invitations to be part of this madness, and some even called us "uptight" and claimed we didn't know how to have fun. But I was sure that this was temporary joy, often ending in disaster and regret for those involved.

We refused to get carried away and instead explored the new and crazy things happening in the city. I would go shopping and buy gifts for my family, which was my source of happiness. We also treated ourselves to dinners in upscale restaurants if we wanted to reward ourselves. As I said, these are choices in life, and you choose where to stand.

I started thinking about expanding my business within the city.

I looked around to see what I could do that was close by and that I could manage easily. The first thing that came to mind was to reopen a shop next to mine in the same shopping complex that sold ice cream. The man who opened that shop had invested a substantial amount in setting it up and decorating it, but he closed it after less than a year. I contacted him and asked why he closed the shop. He told me he was busy with other interests and didn't have enough time to manage it. He had entrusted its management to young girls, mostly teenagers, who couldn't handle the responsibility.

I asked him if the shop would be profitable if I reopened it. He said, "Certainly. You own the shop next door, so you can supervise it while managing your primary business." I asked if he still had the shop's equipment, machines, tables, and chairs. He confirmed that he did.

We agreed that I would buy the contents of the shop for a quarter of their original value if bought new. I would pay him half the amount upfront and the rest in deferred checks over a long period, starting once I had begun operations, provided that the deal would be finalized if I could reach an agreement with the mall management to lease the shop.

I contacted the manager of the company that owned the shopping complex and negotiated a six-month grace period before the lease took effect, making the first six months rent-free and reducing the rent for the first and second years. He sent me the contract by mail, which I signed and returned. I began preparing to set up the shop. As I mentioned, the basics were already in place, and I didn't need much. Once everything was ready, I thought about what Americans loved most and decided to offer a type of ice cream called yogurt, which is completely fat-free. This was a craze among Americans, given the prevalence of obesity due to their diet dominated by fast food, with only a few people being mindful of what they ate.

I contracted with the most famous company that provided this type of yogurt to be the official supplier for the shop. I contacted the girl who had managed the shop before; I knew her because I was a regular customer. I hired her as the manager, and she, in turn, hired other girls aged 16 to 20, most of whom were still in school.

When we had everything ready and planned the grand opening on a Saturday—the main shopping day in America—I launched an advertising campaign and distributed flyers with discount coupons. I assigned one of the girls to hand them out to people leaving Walmart, which was in the same shopping complex and brought a radio station to broadcast from in front of the shop. They invited people to come and try our products. When we opened, the line extended over 15 meters outside the shop, with customers eager to try NY Yogurt. This was the name I chose for the shop, which had two meanings: the initials of my name and my wife's, and for Americans, "NY" stands for New York. We didn't have to explain the shop's name, especially since New York was known for its yogurt.

Along with the shop manager, we had four girls working, but they couldn't keep up with the customers crowding the entrance. This continued most of the day, and I had to step in and help during peak times.

The summer passed very well, but when winter came, business dropped significantly because South Carolina has a climate similar to the Middle East, experiencing all four seasons. The girls became lazy about coming to work, and I discovered many issues. There needed to be a key person to manage everything and solve problems, especially since I later discovered that the woman managing the shop was an alcoholic who lost control when intoxicated, causing many issues with customers and other employees. I had to let her go and appoint one of the assistants in her place.

I also noticed that the day's revenue from all this work and the number of customers did not exceed a few hundred dollars, while a single customer at my primary shop could bring in much more. My main business also suffered because

I spent a lot of time-solving problems at the ice cream shop and managing the girls' issues. I tried hard to find someone nearby to take over the shop from me but couldn't.

I decided to close this chapter, considering it a failed experience and a new lesson in life that cost me several tens of thousands of dollars. Before the two-year lease ended, I closed the shop's doors.

While my ambition was beyond my current situation, my constant search for a new venture that would elevate me to the level of a businessman, befitting my capabilities and potential, inspired me. One day, while following business developments, I noticed the rise of leasing—a concept called leasing in the business world. Large companies across the United States were opening offices in various states, acting as intermediaries between those needing equipment, machines, and high-value items and the manufacturers who leased them. Leasing often proved more profitable than selling these items.

I read and researched this topic extensively. After being fully convinced of the viability of such ventures, which were not common in our state, I decided to contact one of the largest leasing companies. When I spoke with the vice president of the company, which was publicly traded on the New York Stock Exchange, he told me that the company's president would be visiting the South, specifically Atlanta, Georgia, at the beginning of the next month. He could visit my city and meet with me. We scheduled a meeting, and I met with the president when he came to our city.

He laid out a plan for me to invest $100,000, which covered everything from the subscription fees to establishing my own company under their name through a franchise system. This included setting up offices, hiring and training staff, and integrating into their network to find clients and suppliers.

This move would significantly elevate my status in every sense of the word. I signed a memorandum of understanding with the man, giving me a three-month trial period to evaluate the project and decide whether to continue or withdraw.

Attending fashion events in Las Vegas Convention Center in September 12th 1994

Middle of Time Square, NYC - June 13th, 1993

Chapter 7 - Return to Amman

Eid in Greenville, SC 1995 in front of our old home.

Who said that life passes without problems? And who lives their life without them? God Almighty created us and gave us the keys to happiness, or at least that's what we believe. However, perfect life or complete happiness remains contingent on one condition. There is always something missing that completes this perfect life. You find that this condition or thing controls a large part of our thinking, and sometimes, it goes beyond thinking.

It is what makes the picture incomplete. I have not found a person in this universe whose life is perfect, with all elements complete. It is a wisdom from God Almighty, often for two reasons. The first reason is to keep us running in this life to solve this problem, as humans by nature do not accept the reasons for happiness in their hands but always search for the complete picture. The second reason is to cause a fundamental change and reconsideration of that life.

This introduction is to explain my belief at that time that my life was complete. Here I am with a wonderful family, thank God, and a large, sprawling house with all the amenities. We even have two cars and a job that brings in good profits. Even after my significant loss in the yogurt shop, I signed with the new company, where I would be the general manager after three months.

But as I mentioned earlier, it is unlikely for all elements to be complete. Our decision to move from Saudi Arabia to America was based on the visa we obtained from the consulate in Dhahran. They told us we could convert that visa to a residency because my wife's entire family has been living in the United States since the 1950s. They are not only naturalized citizens but the third generation is born in America. There should be no difficulty in converting a visitor visa to a residency, especially since my wife spent her entire childhood there. We relied on God and settled in America, renewing the visa with the hope it would convert.

However, immigration laws in America are constantly changing. Despite this, we were treated like citizens with all rights and duties. Anyone who has lived in the United States knows how easy life was before September 11, which turned the situation upside down. During this time, I was building my business excellently, achieving far more than I had hoped when I left my job in Saudi Arabia. I was also moving into a new phase, one I had never even dreamed of in this new job that would add to my successes, whether in the stores, the stock market, or even my family life.

Yet, I felt something was missing. Our papers and residency in America were not complete. Before taking my next big step, I needed to ensure it was safe and that I was standing on solid ground. Despite our failure to obtain residency and spending a lot of money on lawyers, all attempts failed, especially when the main lawyer handling my case in Atlanta, Georgia, fell ill with a serious illness. An Indian lawyer working for him took over, but despite living in America and graduating from its universities, his third-world mentality still governed his actions, leading to rejection by the immigration department.

I was forced to hire Mr. White, an immigration lawyer from our city, who was also the mayor. An American priest, a customer of mine, introduced me to him. I formed a friendship with Mr. White, who said we only needed to pay a fine and conversion fees for the visa, which exceeded ten thousand dollars at that time. I agreed to pay instead of returning to Amman to get the papers from the embassy and coming back, especially since we had no one in Amman to go to.

We paid the amount, but after reviewing our papers, they found that the Indian lawyer had not completed the appeal documents within the specified period, so our conversion request was rejected. The lawyer informed us that our request was denied and that we had to go to Amman to settle our situation.

At that time, our eldest daughter was twelve years old, and the youngest was nine. The girls had started to become aware of the open life in American society, noticing the significant difference between our conservative Islamic life and the American way of life. Our closest friends and their friends were an American white family living across the street from us, with daughters the same age as our eldest and youngest daughters and even a son the same age as our son. They were inseparable. Our children noticed the contradictions between what we told them in our upbringing and preaching and the lives of these friends and others in the street and school.

This raised many questions for them that we struggled to answer. One evening, I came home from work to find my wife surprised by our daughter's question. Her dear friend, who spent most of her time with her, had asked her the question, and she didn't know how to answer it. I told my wife, "You know, it's time to reconsider our entire life in the United States. Let's go to Amman, settle our papers, and live there for a while so our children can learn the language, religion, customs, and traditions. The time is right for this now because, in a few years, it will be too late."

We agreed that at the end of the year after the season ended, I would go to Amman first, prepare everything, and then they would follow me after the school year ended. Certainly, such a decisive decision required thorough consideration from all sides, whether from the work perspective or the home perspective. It was not easy, especially since I was at the peak of my success. The first thing I did was contact the director of the company I had signed a preliminary agreement with. He took the news graciously, wished me luck, and asked me to send a fax requesting cancellation. He also asked me to contact him first upon my return to reactivate the agreement, as I told him our absence wouldn't be long.

The second thing I did was start preparing to sell my store, as I found several buyers. I contacted the manager of the real estate company, the owner of the shopping center, but he completely refused the idea. He told me, verbatim, "Look around; you will find that all the existing stores are branches of chain stores or sequential stores, and you are the only individual tenant. We have rented to you for ten years without any problems or delays in rent payments. If someone else takes over, we don't know how they will be, and we don't want to take that risk. If you want to leave the store, so be it, but don't think about selling it. We will rent it to a chain store like the others."

When I realized that this decision was final for the company, and since this man had become a friend and would not lie to me, I had to reconsider the whole matter and plan to exit the store in the most beneficial way. It was August at that time, so I had four months to finish dealing with the store and sell everything in it. I informed the company that I would not renew the contract for the next period and stopped paying rent in protest of their decision to prevent me from selling the store.

A company in Chicago specialized in liquidation (liquidating) stores and constantly advertised this service. I contacted them, and it turned out that they take a net 25% of the proceeds from the liquidation. I thought to myself, why should I lose such a large percentage? I asked what they do for that fee, and they explained in detail, sending me information and a video about their work.

After reviewing the contents, I decided to take these steps myself without paying that percentage. My first step was to put up a large sign at the front of the store and on the street front, saying there were big discounts because the store would be closing. As soon as my customers read it, they flocked in, unable to believe what they were reading—that Elegant Man was closing its doors forever.

Some of the ladies who used to come to buy for their men, which is very common in America, came and severely reproached me, feeling deeply disappointed. I knew many of them by name and was asked how I could close such a store. Many expressed their sorrow, hugging me and apologizing as if they were the reason contributing to the store's closure. Truly, some were very attached to my presence and my store's existence to the extent that they often made me feel guilty, but the decision had been made.

I made settlements with all the companies that supplied me. As the end of the year approached, my sales reached record highs after I adopted an intensive advertising policy on radio stations and offered significant discounts to all customers, not rejecting any deal. By the end of the year, I had sold everything in the store, even the small tools I used in the shop. The financial outcome was excellent by all standards. I achieved an increase of about 50% over the selling price I would have asked for had the shopping center's manager agreed to it.

But I always believed that when God Almighty closes one door in your face, He opens a thousand others instead.

At the end of the year, we set the travel date for late February, with my wife to follow in early June after the children finished school. I had to try to finish as many pending matters as possible before my departure. I made a settlement with the lawyer representing me and the company owning the shopping center after I sent them the store keys by registered mail at the end of the year. The settlement was that I would pay only 25% of the due rent.

I remember when I went to hand over the store license to the state sales tax department, where we paid sales tax every month collected from customers, the employee was surprised. He said, "I know your store well; it was very successful." When he looked at my record and saw I was always on time with the tax returns and payments, he said losing my store from our city was unfortunate. The surprise came when, after giving him two checks representing the last two months of payments, he returned one check and said, "This is enough for the two months. Isn't the loss that you closed your store?" He then said the state remained stronger than you and returned the larger check, which was about a thousand dollars at that time. I thanked him, and he told me, "Anytime you need help, I'm here to serve you."

The period between finishing the sale of the last item in my store and handing over the keys until the travel date was dedicated to completing all pending matters to reduce the burden on my wife during my absence. She would have to handle many things, such as preparing four children for school and organizing the house and its contents for shipping to Amman.

One of the hardest things I did was sell my favorite car in the whole world after having it for more than six years. I was very sad handing over its keys to the buyer. I had taken great care of it, subjecting it to continuous maintenance, mostly at the same company, so the car was in very good condition when I sold it.

I also listed the house for sale and gave a power of attorney to one of my close friends in case it didn't sell in time because houses are not as easy to sell as cars.

Amman, Once Again

Time has flown by quickly, and before I knew it, my departure was drawing near. I started thinking about embarking on a new phase of our lives; we were about to turn a new page and undergo a new migration in this life. This time, I would return to Jordan, specifically to Amman—the city that witnessed the crazy upheavals in my life. Here I am, returning after 14 years of absence.

The night of departure arrived, and my friends and family came to see me off, filling the large house to its brim. They couldn't believe how I could leave everything I had achieved behind and embark on this journey, especially since many of them had spent even longer years without achieving even a fraction of what we, the newcomers, had.

I remember many of them saying that Abu Firas wouldn't last more than a month in Jordan. One said he wouldn't last three months, while my brother-in-law claimed that stubborn Abu Firas would persist for six months in Amman. As I listened, my brother-in-law asked if it was really conceivable that I'd stay for six months. I told him the truth: I intended to stay for six years. Everyone laughed, thinking I was joking, considering all those who came from America to Amman didn't last more than a year before returning.

The farewell at Greenville Airport was stormy. There were my wife, children, relatives, and friends, bidding me farewell with tears and many hugs as if they would never see me again, as if I were going to the ends of the earth. I had a strong desire to raise my children in an Arab community where the language, customs, and predominant religion were Islamic, guiding all behaviors.

I wanted my children to know they have relatives—uncles, aunts, and a grandmother—all from their mother's side. They knew nothing except what I told them, which was different from what they saw in reality. They had roots, and I, too, for a moment, almost forgot where I came from, who my people were, and the details of their lives, and that they, too, had a homeland we were forced to leave.

All of this propelled me towards the time for change, even at the peak of my glory. My children, especially my daughters, aged 12 and 9, were beginning to be influenced by American life. They noticed everything, especially the limitless openness where nothing was considered improper.

My journey was direct to New York, specifically to JFK Airport, from where we would board a Royal Jordanian flight directly to Amman. As soon as I arrived at JFK, I headed to the Royal Jordanian gate. Everything was straightforward, as I had grown accustomed to airplanes and airports. I wondered if this might be my last time at an American airport or on American soil. Could this journey be the eternal one with no return? I loved this country and these people and had grown accustomed to the life, freedom, language, and people here. America the mother of the world, where everything was easy, and people smiled wherever you looked.

We had everything here—money, family, home, cars, stability, security, peace, and independence. It wasn't the same feeling I had when I boarded the plane coming to America from Dhahran Airport. I was happy when I left, and I don't know why I felt sad as I bade farewell to the last piece of American land, maybe because I was alone without my family, whereas I had come with them.

And here were the staff and passengers, all heading to Amman, all speaking Arabic. I never really snapped out of these thoughts as I sipped my favorite coffee from Starbucks, which I had bought at the airport café—a place I considered one of the most important inventions of our modern era, even if many disagreed.

And then, the announcer at JFK Airport declared that passengers on the Royal Jordanian flight to Amman should head to gate number... Yes, that was my flight, my journey!

I woke up from my dream and walked to the gate with these people. After completing the usual procedures, I boarded the plane. For some reason, at that moment, I felt a strange sensation as if I were already in Amman, and as if those 14 years had never passed, hearing everyone speaking our dialect.

Especially when the flight attendant came over after I settled in my window seat—as I had requested—and asked me in a Jordanian-Palestinian accent what I would like to drink. I don't know how, but that strange feeling disappeared, and I felt safe.

The long hours we spent in the air were, for me, hours spent pondering what tomorrow might hold for us—this great concern that we all fear. What has changed in Amman, Jordan, and the always turbulent Middle East? Could we live there, or would we go to Palestine and live there? Could my family live and adapt, whether in Jordan or in Palestine and would we be allowed to if we decided to do so?

Despite those anxieties that took me back and forth, I strongly believe that God always creates reasons for our days to be beautiful. I have always clung to this faith that what is destined will happen to us in the end, and we are just executing it. I always reassured my wife, who was always fearful of the future. I comforted her by saying, "We came to America not knowing the language, customs, or people. We were strangers in every sense of the word in this society, but we managed to achieve a lot with God's grace and our parents' blessings. Now, we are migrating to our land, country, and people, and thankfully, we are rich in experience, culture, life, and money, so don't worry about tomorrow—it will be better, God willing. And if we succeed in our lives in America, we will succeed anywhere, God willing."

With these words, which often cured her of all doubts and obsessions, the hours from New York to Amman were strenuous and tiring. We counted the hours as they passed, hour by hour until the 11-hour flight directly between New York and Amman elapsed. Signs of relief began to appear on us. I felt a shiver run through my body when the pilot announced in Arabic to fasten our seat belts as we crossed Palestinian territories and approached Queen Alia International Airport in Amman.

As soon as the plane touched down in Amman and the captain welcomed us to Amman, my heart began to beat faster. Here we are in Amman, finally. As we gathered our belongings and moved out of the plane into the corridor leading inside the airport, where stern-faced security officers carrying communication devices inspected everyone coming out of the gate, I smiled inwardly and thought, "Yes, we have arrived."

I finished with a stamp on my passport, which was about to expire after the security officer who stamped it asked me, "Where are you going?" I told him, "God knows, my relatives are waiting outside in Amman." He nodded his head and said in a commanding tone, "Don't forget to renew your passport," to which I nodded in agreement.

I remembered, we are in Jordan; everything here goes in a different tone. You don't see smiles or hear someone saying words like 'go ahead' or 'please.' As soon as I picked up my bags and went out where everyone was waiting, I found my friends Nadeem, whom I hadn't seen for more than 14 years since I was in Amman and we were colleagues at the Jordan Kuwait Bank, and Abu Alaa, whom I met while I was an active member of the Banking Union. I maintained friendships with them even while I was abroad, and also the father of my dearest friends in America, Mazen's father, Al-Haj "Abu Nabil"; God rest his soul, who always stood by me. He visited me at my store, and we had a special relationship. My friend Mazen gave me the keys to the villa he owned in the Tareq area, also known as Taborbor, which had only an Indonesian maid and an Egyptian guard. He told me to live there until I decided what I intended to do in Amman.

The three came, each one in his own car, and each tried to get me to ride with them, but of course, I rode with Haj Abu Nabil out of respect for his age and for him coming to the airport to welcome me. My friends followed us because we were headed to Mazen's house.

The car drove through all these new streets in the new areas of Amman, which I did not know, even though I used to pride myself on knowing every corner of Amman when I lived there. Haj Abu Nabil explained their names to me. Amman, which was growing not just naturally but also constantly experiencing waves of migration triggered by the instability that affected neighboring countries, bringing population waves seeking refuge in.

Jordan

Amman had changed a lot, which I confirmed to Haj Abu Nabil as he showed me the streets, buildings, and new areas until we reached the Taborbor area, which was also new. We arrived at my friend Mazen's house, which occupied a large area and had a large garden cared for by the Egyptian guard. Mazen, the self-made friend who became a millionaire at the age of 25, had bought that house at his parents' wish as a status symbol while he lived in America, coming sometimes in the summer.

We arrived with our friends, who were following us in their cars, and stayed up late after the Indonesian maid in the house served us dinner brought by my friend's sister from her nearby home.

I woke up early as usual and went out to smell the morning air of Amman, which is unlike anything else, truly having missed it. I went out to the garden to inhale the fragrance of the early dawn hours, which I am enamored with wherever I am. Only the smell of falafel and hummus, which my friend's father brought early after the maid prepared a large breakfast table for us, interrupted it.

Return to Amman

I had to set my priorities for what I would do, which was a lot. I was content on the first day to go out with Haj Abu Nabil to get to know more about Amman. Sitting next to him, a veteran driver, was a unique experience as he taught me the meaning of driving a car on the streets of Amman.

Suddenly, I remembered how people were tense, racing in the streets, wanting to get there first, even if they had nothing. But the congestion, stares, and sometimes curses prevailed on the streets. What was I to do in this strange mix, coming from America, where order, prioritization, smiles, and comfort characterized everyone?

I decided to adventure on the third day and rent a car through a friend because I had many issues to resolve. I still did not know the streets or places, but in the end, I considered myself a son of Amman and had to experience it.

My friend explained the names of the main streets that connected the capital's outskirts, so I wrote them down on paper, and thus, I gradually got used to them. I would ask people if I lost my way—and often did—.

The important thing was that I knew the way back home, but the strange thing was that I found myself driving like them. If you drove according to priorities, as in America, you would remain at the roadside and not move an inch, and no one would pay you any attention.

I was in constant contact with my wife and family to reassure them and to reassure them that my affairs were going well.

I first went to the Arab Bank and opened an account there, depositing my money, and through a friend's wife, I rented a mailbox, so I had an address in Amman.

It was necessary to put an end to the issue of the rented car bleeding money and buy a car instead, especially since I would be settling here in Amman. I bought a white Mercedes also through some acquaintances.

I also began the chases and struggles to solve the problem of the passport and civil status at the Directorate of Monitoring and Inspection, which I suffered a lot. The result was that I lost the family book and the national number, meaning I became a Jordanian citizen with suspended execution.

A major reason for this was the disengagement announced in 1987 between the Palestine Liberation Organization and the Jordanian government, ten years before, and I was in Saudi Arabia at that time.

This is a long and complicated topic; if I wanted to write a book about it, I would, especially my reviews at the Ministry of Interior, where I experienced racial discrimination from the employees as I moved between departments, even knowing the Deputy Minister of Interior and the legal advisor explaining that disengagement does not apply to me.

None of this helped correct my situation. I was also exposed to having to pay sums reaching 5,000 dinars to correct my status, but I refused to pay such amounts, especially since the problem was originally caused by an unintended mistake by an employee at the Jordan Kuwait Bank. In 1984, I gave him my military service book to renew it. At that time, they had invented the yellow and green cards three years before the disengagement. They told the man he had to choose a card to fill out, and when he asked them what the difference was between them, they said they did not know.

Then the man was confused and chose a green card for me because it was a green way since I was traveling.

This was the wrong choice I am paying for now.

I don't know why this reminded me of my reviews at the immigration office in America.

Is it fate and part of every Palestinian's life to be confused among immigration offices around the world?

The important thing is that I did not give up on this new reality and said I would work to change it, God willing.

Palestine after 19 Years of Absence

While I was struggling with the governmental procedures in Jordan, my family was trying to obtain a visit permit for me to travel to Palestine. This effort followed the visit of my younger brother Sabri from our village. I saw him for the first time in 19 years; the last time we met, he was no older than 13. I had gone looking for him as he played in the neighborhood to bid him farewell before I left. Now, he has a son playing in the same neighborhood. When my brother came, one of the outcomes of his visit was that he introduced me to a group of relatives who had returned from Kuwait. I had heard about them but had never met or seen them before.

I began preparing for my trip to Palestine after receiving the visit permit. This event, returning after so many years, was a significant milestone in my life. I had left Palestine as an eighteen-year-old youth, and now I was returning at double that age, no longer a young man but a father of a family of six. I also carried the experiences of more than five migrations with me.

My father passed away while I was far away in Saudi Arabia, and I had not seen my mother since I got married, which was 15 years ago. I hadn't seen my other brothers and sisters either. How would this reunion be? But I had to prepare because this day was inevitably coming as I had set it as the date for my trip to Palestine.

I woke up early, as usual on that day and headed to the bridge cars after gathering all the details and information I needed to make my return to Palestine as smooth as possible. After all, it was my first time. The bridge car left Abdali station in the morning, the same station I had arrived at 19 years ago, coming from

Palestine. Now, I am returning to Palestine from this station after many years and many life changes. I asked the driver not to let anyone sit next to me in the front seat after paying him the extra fare because I wanted an hour of reflection. The distance between Amman and the King Hussein Bridge, or the Allenby Bridge as the Isreals call it, was a time for me to soar high in my thoughts. How would my mother and the rest of my family react when they saw me for the first time after all these years? As the car cut through the Jordan Valley road, which was now blanketed in spring from both sides, I thought to myself that this was the best time to be in Palestine, in the spring.

After the procedures on the Jordanian side were completed, despite one of the security officers trying to make an issue of the green card and passport, everything went smoothly. We boarded the bus, crossing the Jordan River to the Palestinian side of the bridge, to face the Israeli procedures, which were usually complicated, lengthy, and stifling, including thorough scrutiny and numerous questions.

One of the most annoying encounters was with a blonde female soldier, likely from Russia, who asked me in broken Arabic while inspecting my visit permit if I had an ID. I replied that I used to have an ID, but it was taken from me. She continued scrutinizing the permit, hoping to find something, but in vain. Then she said, "You don't have an ID; you need to consult the authorities." I responded, "Okay." She stamped the permit, allowing me to pass. After completing the rest of the procedures, I exited. The first thing I encountered was a taxi driver, whom I recognized from his accent as a native of Hebron, who asked me in his distinctive Palestinian accent, "Do you need a taxi, brother?"

I said, "Yes."

The driver: "Where are you going?"

Me: "Ramallah."

The driver: "Get in."

Me: "How much do you want?"

The driver: "150 shekels."

Me: "Okay, what if I want you to take me to my village?"

The driver: "What's the name of your village?"

Me: "The village of Abwein."

The driver: "Oh, I know it. Get in."

Me: "How much do you want?"

The driver: "200 shekels."

Me: "Okay, but I have one condition."

The driver, with his Hebron accent: "What's the condition?"

Me: "You need to help me find our house because I don't know it."

The man laughed in the characteristic Hebron manner.

The driver: "How can someone not know their own house?"

Me: "I don't know because I've been away for a long time, and our house has changed since then."

The driver: "How long have you been away, brother?"

Me: "19 years."

The driver, raising his eyebrows: "That's a shame, man. Who stays away for that long?"

Me: "Circumstances and exile dictated it."

The driver: "Get in, get in, you live, and you learn."

I got into the car with the man, and we headed to Palestine. My God, this is real. The car was moving through the Jordan Valley, passing Jericho and climbing the barren mountains that separate the valley from Jerusalem. The shantytown houses, made of corrugated iron sheets, were still standing on both sides, unchanged.

Finally, the car took a bypass road around Ramallah, passing by the settlements built by the occupation. The driver often cursed the Jews and their day, but sometimes he would say, "When they made these roads, it made things much easier for us." We passed through 'Ein al-Haramiyyeh to Sinjil and Jaljilia, and there was Abwein, my village, coming into view. Yes, I was entering it after dreaming of this moment many nights. I had seen it in my dreams; it was the same village, unchanged, the street was the same street. We hadn't gone far when I saw a young man standing in front of his house. I asked the driver to stop so we could ask this young man about the house of my eldest sister, Umm Muhannad, whom I had last seen on my wedding day when she was passing from Kuwait to Palestine. Her house was described to me as being at the entrance of the village.

As soon as the driver stopped, I got out of the car and said to the young man, "Hello."

He replied, "Hello."

I asked him, "Where can I find the house of Umm Muhannad?"

The young man looked at me with great astonishment and asked, "What do you want from her?"

He stared at me intently, and I was puzzled by his hostile tone. Then he suddenly shouted, "Are you Uncle Younes?"

I replied, surprised, "And who are you?"

He said, after embracing me, "I am Muhannad, Uncle," and started shouting at the top of his voice, "Mom, Mom, it's Uncle Younes! Your brother is here!"

My sister came out, not even noticing that her head was uncovered, not knowing what to say. Sometimes she ululated, sometimes she collapsed on the ground, and sometimes she crawled towards me. We met halfway, and she threw herself at me, hugging and kissing me. Her voice choked as she said, "Thank God for your safety, my dear brother." Tears welled up in my eyes. Those moments were among the most dramatic in my life. How could they not be when my sister and I had a very special bond, growing up together before my emigration and before her marriage and subsequent emigration to Kuwait?

She could hardly contain herself as she told Muhannad, "Give me my headscarf and close the doors. We're going to your grandmother's house." She got into the car with me, still staring at me in disbelief. We drove until we passed by a frail, grey-haired man walking on the street. My sister asked, "Do you know who that is?"

I said, "No."

She said, "That's your brother, Mar'i."

I asked the driver to stop, and I got out of the car. The surprise hit him like a lightning bolt when he recognized me. He hugged me tightly, tears streaming down his face. I saw how over three years of imprisonment and torture in Israeli jails had taken their toll on him. Even the driver was deeply moved by what he saw, his voice showing his emotion as he asked where we were headed.

We were headed to our mother's house, which was beside my brothers' homes, after she left our old house. When the car stopped in front of her small house, which my brothers and I had helped build for her since she wanted to live near them but not with them, she saw me approaching. Her tongue froze, and she just hugged me as I tried to kiss her hands and forehead, her tears mingling with the few words she tried to say. She touched my face and said, "Is it really you, Younes? Thank God, I finally see you before I die."

I hugged her and took her inside her house, then went back to the driver, thanked him for his patience, and paid him. He seemed deeply affected by what he witnessed.

In a matter of minutes, the news spread. People came from everywhere, hardly believing it. Before sunset that day, I asked my brothers to take me to my father's grave so I could greet him, offer my respects, and recite Al-Fatiha for him. We went, and it was the first time I visited his grave. I couldn't hold back my tears as I recited Al-Fatiha over his soul. I asked for his forgiveness, even though he was beneath the soil, for any pain I caused him as a child or as I grew up. I also asked for his forgiveness for my long absence, even though he was always present in my thoughts, my prayers, and my supplications.

We then returned to my mother's house, where my youngest brother and his family had prepared dinner for us. After dinner, my brother's house filled with villagers coming to greet and get to know me. It was the first time I saw so many of our relatives and villagers in one place. Naturally, everyone knew me, but I didn't recognize any of them, not even my nieces and nephews, who seemed to have grown up so quickly that I couldn't distinguish between them. These young men and women were my age when I first left because the taste of my exile was different while they were born, lived, and grew up in different circumstances.

But here they all were.

Everyone had heard about me and my small family, and this was the first time they saw me. They all stared at me as if I had been a myth and suddenly became a reality before their eyes.

The night passed perfectly. After the many people dispersed, I stayed at my younger brother Sabri's house, who was no longer as young as I used to call him but had become the head of a family of seven. He had also been imprisoned and tortured in Israeli prisons for over a year for being a leader in the first Intifada.

I woke up early and found that my mother, who I insisted should sleep next to me in the same room, had slipped away to her small house at dawn for Fajr prayer. When I didn't find her, I went to her, kissed her hand and forehead, and sat with her outside the house. Before anyone else woke up, with the sunrise, she made us two cups of coffee. We drank together, and she still stared at me, unable to believe that I was really beside her.

How those were some of the happiest moments of my life, drinking coffee made by my mother in her presence. The dawn and sunrise have a different color and tastes in Palestine. Watching the sunrise and dawn yawn, emerging from the wings of darkness, the sun sneaking between the waves of clouds and fog gathering on these sprawling mountains, which seemed much higher than I remembered, extending long until they touched the Palestinian coasts—the Mediterranean Sea, which we could see from the mountains of our village.

This wonderful spring day made me feel as if I was reborn, blossoming along with the red poppies and oleander flowers that covered the green grass around us and all the Palestinian prairies. I just contemplated and said, "Glory be to God," as if I was reclaiming a long-dormant part of myself.

Waking up early is one of my good habits that I cannot change. I am a morning person, even if I sleep late at night. Every day, I celebrate the rising sun, announcing a new day, no matter where I am in the world. These are the most important moments of my 24-hour day. Every decision I have made in my life started with the spark of those moments, early in the morning while others slept.

After an hour, my brother Sabri joined us with another pot of coffee he made himself. My brother and mother tried to recall what I had missed in those many past years, including memories of my father and how he passed away. May

God have mercy on him. My mother told me in detail what had happened, how he had passed away with great emotion, being a righteous and beloved man who was not tainted by worldly matters, maintaining his piety and fear of God in every action.

They told me the story of how I was never absent from his thoughts. On the night of the Eid al-Adha eve, when all my siblings and my mother gathered at my father's house in his presence, they discussed a family matter. Although the gathering was joyful, my father's happiness was incomplete as he became lost in thought. One of my brothers asked him, "What's on your mind, Hajji?"

My father sighed and said, "Isn't it a shame that your brother Younes is the only one not here? He is the only one absent."

Silence fell over everyone, and my mother said in a choked voice, "He has always been away from us. May God bring him back to us soon."

At that time, I was in Saudi Arabia.

They also told me many stories about the prison and the attempts by Israeli settlers and the army to confiscate our lands in Gharaaba (a high mountainous area where my father owned much land). My father, along with the villagers, resisted the Israelis, filed a complaint with the Israeli Supreme Military Court, and managed to regain the land after the Israeli settlers had fenced it off with a metal barrier.

Naturally, I took a tour of our village, which I had left 19 years ago, on my first day. Yes, things had changed. Everything had changed except for the streets, which were still small and potholed just as badly. I didn't understand why the municipal council hadn't improved these streets, unlike other villages.

But the neighborhoods had changed. Everyone had left the old town and migrated, building new houses, as did their children, just like my brothers did in the new area of the village. The people there didn't resemble each other anymore;

everyone had changed, and so had I. Yes, I had aged 19 years, and I was no longer that young adolescent who people admired. I had become a middle-aged man.

Gray hair started creeping into my head, and I had gained weight, even developed a belly, whereas I used to be fit and well-proportioned. The truth is, I hadn't paid much attention to this until we happened to meet a woman, the sister of a friend of mine. Her husband had left her after three months of marriage, and she was once known for her beauty and rebellious nature. I didn't recognize her, but she shouted when she saw me with my brother, "Younes, what happened to you? You've grown, and so has your belly. You used to be a model, but time has changed you."

Of course, I laughed, and quickly, my brother told me her name. I remembered immediately and said to her, "You still look the same, mashallah." This was a compliment, though the truth was quite the opposite. This encounter opened a big challenge for me to recognize at least some of the people.

Everyone knew me, not because of anything special but because they heard that Younes had returned, and since I was walking with my brothers, they assumed I was the long-absent brother. Even the people of my generation, I couldn't recognize any of them when we met.

My God, had I aged just like them, becoming bald and with a big belly? Surely, I must have looked like them now. Even my brothers walking beside me didn't seem like my brothers any more, or so I thought. Or was it that time had taken its toll on us all?

I needed my brothers to prompt me when we met someone, saying in surprise, "Hey man, don't you recognize me?" I would reply, "Oh man, you haven't changed much; you're so-and-so." This would lighten their mood, making them think they hadn't changed. Is it human nature to resist the idea of aging?

With my brothers' help, this strategy worked to some extent, making me appear less ignorant of those I didn't know. It was as if I had quickly filled my thirst for seeing people. Imagine being thirsty, seeing water, drinking, and then no longer needing it. I felt no need to know everyone or every place. Why would I, knowing I might not see them again?

People would likely ask me the same question again, "Hey man, don't you recognize me?" By then, my brothers might not be around to prompt me. The truth is, I wouldn't remember what I had learned, and the problem is that everyone believes they haven't aged or changed, including me. But the reality is we have all aged and changed.

I remembered an old man, the father of a friend of mine, whom I met at my friend's house in Greenville, South Carolina. When he returned from a visit to Nazareth after 40 years of absence, I asked him how he found Nazareth.

The old man sighed and said to me, "You know, Abu Firas!"

I waited for the man to continue, who took a deep drag from his cigarette and said, "Imagine the following: you once knew an elegant, sweet young woman, fully feminine. Then suddenly, you are away from her for 40 years. During those years, you continue to imagine that young woman, with all her beauty, elegance, sweetness, and everything wonderful about her. When you return, you find that she has become an old, worn-out woman, her body and face weathered by the sun and time, giving her a color without color and a taste without flavor. That's what I found Nazareth to be like."

The man's words and his sigh lingered within me. Despite the celebratory atmosphere my family tried to create during this visit, this feeling of unease dominated me. I don't know why I felt this way throughout my visit, despite my attempts to visit the places I was attached to, places that had moved me deeply. Most of them had either been demolished or eroded by time.

One of the places I was determined to visit was a spot in the wilderness about a 15-minute walk from the village called "Al-Karakaf." It used to be a paradise in my eyes when I was a child. It was filled with vineyards, fig trees, and olive trees. My father owned a large part of the area and kept it in pristine condition, considering it was a stone's throw from our house.

He even took care of the wild trees there, such as hawthorn and oak. I had a special bond with a large oak tree in the middle of our land. In a moment of childhood fantasy, I believed this tree to be the mother of all trees due to its grandeur and dominance over the others. A black grapevine climbed and intertwined with this oak, growing beautifully together. I had set up a cozy spot at the top of this oak, placing a piece of bedding there to sit for hours. From the highest point of the tree, I had a wide view of my surroundings. I savored the black grapes directly from the vine that climbed the strong oak, much like me.

My happiness was immense when I learned from my father that his destination that morning was Al-Karakaf. I had a unique bond with that oak tree. Even as I grew older, it remained my friend. I would take a book or story and a water flask, reading from the top of the oak.

I decided to visit that area, and I was shocked by what I saw! The flat, red earth, free of stones, once as smooth as the palm of a hand, the neatly arranged stone terraces, and the tall, dense trees reaching for the sky were all gone. I couldn't comprehend it and doubted if this was the same place I remembered. Weeds and tall thorns covered everything, even competing with the sad, ancient trees still standing or what was left of them.

The terraces, once arranged in a marvelous geometric pattern, were gone. I remembered trying to build like my father once did, who laughed and tried to teach me, saying, "You need to put the big stone at the bottom, then the smaller ones." But I failed as my father laughed and said to me, "Stay smart in school; you don't need this work."

I found those terraces had collapsed, their stones mixed together, the land merging with no clear boundaries between them. I couldn't help but imagine my father, may he rest in peace, who had poured his sweat into every handful of soil and every stone in this land as he worked on it.

I felt a severe lump in my throat, and tears welled up in my eyes as I saw all this. Even my friend, the oak tree, was reduced to nothing but the remains of a massive trunk, cut down by someone for firewood after they had ravaged it and burned a large part of it. The hand of neglect and destruction had reached even our old house, part of which was demolished by bulldozers to widen the road in front of it.

After my father, may he rest in peace, passed away; we all left this land and house, engaging in anything but its upkeep. I can't blame anyone; I was the first to leave, and my brothers did the same. But was it time, exile, occupation, or the hardships of life? Still, I couldn't help but repeat, "May God have mercy on you, Father." Yes, they were the generation that turned this land into a life, a homeland, and a history.

I don't know why, but I collected myself in those moments and thought, I don't want to spoil all the memories in my head. I need to leave. I carried my great disappointment and headed back.

The next day, I set off for Ramallah, hoping to ease the harshness that had befallen me the previous day. Ramallah had witnessed important phases of my life. Not much had changed even after the return of the Authority. Yes, some buildings had started to appear, and new streets had been paved due to geographic expansion.

I went to look for my old residence and found the house abandoned after the death of the lone woman who lived there. Her children had all stayed in America, and there was no one I could talk to. I walked back to the city, remembering the road I used to take daily, passing by shops I once knew and greeting people by their names.

All the scenes had changed. I passed by a taxi office; the owner's son had been one of my closest friends, and we often traveled together in their cars. I decided to go in and ask about him. The owner was not there, but a man was working. After asking about my friend, he said that he had gone home for lunch but had spoken to him a few minutes ago, and he was on his way back to the office. The man invited me to wait inside, so I decided to place a chair outside the office and sit with him. I learned that his father had passed away, and he was now the owner of the taxi office with a fleet of cars.

The last time I saw him was in Amman when his father had sent him to study medicine in Italy. He returned after six months, declaring he couldn't master Italian or medicine. He stayed with me in Amman for a few days before returning to Ramallah, preferring to stay with his father in the business he understood well.

I had not finished my cup of tea when a taxi from the office stopped in front of us. A bald man with a belly got out, and the man I was with said, "Here he comes." I thought, could this really be him? The one who used to take care of his long hair and appearance? Could this be me too? Have I changed this much?

The strange thing was as soon as he stepped out of the car, he immediately recognized me. Had I met him elsewhere, I wouldn't have recognized him at all. I spent the rest of the day with him. He took me to lunch, and we talked and laughed about the past and memories until late into the night.

I told him I wanted to return to our village, and he said, "Okay, I'll take you." But I replied, "No, you won't do that. It's a long trip. Just take me to the village taxi stand, and I'll take a service taxi or the yellow bus from there."

Indeed, he took me there after we asked about the Abwein taxi stand. Then, I boarded a taxi that only needed one more passenger. After bidding farewell to my friend, who asked me to visit him again, I promised to do so if time allowed.

I got into the taxi and said, "Peace be upon you," after the driver closed the door on my side, signaling our departure to the village. The car was full, and I assumed that everyone was a worker finishing their late shift. I examined the faces around me, hoping to recognize someone and start a conversation, but I found no one familiar. For a moment, I even doubted that I was in the right car, so I asked the driver again if this car was headed to Abwein. The man confirmed it.

That was the last thing I said in the taxi as silence enveloped everyone. I was very surprised that no one spoke to me or recognized me. I never felt more alienated in my life than during those 45 minutes between Ramallah and our village at night.

I decided to contemplate the darkness that enveloped the olive trees we passed by. The only thing that broke those moments of contemplation was our arrival at the village next to my sister's house, where she had invited me for dinner that night.

As I was about to get out, the man sitting next to me shyly asked, "Aren't you Younes?" I looked at him, full of reproach, and said, "A bit late, isn't it?" I closed the door, and the car drove away from me.

I don't know why I felt deeply disappointed as I walked the distance between the street and my sister's house

. I had to visit Jerusalem.

Yes, Jerusalem is the only place that doesn't change and will never change. It has been there for thousands of years, with thousands of generations passing through it. I had to prepare myself and go alone to Jerusalem, which means a lot to me both personally and as a city that belongs to all people and all religions.

I drank my morning coffee, ate something light at my brother's house, and took the car to Ramallah. From there, I headed to the cars bound for Jerusalem and boarded one. We stopped at the Qalandiya checkpoint, which was still a checkpoint in those days, not like a border point as it is now. The heavily armed Israeli soldier scrutinized my permit and the IDs of the other passengers. After that, we continued our journey to the car stand near Damascus Gate.

As soon as I got out, I was face to face with Damascus Gate and its massive gate. Seeing it filled me with peace and tranquility. Truly, Jerusalem had remained unchanged for hundreds of years, so how could it change in the 19 years I was away?

There it was, with its high, majestic walls and huge stones. There were the sellers of bread rings and falafel and the kiosks inside the walls near Damascus Gate. The peasant women from the neighboring villages of Jerusalem were still lined up, sitting and selling all the produce that the Palestinian land generously offered.

This might be another generation, perhaps their daughters, for this work is passed down from generation to generation. There was the descending staircase to the old, covered markets, guarded by a group of green-capped soldiers, always ready with their hands on the trigger. They were young, another generation whose origins we didn't know—perhaps from an African country, a communist country, or somewhere else in the world. They scatter us across all countries of the world while they gather on this sacred land from every part of the world.

This situation won't last long for them. History and Jerusalem have taught us that the people of the land have changed, and soldiers of history have trampled its streets since dawn. But in the end, it returns to being Arab. I am certain that even if they build thick walls and crowded settlements around it, the

Lord of Jerusalem is stronger than them. History's inevitable change means no occupier remains forever, even if they hold power now and stay for hundreds of years.

The old markets exuded the aroma of falafel, spices, and history. People crowded those old, covered streets, and your shoulder often brushed against someone else's, whose origin you couldn't tell. People from all over the world walked there—blonde, yellow, black. Passing by Jaafar's knafeh, you couldn't help but taste it.

I then headed to Al-Aqsa Mosque after asking for the nearest way. I walked through the narrow, covered streets. I noticed the Israeli flags prominently displayed on a building, heavily guarded. Curiosity led me to ask a young man standing in front of his shop near the building, and he replied angrily, "That animal Sharon came and seized it. See the soldiers guarding it and him? May God take him." I continued my journey through the narrow streets until a policeman or guard at the gate stopped me, asking, "Are you Muslim?" I replied affirmatively, and he asked for my ID. I gave him my passport, and he quickly glanced at it and handed it back.

Finally, my feet stepped onto the courtyards of Al-Aqsa and the Dome of the Rock. The sky suddenly opened up, filled with sunlight, and the Dome of the Rock shone brightly before me, dazzling even if you had seen it a hundred times before. This light and the golden dome gleamed, reflecting in your mind as it did from the sun's rays. You find yourself staring for a long time before realizing you are in front of the Dome of the Rock, in the presence of Al-Aqsa Mosque.

I spent over an hour inside the Dome of the Rock, sometimes praying and sometimes contemplating the sanctity of this place. Then, I went to Al-Aqsa Mosque, where I stayed for another hour, praying and reflecting. The mosque sits on a hill overlooking the scattered parts of the surrounding towns of Jerusalem.

After that, I headed to the Church of the Holy Sepulchre and then to Jaffa Gate, the gate that once separated East Jerusalem from West Jerusalem, which the Israelis had changed significantly on that side. Then, I returned to Damascus Gate, where I bought bread rings, falafel, and boiled eggs. I also bought a cup of tea, as I was very hungry, and sat on the stairs of Damascus Gate for an hour, eating my bread ring, drinking tea, and watching all the people entering and exiting the gate.

I then went to Salah al-Din Street, passing by the shop where I once worked. It looked very old, so I didn't enter.

Then I returned, with the sun about to set, and took the car back to Ramallah and Abwein.

Settling in Amman

This was the last day I spent in Palestine; afterward, I decided to return to Amman. This visit was supposed to be an opportunity to determine the future residence for my family and me when they return.

I felt like a stranger in my own country and did not feel that I had become a part of it again. I truly do not know why I no longer felt that I belonged there.

The decision was to return to Amman. I cut my vacation short; instead of staying a full month in Palestine, I reduced it to only ten days due to the signs I saw, and I decided to return and start my new life with my family in Amman.

In Palestine, my homeland, I felt like a stranger. There was chaos in everything: dealing with people, dealing with the newly established authority, which acted as if it was the savior that came to rescue them from the clutches of occupation. I even heard everywhere that anyone who wanted to start any project must include someone from the authority as a partner without any contribution, just to get things done. As they said, it was still chaos; there were no systems or laws, but rather improvisation in everything.

Most importantly, there was nothing I could provide for my children who were raised in America, surrounded by everything.

However, in Amman, the situation is entirely different. There is a state, a government, and a system. You can provide almost anything, especially for my family and children, who need a certain lifestyle at least in the beginning, so that the gap is not too big and the reaction is not negative, affecting their lives and behavior.

I concluded that Amman would be more suitable for us as a family, as well as for any business projects we intend to undertake during the few years we will spend in the Middle East. This would also allow the children to learn their language, religion, and Arabic customs.

As soon as I arrived in Amman, I began the search for a house. I rented a large house in the upscale area of Umm Al-Sumaq, which is close to everything on Mecca Street. I started preparing and purchasing essential appliances and other necessities in coordination with my wife, who was getting ready to ship our furniture after I sent her the container to our home and made the necessary arrangements. After the children finished school, she and the little ones began packing their bags, preparing for a new phase in our lives after we set the travel date and booked them a one-way flight to Amman.

My joy was immense as I prepared to reunite my family once more, this time in Amman. After the Royal Jordanian plane landed, I was accompanied by several friends and Haj Abu Nabil, who insisted we go to my friend's house, where I was still staying.

We stayed there for a week to rest from the journey. During that week, I took my family on tours around Amman. I also took them to see the house we rented, which they loved, and we decided to move in despite our furniture not having arrived yet. We bought the basics to get by at this stage and moved into our house in Umm Al-Sumaq. We lived on those basics until the container with our furniture finally arrived.

Despite the many difficulties we faced, we managed to overcome them and complete our home as we wanted. That period was hectic and packed with prioritizing and arranging our lives. Beginnings are always difficult and challenging, but if we endure the initial challenges, there is no doubt we will cross the bridge to a better life.

I had always been used to overcoming this stage in life. Yes, I had the experience of how beginnings come in a thousand shapes and forms, and if you are not strong, beginnings can break you. But this time, my burden was heavy because I was responsible for a family of six, unlike previous times. However, my faith in God and strong will always drove me.

First, during this period was to find schools for the children, especially since I noticed my daughters feeling frustrated and disappointed with the general situation in the country and being uneasy with the idea of being in Amman, feeling alone without friends. I asked them to be patient and to endure until the school season began after I finally chose schools for them, despite the high cost of private schools in Amman, which was a new issue for us since schools cost us nothing in America. I ensured the schools were similar to what they experienced in America to avoid drastic changes, allowing them to adapt gradually.

The biggest challenge for me was to start my project after arranging the basics for the family, especially since those arrangements consumed a significant part of the capital I brought with me. Simultaneously, I was working on correcting the issue of the national number and citizenship, which also consumed a lot of money and time. It seemed written that I would not find stability, as I always faced issues with identity and citizenship wherever I went. The curse of the Palestinian identity followed me. How could I start my project when things were not clear yet? I traveled with Jordanian citizenship and identity documents, but with a stroke of a pen, I was left without an identity, citizenship, or even a national number.

My initial idea for the project, even before leaving the United States, was related to tourism, specifically non-traditional tourism. I contacted a large American company that organizes international exhibitions and conferences. I offered to represent them in the Middle East, and they agreed in principle since they had no offices outside America. I told them I would continue to contact them via email if I settled in Jordan.

Shortly after my arrival, I started inquiring and understanding the local market. I found a specialized tourism institute offering a three-month course, which I joined. I sat in class once again, attending regularly and participating, although all the other students were much younger than me. I wanted to understand everything in this field, especially domestic tourism. This was before my family arrived in America.

For me, things were very easy, especially since I had spent more than half of my life traveling. I graduated with honors from the course and naturally received special treatment due to my age difference from the other students. I attended in my car and in full elegance!

At the time, I was exerting my efforts to find a place to start my tourism project or even buy an existing project so I wouldn't have to obtain new licenses. I considered buying a travel agency or a struggling company to restructure it so it could get the agency from the American company.

One day, I saw an advertisement in a widely circulated local newspaper about the sale of an international beauty agency. I decided to make a phone call to learn more details. A young man answered, introducing himself as Hisham, the responsible person, and suggested we meet face-to-face. We scheduled a meeting for the next day, and he gave me the time and place.

The next day, I went to meet the young man. I learned from him that the agency was for the American company Avon, which I knew well because I used to trade its shares while living in America. I knew it was a very prestigious company. I thought, why not see this opportunity?

Hisham explained to me that I was the 13th candidate, with twelve other companies in Jordan having already applied to purchase this agency. He told me I needed to submit a Letter of Intent to the company, which typically includes personal and professional achievements and questions about why I want to manage the agency and your vision for its development, as well as information about financial solvency.

This was a big challenge for me. I found myself competing with twelve companies, all of which were already established in the local market, some with significant experience. Meanwhile, I had recently arrived from America with no company and no experience in this market. I thought carefully about it and decided to participate despite the unequal competition. The spirit of challenge within me made me think, what do I have to lose by entering the competition? There was a slim chance I might win among these giants, and I could pursue my primary project simultaneously.

I resolved to try my luck and enter the competition. I immersed myself in gathering as much information as possible about Avon. I already had considerable knowledge about the company and its unique business model, which was taught in universities. I studied their methods in various markets.

I began drafting a roadmap of what I intended to do if I won the competition. I spent two full days writing the Letter of Intent, originally in Arabic, which I was proficient in. I then enlisted the help of my 13-year-old daughter Lara, who was fluent in English, to translate the letter professionally.

After crafting the letter in a commercial format, we printed it professionally. I took it to Hisham, who asked to read it. After reading it, his eyes widened, and he told me it was the best letter among all the others, incomparable because many of them did not understand the concept of a company like Avon. He told me he would send it along with the other letters via express mail and would inform me of any updates.

Not long after, Hisham contacted me, saying an Englishman had arrived in Amman and would interview each group member individually. He scheduled my interview for the next day at 9:30 AM in his office.

I prepared myself with the information I had gathered. Although I knew little about the beauty industry, I didn't know the difference between lipstick and eyeshadow. My expertise was in numbers, banking, and men's clothing, among other things. Beauty and women's topics were a different world for me. So, I had another idea to bring my wife along for the interview. Like most women, she knew the intricate details of this world.

Indeed, this idea had a positive impact throughout our five-hour session with Max, the Englishman in his late fifties, who had a very comforting demeanor. From the first moment, I felt I knew him. This feeling often occurs when meeting certain people for the first time, and the opposite can also be true.

I introduced myself and my wife. We talked extensively about many aspects of life and our professional journeys and even exchanged jokes. We conversed with ease, like friends, and I didn't feel it was an interview. The discussion about the company was brief. I shared information about Avon, which he seemed to hear about for the first time. My familiarity with the company stemmed from trading its shares and following it on the New York Stock Exchange.

Max took notes in his notebook. We drank tea and coffee until 2:30 PM when Hisham invited us to lunch, but we politely declined. I shook Max's hand as we said goodbye, and he held my hand firmly, saying we would meet again soon.

I learned that the session left a positive impression on Max when Hisham called that evening, telling me Max felt very comfortable with us and couldn't stop talking about us during lunch. He also told me our session was the longest among all candidates, some lasting only 30 minutes. Max had selected five candidates, including me.

Ten days later, Hisham called again, saying the competition had narrowed to three candidates, with Max confirming I was one of them. I replied that we should wait and see what happens.

Chapter 8 - The Golden Era

Night of Principles and Dawn of a New Project

It had been a long time for us, and one summer night in Amman, my wife and I sat on the balcony of our house discussing our options, especially since we had received the residency permits from the American embassy as promised. We debated the matter of our return to America, and after doing our calculations, we realized that the amounts we would spend on private schools in Amman could instead be used for our tickets and return expenses, especially since our house hadn't sold and was still available.

Additionally, there were daily complaints and grumblings from our young daughters. I still remember walking into their room one day and finding them crying. I asked them what was making them cry.

My eldest daughter said, "We want to ask you, Dad, what great sin did we commit to deserve being punished by bringing us here?"

I hugged her and said, "You have committed no sin. I just wanted to teach you your original language and for you to know who you are. Beginnings are always tough, but I promise if you don't like it here, we will return, God willing, and it won't be long." The school year had not yet started for them, so these days were perfect for our return. We considered our time in Amman a sort of vacation because, in the end, there is no comparison between the lifestyle here and there.

We decided to return to America and start anew, and how much easier it is to begin there compared to here. We also decided to sell our house's furniture and buy new ones there. I started writing an ad to sell our house furniture to put in the newspaper the next day. Just then, my cell phone, which I was holding in my hand, rang. It was an English female voice on the other end asking if I was Mr. Younes. When I replied yes, she introduced herself as Max's secretary, the Englishman, and said she was calling from Britain and that Mr. Max wanted to speak with me.

Max spoke to me as if we were friends, despite the typical English coldness, but he spoke warmly and said after the introductions that the meeting with us had left a lasting impression on him and that they had chosen me to represent Avon in Jordan. He added that he would send me a copy of the invitation, and the other copy would be sent to the British embassy so I could come to their headquarters in Northampton for a full week. He would send the program for the week-long visit with the invitation so we could get to know each other better. My meeting with him would be on the last evening over dinner with the big director responsible for all of Europe and the Middle East. Afterward, the final decision would be made if we liked each other.

I don't know how happy I was at that moment. Firstly, I had won over 13 competitors and was a candidate to take that agency. Secondly, this meant that our return to America would be postponed, at least for now. I hugged my wife and told her this would change our lives forever. I took the ad I had written and tore it to pieces.

I started preparing for the trip after receiving an email from Max with the details and began the process of obtaining the visa, which the embassy was initially hesitant to give me. However, Max sent them an email, a copy of which he sent me, which expedited the process, and they granted me the visa quickly. Not long after, I began preparing for the trip to London. As soon as I arrived at London Airport, I was met by someone holding a large sign with "Avon" and my name on it. He escorted me to a limousine, opened the back door for me, and sat in the back seat of the car, which then drove through the streets heading to Northampton.

We arrived at the main gate of Avon's headquarters, which is located on a beautiful riverside site occupying a vast area. As we reached the main entrance gate, it opened for us, and the driver stopped, rolled down my window, turned to me, and said, "Here is your flag, sir." I turned and saw them raising the Jordanian flag on the main flagpole alongside the British flag and the company's flag. I was surprised and didn't know what to do in this situation. The man noticed my hesitation and said in his elegant English accent, "If you wish to salute it." I saluted the Jordanian flag, knowing well that Jordan had stripped me of my national number, and I was no longer Jordanian, but here I was representing Jordan, and this was my flag.

After the car passed through the main gate, it stopped in front of the company's main lobby. The driver quickly opened my car door, and as I took my first steps, I saw an illuminated electronic sign with large letters welcoming me: "Welcome, Mr. Younes, our candidate representative for Jordan." Then, one of the employees approached and handed me a bouquet of flowers, saying, "Welcome."

Our friend Max was also in the main lobby to welcome me, and we had English tea together. He told me that he would pick me up from the hotel at 8 PM that evening to take me to dinner. He instructed the driver to take me to the hotel, where they had booked a luxurious room for me. After the receptionist handed me the room key, a hotel employee brought my luggage and opened the room door for me. Inside, I found a basket of Avon products as a gift with a welcome message from the senior manager of Northampton.

Even after dinner and the evening gathering, which included Max and a person named Ashley, who would later be my guide and mentor, and the sales manager Edwina, in a classic English restaurant not far from the city center, Max drove me back to my hotel room. After finishing a thorough English protocol day, I felt an unparalleled joy, something entirely new to me.

I couldn't help but remember the days when I used to walk from Jabal Al-Nuzha, starving because I didn't have even a few coins to take the bus or buy a falafel sandwich.

I spent a whole week in Northampton, following a meticulously prepared program. Avon had assigned Ashley, whom I had met on the first night, to accompany me daily. He would arrive at the hotel, which was not far from the company headquarters, at 9 AM each day to take me through the planned steps.

One of the highlights was a visit to the factory to see the manufacturing processes of all Avon products. I also visited the executive administration and was highly impressed by the advanced, organized technological stages that orders go through without human touch—from entering the computer to being picked and packed in the warehouse, regardless of order size, all automatically. The computer even determines the size of the cardboard box needed, prints the label with the address, and sorts it by region, ending with drivers who deliver the orders to representatives automatically, without any human intervention, despite the product line exceeding 1500 items.

My visit also included field operations, observing how the company's field system works and how the administrative regions are divided. I even spent a day with representatives visiting many homes. The week was full of activities, and I interacted wonderfully, making it one of the best experiences of my life, enhancing my expertise and introducing me to the new field of direct sales, which is Avon's core business.

At the end of the week, as scheduled, I was to meet Jerry, the general manager responsible for Europe and the Middle East. This was a memorable experience in itself. Max called me the day before the meeting and told me that Jerry had invited me to dinner at a very upscale restaurant in the famous English countryside. Max would pick me up in his car at 8 PM because the drive would take 30 minutes, with our appointment with Jerry at 8:30 PM.

I asked about the dress code, and he said, "Smart casual," meaning a jacket but no tie to avoid making the dinner too formal. Max arrived on time, and we set off. We found Jerry waiting for us, welcoming me warmly and asking if I was satisfied with what had been offered during the week. I assured him I was.

As we sat down, the waiter asked about the type of wine we preferred. This is customary in restaurants; they don't ask if you drink but rather what color wine you prefer, assuming everyone drinks wine with dinner. Jerry said white, Max said red, and when it came to me, I smiled and said, "Actually, I don't want wine. I'd like a diet soft drink."

The waiter replied, "Certainly." Jerry noticed what happened and stopped the waiter, apologizing to me and asking the waiter to replace their wine with soft drinks. I was very surprised by Jerry's polite behavior and told him it was okay for them to drink whatever they wanted, but I never drank alcohol. Jerry insisted, saying, "We will also not drink wine as long as you don't share it with us. We will share what you drink." I was very surprised by this extreme politeness.

Jerry then asked if my abstention from drinking was for religious reasons. I replied that it was partly religious but also because I had made it a principle in my life since I was young never to drink alcohol. Jerry nodded in respect, and we continued our dinner and evening without talking about work at all, despite my expectation that Jerry would bombard me with questions. We talked and laughed at jokes told by Jerry or Max as if we were three friends who hadn't seen each other in a long time until our evening ended late at night. Max drove me back to the hotel after we said goodbye to Jerry.

That dinner and evening had a significant impact on me, and I often tell this story in my gatherings, saying how the English respect people and principles. I even doubted that Balfour, the man behind the infamous declaration in Palestine, was related to any of them. On the final day, Ashley came at 9 AM for the final meeting with Max, who greeted me with a broad smile and said, "Jerry was very happy with you last night. He had never been so pleased with anyone he met before, and he sends his regards, saying you are our man. If you liked us and felt comfortable with us as we liked you and felt comfortable with you."

These words brought me immense joy. Max then warmly shook my hand and said, "Congratulations, you have earned our trust. We hope we have earned yours." Of course, they had earned my trust since they sent me the invitation to Amman.

The next day, I prepared to travel after agreeing with Max that a limousine driver would pick me up at 8 AM to spend a full day in London since my flight from Heathrow Airport was late. The driver and the car stayed with me all day, guiding me through all the landmarks and things I had heard about in London. I spent a wonderful day on my first visit to that city. Two hours before my flight, the driver took me to the airport, from which I flew back to Amman, carrying wonderful memories and the Avon agency, which was a dream come true for me.

Starting My Own Company

The first task upon my arrival in Amman was to start establishing my own company. It was imperative that I put it under my own name and not hide it under any other name. It was a great challenge to do so to maintain it. Since it was a company, I included my wife's name with mine as a partner in the commercial register.

The beginning was not easy, as expected, due to lengthy government procedures, especially with the complexities related to the national number and the procedures for transferring the agency and relinquishing the goods located in the free zone in Zarqa, owned by Hisham. These procedures took a lot of time and effort due to the deadly routine followed in the processes.

Even these routine procedures govern the ministries and institutions in Amman. However, with determination, willpower, and long patience, I was finally able to establish Younes Freajah & Partners / Avon Jordan with its offices, location, and phone numbers. I also completed the procedures with Hisham, paid him the required amount, and he no longer had any relation to the location.

Additionally, I completed the procedures with the parent company after officially confirming the agency with them and restructured the company internally in terms of decor, employees, and sales. I made attractive offers on the goods from Hisham's time after replacing them with a new order of goods and catalogs from the parent company.

One of the funniest incidents that happened to me was that on the first day, I took over management, the warehouse employee, who was Egyptian, came to me and demanded that his salary be doubled since the company was new. If I wanted him to continue working, I simply told him I did not want him to continue. Consider your work with us to end at the end of the month. I contracted with a new employee, and after training him for ten days, I told the Egyptian young man that we no longer needed him. He could hand over his keys now. I let him go and paid him his salary until the end of the month.

Jerry signing agreement for Avon

The Year of Transformation

From the beginning of the year, I had set an entirely new strategy.

At first, I started an advertising campaign in major local newspapers and magazines to establish my company's name as the official agent for this giant company after I completed registering my name as the official agent in the necessary government circles and institutions such as the Ministry of Commerce, Customs, Standards, and the Food and Drug Administration, as well as the Ministry of Foreign Affairs to distribute it to the embassies abroad.

I also worked on changing the interior decor and highlighting the company's name. I was also able to fully understand the details of the complete daily administrative work in the warehouse, sales, and accounting so that I could take on any employee's job who wanted to leave suddenly or train any new employee.

After the arrival of the new order and the new quality catalog, it was only a few months before all these changes and the new start began to bear fruit, and sales started to noticeably jump until they covered the administrative expenses, which I had been covering out of my own pocket in the first few months.

Avon Jordan 1999

Expansion and Lights

In the first year, I seized every opportunity to establish my company's name. I participated in local market exhibitions and sponsored social activities in schools and universities. Additionally, I organized grand events in the finest hotels whenever we launched a new fragrance. For these events, I would bring in top hair salons and local designers to host fashion shows dedicated entirely to the new fragrance. I would ask designers and hairstylists to ensure the main dress was inspired by the fragrance, its colors, and the design of its bottle.

I requested everyone to share the costs, so the events, despite their grandeur, were relatively inexpensive for me. This was especially true after building strong relationships with managers of major hotels in the capital, allowing me to secure very special rates.

With increasing sales, I began thinking about expanding by opening new branches to enhance our coverage and reach all regions of Jordan. I appointed representatives even in remote areas. Eventually, it became necessary to open branches in these areas, starting with the first branch in Zarqa. I hired an energetic young woman, an engineer living in Zarqa, to manage the branch.

Subsequently, we opened in Irbid, and within a few years, we had branches in all major commercial centers in the country. We even became a staple presence in significant commercial centers like Safeway, City Town, and Abdoun Mall. By the beginning of the new millennium, we had over ten branches and more than fifty regular employees, most of whom were women due to the nature of our business.

This widespread presence brought us considerable popularity, especially for me. I became a well-known figure, and everyone wanted to know Younes, the newcomer who quickly established a solid market presence. People wanted to work with us so much that job advertisements would attract an overwhelming number of applicants, particularly women. The demand was so high that I couldn't interview each candidate individually. Sometimes, I conducted group interviews with more than fifty applicants and then selected a few for one-on-one interviews to choose the ones who met our criteria.

I remember two specific incidents before opening our branches in Zarqa and Irbid. I wanted to see if we had enough audience to justify the costs of these branches. I asked the manager of the Zarqa branch to organize an event to present our products in a hall we rented on the main street known as Happiness Street, a major commercial hub in the city. We invited our representatives, limiting the number to 250 women.

On the event day, I struggled to find parking due to the heavy traffic on Happiness Street. After arriving fifteen minutes late with my companions, I was astonished to find not only the 250 invited guests but over 700 women, filling every part of the hall, sitting and standing. It took us more than fifteen minutes to navigate through the crowd to reach the platform. When I asked the branch manager how we ended up with such a large crowd, she smiled mischievously and said they all came to see and greet me personally.

After finishing my presentation about the company and our plans, everyone gathered around me to greet and take pictures. The same thing happened before opening the Irbid branch.

Even the local press was eager to interview me. Every time we had something new to present, we had to hold a press conference and invite the media. My relationships with the press strengthened after I started giving them generous gifts, leading to extensive coverage of Avon Jordan. This turned out to be cheaper than traditional advertising campaigns.

The Magic of Success and the Power of Compassion

In the second incident, we organized a grand event. We agreed to rent a large hall in the Regency Palace Hotel to present "Woman of Earth," the first fragrance launched by the company worldwide simultaneously.

For this event, I invited Ms. Edwina, the sales manager at the parent company, along with her assistant Sarah. They had visited me before, and this time, I wanted to show her the level of engagement with our company in the local market. I had meticulously prepared for this event, including a fashion show inspired by the fragrance's design and colors, with models styled by the famous hair designer Rajai from Lebanon.

We conducted a rehearsal the day before the event to ensure there were no mistakes. Additionally, I placed an advertisement in the widely circulated Jordanian newspaper Al-Rai, inviting Avon members to attend the presentation. I had coined this name for the representatives after noticing that women did not like or prefer to hear the word "representative."

I even mentioned this at a company conference that year in the UK, which was attended by the company's manager in Saudi Arabia. He was impressed with the idea and asked to implement it in Saudi Arabia.

On the day of the event, a few hours before the start time, preparations began. I asked two girls who worked in the branches to stand at the entrance and present a small sample of the fragrance as a gift.

As the ladies started to arrive, the hall became crowded by the time the event was scheduled to start. There was no more space, even a standing room, so I asked my staff and the hotel security to close the doors. The corridors and halls of the hotel were filled with women. The hotel owner and manager came to see me, raising his hand and saying, "You brought all the women of Amman, Younes Freajah," which made me laugh. I responded, "This is the popularity of your hotel."

We needed another hour to create a passage for the models to walk through after I gave my speech, followed by Edwina, who couldn't believe the turnout. The event began and exceeded all expectations of success. Some attendees watched the show on screens after we reopened the doors.

These were the days when His Majesty King Hussein, may he rest in peace, was suffering from cancer in the late nineties. His illness and anticipated passing brought a period of stagnation, despair, and anticipation to the country, casting a somber mood over the people.

This situation was unbearable for me, so I needed a new idea to change this negative atmosphere, especially among the representatives, considering the late king's immense popularity and love in people's hearts.

I came up with the idea to ask the parent company for their four best-selling perfumes in very large quantities. Once they arrived, I launched a big media campaign, halving the prices and offering a deal: buy nine and get the tenth for free, in addition to the 50% discount. This was the biggest discount we had ever offered since I took over the company.

Sales doubled, and we sold out the entire stock in less than a month. It was a great opportunity for the representatives, who talked about it for a long time and asked me to repeat it again.

Echo of a Journey: Between Amman and Tel Aviv

One day, I received a call from Edwina, a British lady who was the Sales Manager for our company in several regions, including ours. She said to me, "Younes, I am going to Israel in a month to conduct training for the regional managers there for a week. What do you think about accompanying me during this week to benefit from the advanced operational experience of the company there? It would be a new experience for you, helping to elevate your company to another level, especially now that you have a peace agreement with the Israelis and things are going well between you."

I was surprised by Edwina's request and said to her, "Israel and the Jews? I don't think so. It would feel strange. I don't think it's a good idea, and I don't think I am mentally prepared for that."

She said, "Don't rush to respond. Think about it, and I will call you in three days. If you agree, I will make the necessary arrangements. I will come to Amman, stay for a night, and then we can head to Tel Aviv together on the same flight."

The next day, I received another call, this time from Ron, the company manager in Tel Aviv. I had met him several times at the periodic conferences the company held in Britain and never felt any hostility towards him or the ladies who accompanied him at the conferences. I was used to meeting Jews in America, and many of the service providers in my business were Jewish. It's no wonder, as they control many aspects of the economy not only in America but worldwide.

I started to distinguish between ordinary people like us and the stern-faced soldiers who occupy the imagination and existence of every Palestinian. Ron enthusiastically invited me to visit them in Tel Aviv after hearing about my hesitation from Edwina. He added, "Man, we now have a peace treaty with Palestine."

He also said, "We would like to host you in Tel Aviv. I have visited Jordan more than three times and loved Petra very much. I will send you an official invitation." I began to accept the idea, especially after contacting my brothers in Palestine, who encouraged me to make the visit, saying it was an opportunity to visit them. I called Edwina as promised and told her, "Alright, let's do it." She sent me the details and itinerary via email.

As planned, Edwina arrived for a day and stayed that night at the Sheraton Amman, where she always stayed. The next day, according to the arranged schedule, we headed to the airport. After the usual procedures, we went to the gate for the El Al flight to Israel.

As soon as we entered the gate, an Israeli security officer approached me politely, asking to speak with me privately. I agreed, and he began asking all the usual questions known to every Palestinian—destination, purpose of visit, and so on. Of course, I had all the answers ready. He then asked for proof, including the invitation and itinerary, which I had in a file. I expected this but did not expect it to happen here at Amman airport.

After he finished, I sat with Edwina, who confirmed that another security officer had spent a few minutes questioning her as well.

We had only been sitting for a few minutes when another officer, a lady this time, introduced herself as Israeli security and politely asked me to accompany her for more questions. I told her that her colleague had already spent 30 minutes questioning me. She apologized and said it was necessary for our safety. I agreed.

She asked the same questions differently, and I finally said, "If I am not welcome, I can go back home, and that's the end of it."

She replied, "On the contrary, welcome. I am sorry," and handed me back my passport. I returned to where Edwina was sitting.

Not long after, while Edwina was trying to calm me, a third person came and asked me the same thing, beginning with a profuse apology, saying he only had a few questions. He asked the same questions again but differently. I became very angry, grabbed my passport from his hand, and told him I had changed my mind and didn't want to travel. I told him angrily in English, "You ask the same questions, and I give the same answers. I was hesitant about this cursed visit from the start, and now I don't want to go!"

He replied very calmly, "I am very sorry, Mr. Younes, but these are security procedures."

I responded with the same anger, "First, isn't it enough that I need a visa to visit my own country and two hours of security questioning while this British lady with me needs neither a visa nor all this security questioning?"

The man widened his eyes at my outburst and said, "Take it easy; we're done. You can board the plane."

The flight took only about 15 minutes, the air distance between Amman Airport and Lod Airport, which the Israelis renamed Ben Gurion Airport.

Upon exiting the airport, we found a man holding a sign with our names. He was the limousine driver who took us to the Sheraton Tel Aviv Hotel overlooking the beautiful Mediterranean coast.

The first days of that week went as planned. There was a field day scheduled for us to accompany one of the regional managers training the representatives in their homes.

This was to take place inside Tel Aviv. I asked Ron and the Sales Manager, whom I knew well, to go with the regional manager for Jerusalem, especially if it included a visit to one of the houses in the settlements around Jerusalem. I wanted to see these settlements and enter their homes to understand how they think. Ron hesitated to accept my request, saying, "I don't know, I'm worried about you." I told them not to think of me as a Palestinian but as an American.

Finally, Ron agreed but said, "At your own risk." I agreed.

Indeed, I went to Jerusalem with the regional manager, who took me to various areas and homes throughout the city. Finally, we visited a house in the controversial Ma'ale Adumim settlement.

Upon entering the house, I saw these settlers, who were different and religious, introduced as someone from the parent company in America. We sat in their very simple home, and the lady brought us orange juice. I chose to observe, especially since the lady only spoke Hebrew, having been brought from Hungary.

There was no way to communicate with them to understand what they thought except through the regional manager, so I preferred to just observe.

After returning from Jerusalem, Ron informed me that his uncle, the original owner of the company, wanted to host me for a whole day at his farm in the village of Carmel near Haifa.

I welcomed the idea. When I arrived at the hotel, the man called me to thank me for accepting his invitation to visit his farm in Haifa. He promised it would be a visit I would remember for the rest of my life and said he had made the necessary arrangements. I told him I was looking forward to the visit.

Echoes from Mount Carmel and the Complexities of Identity

Ron came to the hotel at eight in the morning, picked me up in his car, and we drove from Tel Aviv to Haifa, about 100 km away. Yes, to Haifa, the beautiful gem as it exists in the Palestinian mind.

I asked Ron to pass by Mount Carmel, which overlooks the entire city of Haifa and its port, and also offers views of Acre and Rosh HaNikra. That view, which I have never forgotten in my life since our school trips when we were still young, and after Israel occupied the lands of '67 and allowed the people of the West Bank to wander around Palestine... Often to lament what they had lost. Ron didn't hesitate to take me to that spot, which brought back the hands of time to my childhood, where that view is still etched in my memory.

After joy and deep sorrow lit up inside me upon seeing Haifa from atop Mount Carmel, Ron continued driving up until we reached the farm. There, that man was waiting for us.

He welcomed me warmly and congratulated me on my brave visit to the Ma'ale Adumim settlement the day before. We drank mint tea, and then he said to me in fluent Arabic, "I invite you first to breakfast with hummus, fava beans, and falafel at my Lebanese friend's place, the best in Haifa."

We headed to the restaurant, where the owner welcomed us in a Lebanese accent. We sat at a table he had reserved for us. When he introduced me to that man, he said, "This is our friend who came from Jordan, but he is a Palestinian living in America."

Of course, I carry that strange mix!

Indeed, we ate hot bread, falafel, and delicious hummus as if I were eating at Hashem's restaurant in Amman. We returned to the farm after he took me on a quiet tour in his classic Mercedes in the village of Carmel, which was definitely built on the ruins of an Arab village and offers a captivating view of the Mediterranean Sea.

As soon as we sat down again and after he asked me about my family, the man started talking openly about himself. He said to me, "Do you know, Younes, that I am more Palestinian than you?" I asked, "How so?" He said, "I was born in Haifa in 1932, and I have a birth certificate and a Palestinian passport.

Do you hold a Palestinian passport?

I also dealt with the Palestinian pound

. Have you ever used the Palestinian currency?"

I said, "Of course not."

I said, "Even your government stripped me of my Palestinian identity. I was born on this land and was forcibly removed from it after growing up on its soil. They gave me a visa and interrogated me extensively before allowing me to visit."

He then let out a deep sigh and said, "Is it possible that peace will ever be achieved between us? And that this land will become ours and yours without fighting?"

I replied, "How will this happen when you elect a bloodthirsty person like Netanyahu as Prime Minister, and you have people who call for our extermination like Sharon?"

He said, "By God, we do not know how these cursed ones came to power. We are puzzled by this."

The intellectual man, who lost his wife to cancer three years ago and is left only with his daughter, who is married to Ron, continued the debate with me. He also worked for General Motors in Detroit, USA, and is fluent in English, in addition to Arabic and Hebrew.

As the sun set, he started grilling two steaks in the American style on a grill that he had set up very neatly in a corner of the farm by the swimming pool. I bid farewell to the man who had greatly affected me, considering that I had gained a new friend after Ron came and took me back to Tel Aviv.

The next day, I went to Ramallah, coming from Jerusalem after taking a car from Tel Aviv to Jerusalem and then to my sister's house there. The following day, I went early to our village and spent the rest of the day until I left, returning to Amman via Lod Airport. And, of course, I went through the same searches and questions as when I was in Amman.

The Golden Era: Balancing Success and Ambitions

All this external success at work paralleled success within our small family. My wife was the cornerstone, managing our home well, so we hired a maid from Sri Lanka to help with basic household chores. She took care of our children, who needed us to be by their side during that time. After transferring our children to a well-known private school very close to our company offices, they would walk to our offices, and I would either take them home or send an employee to do so.

They excelled in their studies, especially after integrating well with the students, many of whom had come from the United States. Their reputation was very honorable among the teaching staff, with whom we communicated daily, especially my eldest daughter, Lara, who was very distinguished and a role model in the school and among her teachers.

We held our heads high at the periodic parents' and teachers' meetings, where they spoke proudly of our children. Despite my great responsibilities and overseeing a vast number of branches and employees, I dedicated the time my family needed to be with them. I encouraged them to participate in all school and sports activities according to their interests.

I also integrated myself with them after being elected Vice President of the parents' council at the school, playing an important role in all school activities and even some critical decisions. I was a source of pride for them when I entered and exited the school, usually in my full elegance and youth in my thirties. We called it our golden period, traveling in all directions during vacations. I took them to Palestine, America, and Egypt.

Our remarkable success on all fronts drew attention in every direction, whether at work or within the family, making us the center of attention. Many people approached us, hoping to form partnerships, alliances, or even friendships.

Despite all this glittering success, I never forgot the goal that brought us from America. I never lost sight, even for a moment, that I came to Amman temporarily and did not plan to stay permanently, especially considering my children's education as they grew older and prepared for higher education stages.

My eldest daughter, Lara, shone brilliantly in her studies, and the rest were to follow. I had a goal in life to see my children reach the highest levels of education, a dream I couldn't fulfill but strived for until my last day. This goal could not be achieved for them in Jordan or any other Middle Eastern country, plagued with local conflicts, problems, and wars caused by its enemies, who surrendered to this bitter reality.

It could only be achieved in the country they hold citizenship in—the United States, the land of dreams and opportunities. My children are intelligent and excel in their studies, and America is the only country in the world that rewards such individuals.

I cannot deny that these thoughts sometimes collide with a barrier preventing us from executing them—the success we achieved in the third world if compared to the openness and economic size of America. But this was our fate, not to settle in one place. We started thinking about moving again even after establishing and settling well in a country that speaks our language and shares our customs and traditions.

However, this innate readiness within me made me give up many advantages to achieve my ultimate goal, which no longer belonged to me but to my children. Aren't they the future, and the bright tomorrow, God willing, is certainly for them?

It was necessary to think differently this time and maintain what we had achieved while also achieving the goal I sought.

Upon visiting the UK for an Avon event, the Jordanian Flag was raised in my honor.

Chapter 9 - Challenges Ahead

Strategic Partnership and a New Chapter in America

Did the circumstances serve me or not during those days?

I had a friend who was introduced to me by another person, and this person had a relationship of kinship and friendship with him.

At that time, I had offered to give the Avon agency in the West Bank to a businessman after I managed to acquire it from Max in Britain, who gave it to me in writing for the Palestinian Authority areas. He had given me the green light to sell the company's products in all Middle Eastern countries that did not have an exclusive agent, but without an official stamp.

I had visited Ramallah multiple times, considering it the capital and the city where my family lives, to find this person but was unsuccessful in doing so.

My friend introduced me to a person named Assi, suggesting that I give him the agency for the Palestinian Authority areas.

Assi frequently visited me at the office, and we started meeting outside the office as well. Our ideas and views on life are greatly aligned. He was an industrial engineer, a graduate from Texas, USA, from a well-known Palestinian family, and a family man. At that time, he was the Deputy General Manager at a large company in Jordan.

We began talking at length and started exchanging visits and invitations, even on a family level.

The conversation evolved from discussing the Palestinian Authority areas to talking about participating in the company's operations in Jordan.

I found that this person might be the right one for us to achieve our goals in life.

When I hinted at my desire to send my children to universities in America and my family's desire to return there, the conversation quickly shifted in that direction. Our new friend seized this opportunity surprisingly quickly, saying, "Listen, Abu Firas, I am ready to enter into a partnership with you in any form and manner you see fit. You set the conditions, the timeline, and the financial arrangements, and I agree to them from now."

When I conveyed the news to my wife and children, they were overjoyed. I knew that the family desired to return to America.

I thought of a plan, a timeline, and financial and organizational arrangements for this partnership, considering the circumstances and mutual interest of both parties, which I presented to our friend, who agreed to it quickly and without reservation.

The plan was to sell Assi 40% of the company and retain the remaining 60%, with the possibility of increasing his share in the future if both parties desired. Our partnership was to start at the beginning of 2001, with me remaining as the general manager with all granted authorities until the beginning of July that year, which was our family's departure date to America. Assi was to remain in his current position, and I would train him daily after work or whenever possible to prepare him to take over the company's management after my departure, with full authority starting from the beginning of July of that year.

We started implementing the legal procedures we had set in motion, and Assi began to visit the company daily. I trained him on everything.

It was necessary to get the parent company's approval on this agreement before we started implementing it, and the company agreed since the external framework of the agency and the company's name wouldn't change, only internal procedures and partner shares. To reassure the administrators at Avon, I agreed to take Assi with me to Dubai, where the company was holding its annual conference.

Before the scheduled date, I had traveled to America and couldn't attend the conference, so Assi traveled alone to the conference.

The financial terms were arranged in an agreement that was implemented precisely. I transferred a large part of those dues to the margin account, which I still owned. I was active in buying and selling, and that period witnessed a significant decline in the market, especially in internet and computer companies, which formed a large part of my financial portfolio.

I bolstered my portfolio with those amounts, which I transferred to protect it from further decline and losses and to restore its value as it was.

Things went as they should, and the first six months of 2001 passed quickly.

America Once Again

In a matter of days, we began preparing as a family to take the necessary steps for our return to the United States and to settle there.

We started prioritizing and deciding what items to take with us and what to get rid of, either by selling or gifting them to our friends and even neighbors. We agreed to pack our belongings into a medium-sized container and ship it back to America.

I made the necessary arrangements, accustomed as I was to move.

The move was no longer within the same country but across continents.

During this time, I had to comply with the wishes of my new partner and the employees who insisted on honoring and bidding me farewell with a party in my honor.

I also requested that it be an occasion to honor some outstanding employees.

The party was filled with emotions. In addition to the shield presented to me, Assi delivered a grand speech, saying that this company would be the tree under whose shade our families would find shelter. He went further, swearing by God to uphold what he had said.

Our arrangements were completed on time.

We packed our belongings and some furniture into the container. We also sold some electrical appliances and other items we no longer needed.

We got rid of many things by giving them away and similar means because that night, we had packed our bags in preparation for the trip amid emotional farewells from family, friends, and everyone we knew who gathered to bid us goodbye. The cars carrying us then moved towards Amman Airport, from where we flew to Frankfurt and then to America.

Upon arriving in the United States and returning to Greenville, South Carolina, we felt as if we had come back to our city, the city we loved, where our children were born, where we had thrived, and which we felt we owed.

After the joyous reception from the family, happy that we had returned from what they called exile, we were invited to stay at my brother-in-law's house until we figured out our next steps.

It didn't take long before I rented a house.

It was at the beginning of the street where our old house, which we had sold at a loss after it remained vacant for more than two years, was located. We had been paying its taxes and maintenance costs.

Challenges Ahead

Returning to our street brought great joy to the children, as they were reunited with their friends, and to us, as we had a good relationship with all the neighbors.

It was as if we had been on a trip that lasted several years and then returned.

We began preparing for the basic necessities we would need before the container we shipped from Amman arrived. We bought the additional items we needed with the help of my brother-in-law and his wife, who provided many things to help us start our lives anew.

We also enrolled our children in schools according to their levels, necessitating enrolling them in three different schools, as American schools are divided by educational stage.

We needed a car quickly to take the children to their respective schools, so I bought one from a friend who dealt with cars.

It felt like we were starting anew.

We were beginning a new chapter in our lives, this time in America, but it was different. We spoke the language fluently, and we had returned to a city and neighborhood we loved.

Our financial situation was different, as we had a good balance in the bank and my financial portfolio, which I had bolstered with a significant amount from the money my partner paid me for his share in the company. We also owned 60% of the company in Amman, which I left to generate a good income.

So, I told myself I wanted to lay a solid foundation before starting a new project, especially since I definitely wasn't looking for a job. I had lost interest in the idea of a job ever since I left my position at the Arab Bank in Saudi Arabia.

I began trading daily on the New York Stock Exchange and NASDAQ after setting up an office in our rented house.

Despite the market downturn at the time, I took the risk and started daily trading, buying and selling stocks even at small margins.

I was content with one transaction a day, buying or selling even for a small profit, as I closely followed the stock trends daily.

I had initially followed the principle of having half my portfolio in giant companies' stocks, which usually aren't heavily affected by daily market movements and the other half in fast-moving tech stocks that are affected by market changes. I relied on these movements to seize buying or selling opportunities, make a profit, and then spend the rest of the day at my favorite place, Barnes & Noble bookstore, or the gym, meeting friends either there or elsewhere, especially since I had bought another car, a classic Mercedes, from a friend, as my wife used the first car for household and children's needs.

September 11

It was the morning of September 11. After my daily routine of dropping the kids off at school and returning home before the stock market opened at 9:30 AM, I was watching the daily program on CNBC, which discussed the news that would impact trading that day, either upward or downward. The time was 9:10 AM.

I saw the anchor relay a news story and image, stating that black smoke was rising from the World Trade Center, known as the Twin Towers. He then said as the camera zoomed in, that a fire had broken out. The reporter came back on and said a small plane had collided with one of the towers. Then the news changed, suggesting that it might have been a large plane with passengers that hit the tower. The biggest shock came as people were busy analyzing the first plane when another large plane struck the second tower with tremendous force.

Challenges Ahead

All this happened as we, like the rest of the world, watched live on television. At that moment, I was holding a screwdriver, working on assembling small tables I had bought from Walmart (ironically, I am writing these memories on one of those tables fifteen years after the event). The screwdriver fell from my hand, overwhelmed by the shocking sight, and I, like everyone else, thought we were watching a Hollywood movie, not reality.

The analyses and discussions about terrorism and terrorists began. I told my wife to pay close attention, predicting they would blame it on the Arabs and that America would never be the same after this.

And that's what happened—everything in America took on a new meaning. Shock and disbelief spread among people, everyone trying to interpret the event in their own way, but everyone glued to their television screens, watching to see what would happen next.

The world saw the collapse of the towers and the burial of thousands under their rubble. A lot of changes and debates ensued, both in America and the rest of the world, marking a new era globally. This period was often referred to as the time before or after September 11.

The quick condemnation did not only target Arabs but extended to anything Middle Eastern. People in America started looking at us differently; our presence among them became a source of suspicion, accompanied by uncomfortable looks and whispers. We had to rethink our priorities and plans, especially since our children in their schools became subjects of scrutiny. Walking down the streets required caution as news of strange incidents involving Arabs, Muslims, and Middle Easterners in America kept coming in.

Economic activity in America froze, and naturally, the stock market plummeted terribly. All company stocks were declining significantly, and I saw two-thirds of my financial portfolio vanish. Everyone on TV was urging people not to sell their shares, assuring them that the market would recover, but widespread panic was the prevailing mood.

It became necessary for me to reassess my plans and put my new project in America on hold, especially after a significant part of my capital, which I was supposed to start with, had disappeared. The prevailing conditions following this massive upheaval in America shifted priorities to survival rather than new projects and investments.

Much has been said and written about that period, but I am writing about its direct impact on me. At the time, the container carrying our belongings and furniture, which we had shipped from Amman to the port of Charleston, South Carolina, arrived.

I was waiting for the documents and the shipping bill of lading that my partner had sent via Aramex, which coincidentally arrived at JFK Airport in New York on the same day as the September 11 attacks. The U.S. government shut down airports and banned aircraft movement for three days, not just in America but in most airports around the world.

Everything came to a halt. My repeated calls to the broker at the Charleston port, who was trying to release the container and send it to me, were futile. He couldn't release it without the necessary documents, and he confirmed that each day's delay incurred significant fines from the shipping company, Maersk Sealand, the world's largest container shipping company.

After three days, airports, including New York's, reopened. I received the shipping documents and immediately sent them to the broker in Charleston, who released the container and sent it to me, but with fines exceeding $850 to Maersk.

I had no choice but to pay the full amount to receive the container with my essential belongings. I felt that I had unjustly paid those fines and resolved to reclaim them by any means.

I searched for the person responsible for our region within the company and found his office in Charlotte, North Carolina, 100 miles from our city. I called him repeatedly and left many messages, but he never responded.

Not giving up, I decided to take another route by looking for his superior in the U.S., but the result was the same—no response. I knew a lot about this giant Danish company, so I decided to send a message directly to the company's headquarters in Denmark, addressing the CEO and the Chairman of the Board. After learning their names, I wrote an email explaining my grievance, stating that their company had forced me to pay $850 under extraordinary global circumstances.

It was a gamble; I did not expect a response from the CEO of a colossal company like Maersk, which owns over 3 million containers traversing the world and controlling the shipping industry. However, to my surprise, I received an email reply from him, first apologizing profusely for the actions of his company and then promising that the regional manager, who hadn't returned any of my calls, would contact me and refund every extra dollar I paid. He also thanked me for using their services.

Within two days, the regional manager from Charlotte contacted me, starting the call with an apology for not returning my calls claiming he was out of state. He asked for my address and sent me a check for the full amount of $850.

I considered that a victory in a period marked by many defeats. I was deeply impressed by the distinguished company and its chairman, who listened to a grievance from an ordinary person 7,000 miles away and acted justly. This, I thought, is why they are the world's number one shipping company.

With the arrival of the container and our belongings, our house felt more complete, bringing a sense of stability. It was time to look for a new business venture or a partner for a joint project.

However, we had to move quickly as our children's school expenses, daily needs, and living costs, including house rent and services and the rising gasoline prices, began to pressure us. Additionally, two-thirds of my capital had evaporated in the stock market following the September events.

For the first time in my life, I started considering getting a job as a temporary solution to cover at least part of our large family expenses.

This was against the principle I followed since I handed my resignation to my manager at the Arab Bank in Saudi Arabia. However, necessity has its rules, and everything is subject to change in this crazy world. So, I prepared my resume, refined it to meet the requirements of the American job market, and started sending it to various companies electronically, as is customary in America.

It only took a few days before my brother-in-law suggested that I work with them at Radio Shack, a leading electronics retail chain in America, which has outlets in every corner of the country, especially during the Christmas season. If I liked the job, I could continue, as the salary was based on a basic salary and sales commissions. He was the branch manager.

I had an interview with the regional manager responsible for the city's branches, who welcomed me and sent me to one of the branches to start.

I had no particular interest or love for electronics but had experience in sales and dealing with customers. Considering myself a quick learner, I believed I could do the job.

My training began, and within three days, I could handle customer interactions on my own. It didn't take long before I became a respectable electronics salesperson. By the second week, I was making good sales, and by the third week, I ranked first in sales among more than seven sales staff at the branch.

I was very disciplined about punctuality and dressed professionally in a formal shirt and tie.

In the fourth week, the branch manager told me that the regional manager was impressed with my work and would come to see me. When I met the regional manager, he said they wanted me to take on a bigger role and offered me an administrative position. If I accepted, they would send me for a month's training in Texas, the company's headquarters, after which I would return as a branch manager with many benefits. This would also come with a three-year contract commitment.

I thanked him for his quick trust and nomination but declined, explaining that no job, however high-ranking, was ever my dream or ambition. A job never granted me freedom or independence. I wanted to be my own master, not bound by the shackles of any job. The job at Radio Shack was temporary for me, and as soon as the holiday season ended, I bid farewell to Radio Shack.

Amman for the Third Time

During those days, even while working at Radio Shack, I was planning with my brother and friend Mazen to establish a company based on the franchise system. The idea was essentially inspired by the creation of what is called a sunroom, also known in America as a Florida room. These are typically rooms built as an external addition to houses, often made of wood, glass, or even aluminum. They are very common, and this large company is present in all states of America. The company we intended to establish would be a partnership between my friend and me, aiming to represent this company in the highest state of South Carolina, with a capital of $100,000.

I was supposed to manage it since my friend owned and managed his own company and many other business interests. While my friend and I were finalizing our company, my eyes and thoughts were still tied to the company I left in Amman, managed by my friend and partner, who had a 40% share in the company. He promised to manage and grow the company his way, using his expertise. I was receiving reports, phone calls, and reassurances that things were going well, even though the situation was not greatly affected by the events of September as it was here. My partner assured me in his almost daily calls, seeking my advice on many matters since I had founded that company and was familiar with everyone around us, whether they were employees working with us or clients dealing with us. I also held the majority in the company, and I had done this as a precaution to see how the company's development process was progressing. If things went well, I would start increasing my partner's share in the company.

The regional manager of Avon Max and his sales manager Edwina were scheduled to visit us in early January 2002 to check on the latest developments in our company. Therefore, it was agreed that I would be with my partner during this visit since it was their first time visiting the company under my partner's management. I was supposed to come from America before our foreign guests from Britain arrived to reassure them that everything was stable even after I had traveled and that things were going well under Assi's management.

While I was hearing reassurances and future project plans from my partner, which he intended to plan and execute, these reassurances greatly comforted me. I booked my ticket to Amman for January 8th, four days before the British delegation's visit to us in Amman, to ensure everything was fine before their arrival. My reservation was for 12 days, the expected duration of my stay in Amman, after which I would return to America to continue the project we had prepared with my friend Mazen.

The big surprise for me came when I informed my partner, Assi, of my booking date. His reaction was unusual; he said spontaneously and surprisingly, "Why did you book? Why are you coming?" His spontaneous and direct questions made many questions jump into my mind. What is Assi saying? We had agreed that I would be with him to welcome the British, and instead of being happy about my coming and standing by him, he was surprised in this notable way.

Amid my great confusion, Assi realized after I asked him, "Don't you know why I am coming?" He said, with hesitation in every letter, "Because I have to go to the West Bank during this period for some land we own." I said, "This is your opportunity for me to take your place during your absence." It was clear he was trying hard to make up for what he had said, but once a bullet is fired, it does not return to the gun, and words are like bullets, especially when they are spontaneous.

Doubt and suspicion entered my mind, but I tried as much as possible to handle the matter and end the call naturally. That call ended with my partner, and for the first time since we became partners, many doubts and questions entered my mind, trying to find an explanation for his reaction when he learned I had booked to come to Amman. What is he planning to do?

My suspicions increased that something was happening and that something was not normal, especially after a call from warehouse manager Wael and Ismail, that young man who was with us in the company to whom I assigned many tasks like advertising signs and printing. They confirmed my suspicions and said that Assi forced them to work on Friday, the official holiday, and despite the thick snow covering the ground, to take out from the warehouses about two-thirds of the goods and load them into cars heading to an unknown destination. He did not allow Wael and Ismail to accompany those cars, so Ismail took a taxi, despite not being one of our employees, and followed one of the cars transporting the goods. He found my partner moving our goods to an apartment in Jabal Al-Hussein.

I was furious and realized that something unusual was happening, especially since Assi had not informed me about this. What is happening, and what is my friend and partner planning to do? I persistently called his phone, but he did not answer until he finally did with a trembling voice. When I asked him where he was taking the goods, he said, "Don't worry, I am taking them to the military institution in Al-Bayader; we have opened a branch there." I knew he was lying and he did not know that Ismail had found out where he was taking the goods. I surprised him and said, "Is the military institution located in Jabal Al-Hussein, Assi?" At that moment, he hung up, and I was certain that a big disaster and surprise were being prepared for me by Assi upon my arrival in Amman.

I still believe that the journey that took me from Greenville, South Carolina, to New York, then to Paris, and finally to Amman was the longest of my life among the many trips I usually make between Jordan and the United States. Even the hours leading up to my trip to Amman passed slowly and heavily. I wanted to know as quickly as possible what was happening in Amman and what was happening to my company because of my partner and friend.

Yes, at one point during that journey, I thought it took more than a week to complete, not just 24 hours, including the transit time at the airports. I never closed my eyes, constantly worrying and anxious. The time felt unbearably slow and tedious, and I couldn't relax until the French plane's captain announced that we should fasten your seatbelts as we approached Amman Airport.

Arriving at Amman Airport at midnight wasn't much easier when a cold breeze hit my face as I left the arrivals hall. No wonder it was January, and snow was still piled up in the outer corners of the airport. I found Wael, the warehouse employee, Ismail, and another young man waiting for me at the airport.

The first thing that came to my mind was to ask where Assi was. They told me he had given them money and told them to go ahead to the airport, saying he would follow. But he hadn't arrived yet.

Despite my disappointment with the man, I assumed he was honest, so I asked them to call him on his cell phone, thinking he might have met with an accident on the way. But his phone was switched off. Wael and Ismail then began telling me about his actions, how he had emptied the company of its goods, leaving it almost empty, and how he had brought in new employees close to him who were handling sales and goods away from their eyes. I remembered how he wanted to fire Wael from the company, and I had flatly refused his suggestion.

I was greatly shocked by what I heard, especially since he had been calling me almost daily, telling me everything was fine. I had no choice but to ask the young men to take me to the company instead of going to the hotel, and it was almost 1:00 AM.

We contacted the guard of the complex where the company's offices were located, and I told him to open the gates for us. When we arrived, we found the guard waiting for us. We headed straight to the company's offices, and to our surprise, the key was that Wael, the warehouse manager, had not opened the doors, even though he opened the company every morning. It turned out that while he had given them money to head to the airport, he had brought someone to change the locks of the company.

At that moment, I was certain that Assi was secretly plotting a major conspiracy to take the company from me and that the threads of this conspiracy were now beginning to unravel. Driven by intense anger, I asked the young man to take us to his house in Jabal Al-Hussein.

When we arrived at his house late at night, we found his BMW parked in the garage in front of the house. That car, which I was the reason he owned after the bank refused to give him a loan and no one would cosign for him, came to me sad, saying no one would guarantee him at the bank. I told him not to worry; I would guarantee him and signed for him at the bank with which I had a good relationship.

We stood in front of his house, and I rang the bell several times, but he did not open the door. I knew he was watching from behind the door and not opening it. We had to return, and it was past 2:00 AM. Later, I thanked God he didn't open the door, for if he had, my reaction would have been entirely different, and the situation would have taken a different turn.

I asked the young men to take me to the Holiday Inn hotel next to our offices after I had asked them to book a room for me there. I didn't sleep a wink that night, spending all the time on the phone with my wife, who was also extremely angry and disappointed by the situation we were put in by someone we considered a friend first and a partner second.

She tried hard to ease the burden of the continuous bad news, sensing the severe bitterness in my voice and the betrayal caused by someone who had sworn an oath to make this company a large tree that would shelter both my family and his. But it was clear that his tongue said one thing while his heart and mind were planning something entirely different.

That night, I was in contact with my friend, the bank manager, with whom I had a close family friendship. He tried to reassure me, asking me to come to see him in the morning even before the bank opened, and confirmed that he hadn't seen anything unusual happening in the company's accounts at the bank.

This was very natural since Assi knew well the friendship I had with that man, so he was careful to make everything appear normal to my friend, the bank manager. He wanted to do and plan things without being seen by him so that my friend, who I was always in contact with, would say everything was fine.

I don't know how dawn broke. After I performed the dawn prayer, I left the hotel, having not slept at all, and didn't know where to go in the early morning hours. I took a taxi and headed to the bank to see my friend, waiting in front of the bank until he arrived. I entered his office, boiling with anger.

He tried hard to mitigate the impact of the events, telling me I needed to hear what had happened from him, that he hadn't behaved abnormally in the bank accounts, only using the traditional methods of depositing, withdrawing, and transferring when needed. He also tried to provide from his account to complete an amount the company needed to transfer funds to the parent company.

In other words, the company's accounts were completely empty, requiring him to provide funds from his account to complete a transfer.

These words essentially fueled my anger even more, especially since I had left the company's accounts with a substantial cash surplus, and the sales reports and figures he sent me indicated that we should have a significant cash surplus.

I couldn't even sit on the chair, pacing back and forth in my friend's office, wanting the threads of this charade to unravel and to understand the truth of what was happening. It was past nine o'clock, and I knew he would come in the morning to open the company doors, especially after changing the locks the previous night. He had to come to open the company. I called the company's main phone number, and the employee who answered confirmed that Mr. Assi was present.

From the moment I left my friend at the bank on Mecca Street to our offices on Medina Street, taking a taxi—these are usually crowded streets that take between 15 to 20 minutes—I was deeply thinking about how to curb my anger when I saw him and what I would do. Would I punch him between the eyes, spit on him, or what? I decided at that moment not to do either and to control my temper as much as possible, to listen to what he had to say, and then act accordingly.

However, I wouldn't turn into a monster and attack him the moment I saw him. I decided to follow the wisdom of an American man I once read about when he said:

"(don't get mad, get even)"

All the employees were surprised when I entered the company; some were happy to see me and rushed to greet me and wish me well. Naturally, the news of my arrival reached my office or the manager's office.

After greeting the employees, I headed to the manager's office, and as soon as he saw me coming in, he got ready and turned from behind the desk—which was originally mine—to shake my hand, saying, "Thank God for your safety." He took a deep drag from a wide cigarette on the crystal ashtray in front of him, but I couldn't control myself and refused to even shake his hand. I sat down while he awkwardly tried to gather himself after my refusal, which was my overt and covert signal of war.

After I turned and closed the door, I sat across from him, reaching for the crystal ashtray and picking it up from where he had placed his wide cigarette after it rolled off. He tried to force a fake smile and muttered, "Thank God for your safety. I'm sorry I couldn't come to the airport yesterday."

Honestly, I wasn't listening to his mutterings as I tried to contain my anger. The only thing I clearly remember is that I picked up the ashtray and raised my hand to hit him with it! But I held back at the last moment and cursed him louder than thunder, something he didn't expect from me. Then I continued shouting, "Now I want to know what you are doing and why!"

He took a deep drag from the cigar he was smoking, knowing how much I hated smoke and cigarettes, and exhaled it away from me after giving a fake smile. Then he said, "There's no need for this, Abu Firas. Everything can be resolved amicably, and your company will return to you after I get my full share. I decided to leave the company, and I want to ensure I get my due when I withdraw. Everything I've done is to secure that."

My tone didn't change even after hearing what he had to say, and I told him there were a thousand ways to leave without destroying the company. We entered amicably, and you can leave amicably. No one forced you to join this company, and certainly, no one will force you to remain a partner.

We had a long conversation that sometimes heated up and sometimes cooled down when I remembered the saying I decided to adhere to. We remained in a standoff, with me trying to understand what he had done and him trying to convince me that he would return the company to me after getting his full share. I was surprised by what he was saying, especially since I was in America, and he was effectively managing and controlling the company after I gave him full authority to handle everything.

We stayed in this state until lunchtime. He decided to go to his home for lunch and didn't feel embarrassed to invite me to join him, to which I replied, "Thank you, but you've already fed me more than enough."

When he went for lunch, I called the young men and told them to change the main company locks, as well as the lock on my office door and the warehouse door. I removed his name from the manager's office door, gathered his belongings into a cardboard box, and placed it by the door.

After he returned from lunch, I prepared the surprise of his life for him. I sat at the manager's main desk. When he entered, he was shocked to see me at the desk, which was originally mine.

I mustered all my strength and said in a loud voice that the entire complex could hear, "Assi, you dog, I am Younes Freajah, and you are fired from Younes Freajah's company. I don't ever want to see your face in this complex again. Don't forget to take your trash with you," pointing to the cardboard box containing his belongings, including the crystal ashtray, by the door.

I don't know what he responded with at that moment because the applause from the employees was so loud that I couldn't hear any reaction from him. I know I heard some threats, as expected, but he left immediately after I told some employees to make sure he left the complex.

I said those words primarily to restore dignity to all the employees he had humiliated during my absence. I also didn't pay much attention to the upcoming battle, which began with the secretary he had hired. I told her to follow her manager and that she was fired. The same went for the sales manager he appointed—I told her she was fired too and to follow the manager who hired her. Then, I stood in the middle of the company and shouted, "Does anyone else want to follow Assi?" The rest were very happy about this.

I told Wael to bring lunch and kanafeh for all the employees because a new era had begun—the era of Younes Freajah. I knew this would open the gates of hell wide open, but I didn't care. At least psychologically, I was ready for it. However, I had to take the initiative.

I began taking practical steps to seize control of everything. I called the branch manager, one of the young men I had appointed before my travels. He had been a sales employee at our Safeway branch, and I promoted him to branch manager after noticing his activity and distinction. I asked him not to allow Assil into any branch from this moment forward and not to give him any information related to the business. That's exactly what happened—Assi lost his mind when he tried to go to the Safeway branch, and the branch manager asked him to leave, saying the instructions came from Mr. Younes that he was not allowed to enter any of our branches.

I also began withdrawing or freezing his signing authority on the company's bank accounts. I sent sealed letters to the malls where our branches were located, informing them that he no longer worked with our company and did not represent us.

Challenges Ahead

The most painful blow to him was when I cut off the mobile phone lines for him and his wife, especially since all his crew knew their numbers. Before my travels, I had given him my and my wife's mobile phone lines with sequential numbers, which I had obtained from a friend of mine who held an important position in Fastlink (now Zain). I don't know how much anger he expressed in his call when he asked if I had cut off those lines.

I confirmed that this was just the beginning and that more significant actions were coming. After these preemptive strikes, I started my journey of assessing the losses and damages he had caused throughout the company, which began to slowly reveal themselves.

For instance, I found that he had randomly imported goods from the parent company in Britain, whether we needed them or not, thus exhausting all the company's credit facilities with the parent company, which amounted to about 100,000 pounds sterling. Then, he took these goods and two-thirds of the goods in the warehouses to an empty apartment owned by his mother in Jabal Al-Hussein.

I discovered that all cash sales in the company were being deposited into a separate account opened in his wife's name. I found out that he had hired two of the most famous lawyers in Jordan to devise a plan to take everything from the company and leave it completely bankrupt, especially considering that the events of September would make me hesitate a thousand times before returning to Jordan.

He had established a fictitious company in the name of a friend and transferred ownership and management of the branches to that fictitious company through fake contracts worth only one dinar per branch. Many other things came to light later.

Thus began the war between him and me. It was necessary to respond and fight with the same ferocity and strength in every direction because defending the company and the wealth I had built deserved all my resources.

While my efforts were directed towards both defense and attack in some situations, steps had to be taken to restore everything to its former state. My goal in coming was not to suspect that my partner would take over the company and its assets or pull the rug out from under me. It was to meet the regional manager and the sales manager of the parent company, who were arriving in two days.

Therefore, it was necessary to act quickly so that my company would not appear shaky and weak and to show that there were no disputes between my partner and me, who had been approved by them at their conference in Dubai.

Things escalated quickly afterward, and we started racing against time. After a meeting with my partner, which also included a group of men he brought along, as well as men from my side, we agreed on a truce. My former partner realized that the path he was on would lead him nowhere and that he had rushed for a solution because he was under pressure, having arranged to partner with a very famous businessman in Jordan to establish a fertilizer factory. As for me, a diplomatic solution was the fastest way to welcome the incoming representatives from the parent company and to move forward with rebuilding the company anew.

One of the first things we agreed on was forming a committee of accountants to evaluate the financial situation and give a general assessment of the company to ensure each party's rights. This was to be done after the foreign delegation left.

My main condition was that he return all the goods to the company's warehouses. How could we present ourselves to the company officials when our warehouses were nearly empty? Additionally, the branches had to be returned to the company without any conditions or preambles because I intended to file a lawsuit for fraud against my partner and his friend, who sold the branches with fake contracts for one dinar each!

After lengthy and exhausting negotiations that lasted until late at night, he agreed to my terms and canceled the sale of the branches, officially returning them to our company's fold. He went to return all the imported goods he had taken from the warehouses. Hours later, he came back empty-handed. I asked, astonished, "Where are the goods?"

He said he would bring them, but. And then he presented a new condition. After leaving my presence to get the goods, he consulted one of the lawyers he had hired for his mission. The lawyer, who had planned and executed everything, advised him to act legally within the powers and authority I had given him before my trip.

His new condition, suggested by his lawyer, was that he would return the goods if I provided him with a security check for part of those goods. He claimed he took the goods to secure his rights in the company, considering that the company was in my name and I owned the majority of the shares.

I was very angry about this new condition, seeing that he had no integrity and couldn't even keep his word from the previous day in front of the men. I initially refused outright, but then a series of proposals and solutions began, especially after meeting with his lawyer in the presence of my lawyer, who advised me to provide a security check. The security check had no legal penalty; it was a civil matter.

His lawyer promised to keep the check himself and return it to me once matters between us were settled. I had no choice but to agree to issue the check to retrieve the goods and place them in the warehouses because the British delegation was arriving the next day.

He returned the goods that day after our meeting, although there were many shortages when the company employees inventoried them. Still, I felt a bit relieved after the warehouses and sales returned to their normal state.

We agreed to behave normally and as if nothing had happened because it wasn't in our best interests for the British officials to notice any significant dispute between us. Assi called me and came to my residence in a furnished apartment in Khalda after I had left the hotel, deeply apologizing for everything that had happened. He explained that his actions were out of haste and fear of not getting his due, especially after being tempted by the agreement with the famous businessman who promised to make him the general manager of a major new company.

The visit from the Avon delegation almost went smoothly, as I did my best to show that everything was normal. Assi's presence and participation in meetings and activities added to the facade we had jointly crafted to make everything appear routine and in order.

However, what I didn't notice was the anxiety that occasionally surfaced despite all my efforts to seem completely natural. Max, the regional manager, who had a special friendship with me since we first met in Amman, sensed this. He had come to meet all the candidates for the Avon agency and always told me when I traveled to Britain to leave two or three days unplanned so he could take me on a drive to the English countryside and northern cities, including Avon upon the River, where Shakespeare was born and where the founder of Avon had migrated from to California before returning and renaming the company after his hometown in 1939.

Max read the hidden anxiety in my features. On the last day of his visit, after we returned from lunch, which Assi attended, Max and I were alone in my office. He stood up, closed the door behind him, and said in his sly English accent, "Why do I feel there's something else I'm reading in your facial expressions, your voice, and even your distracted thoughts? What's really going on?"

I found myself confiding in Max about everything that was happening and what had occurred, much to his astonishment. In the end, he asked me what he could do to help, saying, "You know we gave you the agency because of you personally, so you have my full support for whatever steps you take. We are with you."

I told him that this was my internal battle and that his involvement now might complicate matters. However, I promised to keep him updated on all the details and how things would progress.

After Max and Edwina left, things started to move in a different direction in the search for a solution. I became convinced that a deep rift had occurred, and I began to doubt whether this exhausting, peaceful search would yield a satisfactory result.

While we had agreed to form that committee of accountants, including one from my side or the head accountant who managed the company's accounts before my trip and Assi's personal friend, who had become the official company accountant after my departure, I had reluctantly agreed to this.

Their task was to assess the damage done to the company and its true value after all the tampering with everything I had built before my trip. While the accountants worked day and night, I was also searching in two directions: finding a partner to replace Assi and researching legal options in case we couldn't reach an agreement.

I knew that the local court systems would be a difficult path, taking a very long time and draining the company's time and financial resources. It would also divert my attention from redeveloping and rebuilding the company.

The debate between the accounting committee continued, especially after discovering many things that had happened in my absence. Between rounds of negotiations with my lawyer and my supporters and those with Assi and his supporters, the discussions often escalated to shouting, threats, and attempts to calm things down based on our agreement to resolve matters peacefully.

My position was greatly strengthened when my friend and brother Mazen intervened, bringing substantial material and moral support. This had a significant impact on boosting my morale and curbing Assi and his group's momentum, especially after a heated discussion one night. Assi stood up, threatening and vowing retaliation. When I tried to stand and respond, Mazen held my hand, asked me to sit down, and then stood up, saying to him, "Listen, we are seven brothers, and consider Younes the eighth. I swear in front of all of you that if anyone harms him, not only will my brothers be with him, but the entire tribe will be behind him." He addressed more than twenty people present at the meeting.

After Mazen finished, Assi sat down and moderated his tone, as did those who spoke for him. Everyone agreed that the dialogue should be more civilized to reach a mutually satisfactory result.

Things escalated significantly when Assi presented the security check I had written for him to the court after trying to cash it at the bank, knowing the bank would return it without cashing it. He took the check only as security to return the goods to the warehouses after he had taken them, and he knew the check wouldn't be cashed. But he used it as a pressure tactic to threaten me with jail, on his lawyer's advice. What he didn't know was that I was a few steps ahead of him and smarter. First, because I was a former bank employee and knew all the details about checks, and second because I was accustomed to his and his lawyer's treachery. The lawyer had promised to keep the check, and the bank returned it for two reasons: I hadn't dated the check when I wrote it, and my signature on it differed from the one on record at the bank. These two conditions removed the criminal aspect of the check, leaving it only as a civil matter, meaning there was no criminal intent but rather a civil issue. I never denied that he had a right in the company, but only once everything was settled.

With this treacherous move, Assi destroyed all peaceful attempts between us. I became furious and told him he would pay dearly for this.

While the court set a session for the check issue in a month, my lawyer and I gathered evidence and documents to file a countersuit against him for breach of trust. If proven, this would land him in jail after demonstrating to the court all the deceitful steps he took to steal the company from under my feet.

I knew this would take a long time under local law, but this step was necessary and should have been taken the first day I arrived in Jordan.

Once Assi learned I was about to file a breach of trust lawsuit, he mobilized his supporters to mediate with mine, asking us not to escalate or take the legal route. A delegation representing him came to me, pleading not to take such a step.

I told them, "He started this and brought it upon himself." They assured me he would drop the check issue and that he was under great pressure, causing him to make hasty decisions. I decided to take my time, especially after consulting with my lawyers, who confirmed that the court route was difficult, lengthy, and exhausting. They strongly advised that it was much better to resolve matters amicably.

The night before the court session, we had a meeting at my friend Mazen's office in Shmeisani with more than 15 men from both my side and his, along with the accounting committee. The committee had spent two months deliberating and calculating the figures to determine the values, assets, and discrepancies that had occurred.

After a session that lasted until after 2 AM, filled with shouting and mutual accusations, an agreement was finally reached. With the intervention of everyone present, it was decided that Assi would go the next morning and withdraw the check case, admitting that he had mistakenly submitted the check to the court. He would confess to the judge that he had acted hastily and renounce all his rights to the check. We would then go together to the Ministry of Trade and Industry, where he would transfer all his shares in the company to me. In return, my friend Mazen would act as an arbitrator between us and pay Assi the value of the check when I called him to do so after everything was settled.

This agreement, which was drafted after 2 AM, included other provisions to settle any disputed financial amounts according to the accounting committee's valuation.

That morning, after only a few hours of sleep, we went to the court with our lawyers. The lawyers had briefed us on what to do and what the judge would ask us.

Following the plan laid out by the lawyers, Assi relinquished all his rights to the lawsuit and signed off on it in court. Afterward, we went our separate ways with our lawyers and headed to the Ministry of Trade and Industry. With the help of an old friend from my days in Ramallah who worked at the ministry and made the process much easier, Assi transferred his shares to me. This friend facilitated the transfer, and I received new certificates and a commercial registry confirming my full ownership of the company.

As we left the ministry, Assi said to me, "I have fulfilled my part of the agreement. Now it's your turn to fulfill your obligations according to the agreement." I replied, feigning surprise, "What obligations? (I had decided to play dumb, as they say in our country)."

His face began to change, showing signs of collapse, and he said, "You need to call Mazen and tell him to pay me the value of the check."

I responded, with seriousness evident on my face, "You relinquished your rights to me in court and legally transferred your shares in the company to me. You have nothing left. I have regained my company as it was before, and I will not make any calls."

Assi looked at me in utter shock, starting to mutter, "We agreed, we agreed."

I said, "Yes, and we had also agreed when I traveled to America, and you solemnly swore to maintain this company and keep it as a tree under whose shade both our families could find shelter. Isn't that what you said and promised? Where did that go when you stole the goods, changed the ownership of the branches, and put the sales into your wife's account? Why didn't you honor that agreement?"

You can't imagine Assi's face at that moment as I threw those words at him. It changed dozens of times within a minute, and he completely broke down, especially when I added, "I won't give you the money. Consider it part of the huge losses I incurred because of your actions."

Assi didn't know what to do; he just spun around, touching his bald head, trying to suppress his anger. He wanted to scream in his madness and throw the gravel he had picked up from the ministry's parking lot, where we were standing. Then he returned to plead with me, "Abu Firas, for God's sake, don't play with my nerves any more than this." Seeing the stern, vengeful seriousness on my face, he completely collapsed and began to say, "I beg you, I kiss your hands and feet; don't do this to me!"

I replied, "You did this first. I traveled and left everything in your hands, and you betrayed me and stabbed me in the back."

He started repeating, "But the people who witnessed our agreement..."

I said, "What about them? They are no better than the people who witnessed you say at the farewell party you threw for me that you would protect this company with all your strength. You didn't say you would steal it from me with all your strength."

I believe those 15 minutes I toyed with Assi's nerves were the hardest in his life. I even, in some devilish moments, considered actually doing it. But I smiled and said, "Only God sees us now. I could do this to you easily, and no one would blame me. But know that I am more honorable than you and not a traitor like you. I was raised with honesty and integrity. Despite feeling utterly wronged, I am a man and respect the words of men. I just wanted you to feel, even a little, what I felt in the past days."

"Go to Mazen and get the money from him," I called my friend Mazen and told him that everything went according to the agreement and that he should pay him.

I decided to reorganize everything, as they say, now that I was in full control and the company was entirely mine without any partners. After the accounting committee we appointed completed their statistics, it was up to me to recover everything I had lost. Despite the exhaustion of cash flow and its depletion after paying off the remaining dues to Assi as per the agreement with the committee and the group of men who witnessed the agreement, I had to put this behind me to start anew without any headaches. I intended to make this shake-up a source of strength rather than a setback.

I began by addressing internal matters, ensuring no employee remained loyal to Assi. I replaced all of them. I had no choice but to restore the company to its full strength. I started with the branches, reorganizing them after instructing the branch manager to get rid of all the lazy employees and replace them with proven salespeople. I also reorganized cash incentives, prizes, gifts, and certificates of appreciation to create a competitive environment among them. The same applied to the sales managers in direct sales after I worked on developing a competitive program among them.

I ignored the rumors spread by my former partner and the dismissed employees loyal to him that the company was on the verge of bankruptcy and would close its doors in a few days. These changes began to bear fruit, especially the generous offers in the branches and for the direct sales members, bringing back the company's sparkle and activity.

At the same time, I stayed in constant contact with Max, the regional manager, keeping him updated on all developments as I had promised. I also communicated with Edwina, the sales manager, to help me launch a new initiative for the regional sales managers. We agreed to prepare a sales conference and workshop in Amman, attended by training managers from Britain, Saudi Arabia, and the UAE, scheduled for the second half of June after my return from the United States. I had decided to travel there to bring my family back after the end of the school year.

After setting things in order in Amman, I had to travel to the United States to be with my family and wife, who was also struggling to manage our four children, especially since the girls had entered their teenage years. This was no easy task.

I booked my trip to America with a two-day stop in Milan, Italy. I had arranged to visit an Italian cosmetics company, meet its owners, and negotiate a deal to represent them in Jordan. The goal was to supply our branches spread across all the shopping centers in Jordan and to strengthen our position among competitors. After spending two wonderful days in Milan, which I needed after the five-month struggle, and accomplishing my objective, I continued my journey to New York and then to Greenville, South Carolina.

The reunion with my family was emotional after this absence. They had been worried something might happen to me despite my daily calls to reassure them about what was happening in Amman. Upon my arrival in Greenville, preparations for the return to Amman were in full swing. Although we hadn't even completed a year back in America, here we were, preparing for another reverse migration. This migration was not by choice but by necessity, unlike previous migrations.

Our children had already adjusted to their new schools. Our youngest son, Nadeem, whom I remember being so scared when we returned last year and took him to school for registration, had now settled in. All his siblings were at the same school, and we had a good, friendly relationship with the principal and staff.

At that moment, Nadeem, holding my hand as we entered the school to join the third grade, repeatedly reminded me to tell his teacher that he didn't know English well, hoping they would be gentle with him. I looked at him, hugged him, and said, "Don't worry, my man. I'll make sure they take care of you, and you'll learn quickly and speak better than them."

After having learned English well and having reintegrated, Nadeem and his brother Firas, who had no difficulty with either Arabic or English due to his older age and familiarity with both languages, were doing fine. As for Leana, who had started high school, there was no problem since she would attend a private school that followed the American SAT curriculum.

Our real challenge was with our eldest daughter, Lara. Lara had completed high school with excellence, and she was the main reason we had returned to America in the first place.

She was always the top student, and I encouraged her to aim for admission to one of the most prestigious universities in America, Georgetown University in Washington. This renowned university has produced many top leaders in America. I always supported her and helped her strive for a scholarship there. We were both deeply saddened when she received a letter of rejection from the university, informing her that they could not accept her despite her extraordinary efforts to secure a place at such a prestigious institution. We knew well that admission to these universities involves specific factors and criteria despite the high cost of studying there.

Challenges Ahead

Our consolation was that Lara received an acceptance letter from Furman University in the same city, one of the finest and most prestigious universities in South Carolina. The acceptance came with a scholarship that covered all her study expenses, including housing and tuition fees.

As we began preparing for the return to Amman with the rest of the family after organizing everything, I had to ensure that Lara's transition to the university would be smooth and easy. The university semester was set to begin in mid-August, and we were still in June. We agreed that Lara would stay with her aunt's family, her cousins, for these two months until she moved into the university dormitory. Her cousins were her age and her best friends.

I arranged for Lara to have a car for her transportation needs, especially since we agreed she should find a job and work during these two months. I went to a friend and bought her a Honda Civic. We were overjoyed that our firstborn would be attending university.

I was determined to support Lara with all my might. She was, for me, the hope that I could achieve what I had not been able to accomplish in my life. She was the role model for her siblings, who looked up to her and followed her example. I spared no expense in anything that would help build her character and self-confidence. I entrusted her with many tasks to nurture this tendency in her, and I often took her along on many of my business trips. I introduced her to all my friends, acquaintances, and everyone I interacted with through my work, which honed her personality and gave her a distinguished presence.

After securing a car for Lara, who also found a job at a nearby hypermarket close to her aunt's house, we arranged for a shipping container and loaded our belongings again. Despite the heavy rain that day, we managed to load the container safely.

We prepared ourselves for the journey back, which was supposed to be

Greenville/New York/Rome/Amman. It could have been a typical journey from the small Greenville airport to New York and then continuing to Rome and Amman with my family, were it not for the tension that permeated all the airports in the United States, especially for us Middle Easterners, as they called us. The period was short after the events of September, and there was a visible hardening and alertness in all aspects of life, particularly at airports.

Given that our final destination was a Middle Eastern country, it was always noted on our boarding passes for security to give us extra attention at the airports. We came to refer to it as the "preferred list" or VIP list, not only being treated with extreme caution but also being subjected to meticulous searches, our bags and personal items thoroughly inspected, often causing hours of delays—something we were never used to before.

After packing our bags and heading to the airport, we stood at the United Airlines counter for our domestic flight to New York. The elderly man behind the counter, who was over seventy years old, entered our ticket information into the computer, revealing our final destination Jordan, a Middle Eastern country. Consequently, our names, despite being a family, were on the "preferred list," meaning rigorous inspection and suspicion.

I was surprised, first, at how this elderly man was still working at his age with such slowness despite the long line behind us, and second, at his insistence that the entire family undergo thorough inspection, including our bags and personal items, wondering how much time this would take.

But we had to comply.

They began inspecting our ten hand luggage pieces right before our eyes. As we were departing, each of us had our necessary items, while the rest of our belongings had been sent by sea in the container. All this time, the security personnel were working leisurely, and I kept telling them our flight would leave without us. They sternly told me to let them do their job. After they finally finished and sent our bags to the plane, we proceeded to complete our travel procedures.

We were also subjected to thorough personal searches. When it was our turn, we were separated and underwent meticulous inspection. It felt like we would never get out of this predicament. During their inspection of my personal bag, they found a small set of screwdrivers in one of the pockets. It was a promotional gift from a famous cigarette brand called Baisik that someone had given me long ago and which I had completely forgotten about.

The security officer, discovering these small screwdrivers, acted as if he had found something significant and started questioning what they were and why they were in my bag. I explained that it was a simple promotional item from an American cigarette company he surely knew well, and I had no idea how it ended up in my bag. I suggested he throw it away to expedite the process or take it from me and confiscate it, but he was tense and refused.

I then suggested giving it to my daughter Lara, who was standing outside with our relatives who had come to the airport to see us off, pointing them out to him. The officer's mood brightened at this suggestion. After handing the item to my daughter, the airport announcer made the final boarding call, stating that the United flight to New York was closing its doors.

After we were finally released, my wife, children, and I ran towards the plane's gate, only to be told by the attendant that we were late and the plane was already on the runway.

At that moment, I lost my temper and went mad. I shouted hurtful words at her, asking what we should do. We spent more than three hours being inspected. None of that mattered; the employee reiterated that they had no control over federal government work and said we had to return to the United Airlines counter at the beginning of the airport to find alternatives.

We retraced our steps, passing through those barriers that had taken us hours, back to that accursed counter and that elderly man who was still responsible for finding our alternatives. I sought refuge in God from losing my temper and tried to remain as composed as possible. I told him, "Listen, you are the reason we missed our flight, and now you need to find us an alternative." Despite my shouting, he took his time and eventually told us there were no other flights from this airport to New York that would allow us to catch our flight to Rome.

I asked, "What's the solution then?" He looked at me very coldly and said there was a flight from Charlotte, North Carolina, which was 100 miles away, leaving for New York in four hours.

I asked, "Okay, fine. How do we get there with 10 bags?"

He arranged for us to be transported in a van, with our bags, to Charlotte at their expense. Despite the frustration and anger I felt about our exceptional treatment, there wasn't even time to think about it. I just wanted to get to New York and leave America as quickly as possible, especially since Edwina and her assistant Sara had already arrived in Amman from Britain and were starting to arrange the conference.

When we arrived at Charlotte Airport, my wife, children, and I began to run with our bags toward the counter. They insisted on inspecting our bags again, despite them having marks showing they were inspected at Greenville Airport. After much shouting and strong protests from me, the employee let my wife and children through, allowing them to pass the inspection barrier while I stayed with the employee. He discovered that one of our bags was five pounds over the weight limit.

I asked, "What do you want me to do? Take the excess weight and throw it in the trash?" He said that wasn't allowed. I suggested taking the excess and putting it in one of the other bags, which were well under the weight limit. He said there wasn't time, as the other bags had already been sent. I asked, "What's the solution then?"

He said I had to pay for the excess weight. I asked, "Fine, how much?" He replied, "330 dollars." Enraged, I asked why I should pay such a large amount for just five pounds. He said it didn't matter; either I paid or he would throw me and my family off the flight.

I had no choice and had to decide quickly, so I said, "Fine, I'll pay." Despite my extreme anger, which I tried hard to control, I handed him a credit card issued by a Jordanian bank. Once he processed the payment, he handed me the receipt to sign. I signed it with a different signature than I usually used, and he allowed me to join my family.

In my view, this amount was taken from me unjustly, so I decided to take my revenge in my own way. As soon as I arrived in Amman, I went to the bank and reported that the card had been lost the day before we left Charlotte Airport and that I was not responsible for any purchases or charges made on that card. This way, I never paid that amount at all!

The ordeal wasn't over yet. Although we breathed a sigh of relief as my family and I finally sat in our seats on the plane, the moment we set foot in New York Airport after arriving from Charlotte, we started running towards the Alitalia counter to catch our flight to Rome and then to Amman. Running through airports is challenging, especially with children in tow and in large airports like New York, Chicago, or Atlanta.

When we finally reached the counter, and it was our turn, the big blow came from the employee who looked at our tickets and said there was no reservation for us; all our bookings had been canceled. I almost grabbed the man by his collar, exclaiming, "What are you saying? Do you know what we went through to get here, and now you're telling me our reservations are canceled?" He replied, "I can't do anything for you. We didn't cancel your reservations; United Airlines did after your flight left without you. You have to go back to them to sort this out."

Shuttling back and forth between the counters, which were in separate terminals—one domestic and one international—didn't help. Finally, I couldn't take it anymore and asked for the Italian airline station manager. When he arrived, I said, "Look, these are your tickets. United Airlines has nothing to do with them. You need to find a solution now." I started yelling at the top of my voice, saying that neither I nor my family would move until a solution was found.

Amidst all the shouting, the manager called security. I turned around to find a tall, broad-shouldered officer standing right behind me, introducing himself as an FBI agent. He ordered me to lower my voice, or he would take me downtown (an American expression meaning to the police station for arrest) for causing a disturbance.

Realizing the seriousness of the situation, I began explaining what my family and I had been through before arriving here. He asked me to sit down with my family and assured me he would solve the problem.

Following his instructions, I sat down while he talked to the station manager. He then came to me and said the manager was now working on a solution. "The important thing is to stay calm, and you will be flying tonight."

A few minutes later, the station manager called me over and told me they had booked my family and me on a Swiss Air flight in business class to Zurich. From Zurich, we would board a Royal Jordanian flight to Amman.

When we boarded the Swiss Air flight, everything was different—the seats, the service. We finally relaxed after all this long ordeal. We reached Zurich and then boarded the Royal Jordanian flight, where the experience differed greatly between the two flights. But we finally arrived in Amman and headed to the house

I had rented before my trip to the Rabieh area.

Since our arrival in Amman, preparations began for the sales conference and training course for the regional managers, including those I had appointed along with Edwina, the sales manager at Avon, before my trip to America. We selected 15 women and girls from various regions across Jordan, along with participants from Saudi Arabia and the UAE. The conference and training course were scheduled to last an entire week.

We needed to set up a venue that could accommodate everyone, so I rented an office on the fourth floor of the complex and fully equipped it to meet the needs of over 25 women, with myself being the only man among them. This presented its own challenges, especially ensuring that 15 Jordanian women would arrive and leave at the same time.

The remaining participants were accustomed to organization and work, particularly known for the precision and orderliness of the English, with Edwina epitomizing these traits. It was necessary to remind the Jordanian participants of this before each day concluded. Additionally, arranging for their entertainment and meals was another challenge.

This wasn't my only concern; I also needed to prepare and set up our new family home, as all our household furniture was still in a container at sea. I had to at least provide the basics for sleeping, kitchen tools, and entertainment items since we were on a school break and the academic year had not yet begun. I needed to find private schools for the children to enroll in.

The support of my wife during this period, through all our steps and especially in settling our home, was a crucial factor that helped us get through this period peacefully and put everything in its proper place. The conference and training course concluded successfully after a busy week. Edwina and I celebrated the graduation of the regional managers with a dinner hosted by Avon at the

Sheraton Hotel in Amman.

Once our furniture container arrived in Amman, we completed setting up our rented home. Despite the high cost of clearing the container from Amman Customs, due to some mishandling by customs employees, I had no choice but to accept it and add those losses to the other losses incurred since I met my former partner.

However, things started to move in the right direction. The company's operations and sales were flourishing, and I had full control over the network of regional managers and employees across eleven branches spread throughout the Kingdom, totaling over fifty women and girls. Managing the fluctuating moods of these women, as moodiness is a prominent trait of women in general, required tremendous effort.

Chapter 10 - Stability, Family & Legacy

Haj Abu Rasmi - The Pillar of Our Family

In those days, we were devastated by the news of the death of my father-in-law, Haj Abu Rasmi, my father-in-law, in America. The impact of his passing on us was immense. May God have mercy on him; he was like a father to me, and I held great respect and appreciation for him.

We shared a very good relationship. So much so that when we went to bid him farewell before our travel, he was suffering from Alzheimer's due to old age. When I approached him, greeted him, and started speaking to him, he smiled a contented smile and held my hand tightly after staring at me for a long time. His son asked him, "Do you know who this is, Father?" He replied without hesitation, "How can I forget Younes Freajah? May God be pleased with him." Despite losing his memory and not recognizing anyone, not even his wife or children, he remembered me. Tears filled my eyes as I looked at him and recalled how strong he once was. I remember when I proposed to my wife through his friend.

I also recalled when all his children came from America, and all his relatives from Palestine gathered. It was the beginning of his illness, and they were all in our first house in the Um Al Summaq area. He left more than 20 of his children and relatives and came to me, holding the key to his house and the key to the building he owned in Al-Ashrafieh. He said in front of this large gathering, "You are the only one among them I trust and give the keys to my house and the building. This is a trust; do not give it to anyone else."

He said this amidst the silence and astonishment of those present. Yes, this man, may God have mercy on him, was a significant and distinctive figure in our lives, present and even future. His foresight was the main reason the entire family obtained American citizenship. He was the first to emigrate to America in the 1950s.

When I asked him, "Father-in-law, why did you emigrate? You, praise be to God, did not need it." He would confidently reply without waiting for thanks from anyone, "My son, it was not for me but for you, your children, and your grandchildren so that your future would be better than our present. My son, these Arab countries and their leaders clinging to power are of no use, and there is no hope in them. Do not rely on them!"

The Generational Gap and the Weight of Decisions

This man belonged to a generation that is rare to find, a resilient generation that carved itself out of rock and built itself up until it became towering and a patriarch of a large, extended, educated family. Among them are doctors, engineers, businessmen, and managers. He built his kingdom around him quietly, without fuss, and with remarkable piety and strange uprightness.

I don't know why I saw in my uncle the image of my father, may God have mercy on them both, even though they never met.

My father stayed and struggled in the mountains of Palestine until he was buried there, while my uncle, Abu Rasmi, emigrated and was buried in the land of exile, fighting beyond the borders of Palestine.

He left his village, which he had rebelled against, for a nearby village where he saw a bit of himself. But his ambition and vision were greater than those around him. It pushed him to leave Palestine, and even after arriving in Amman and moving from place to place, he was not content with a small migration.

He preferred to go to a broader and larger space, and at his first opportunity, he borrowed the price of his ticket and emigrated to America. At that time, people did not know much about that new, emerging continent. He also knew nothing about that land, yet he left his small family and emigrated to that vast, expansive land with a strange language.

He challenged all those circumstances, carrying his bundle that contained everything he could sell, sometimes on his shoulder, sometimes on his back. He knocked on doors and faced rejection, disdain, and sometimes reprimand, but the determination and will to create a better tomorrow for his family drove him on.

I was close to his spirit and heart, despite his initial hesitation, because I was a stranger to him. But soon, these hearts grew fond of each other, and he treated me like his own children, sometimes even more. I was like his confidant, and he often complained about his children not achieving the ambitions he had set for them.

However, this is a historical dilemma; fathers always complain about their children because the truth is that fathers always want their children to be better than them.

Haj Abu Rasmi lived for over a hundred years without suffering from any modern diseases like hypertension or diabetes. He died of old age and forgot everything except the Quran. Whenever someone mentioned the beginning of a verse from the Quran, he would finish it completely. When his soul departed to its Creator, he was in a state of complete testimony, and at his burial, no one could unclasp his finger from its testimony position, and he was buried in that state.

May God have mercy on you, Abu Rasmi. You lived your life as an exceptional man, and even in your death, you were exceptional.

The Burden of Protective Instincts

Shadows of September 11 Events

We faced another problem during that period, as we left our daughter behind to complete her studies at the prestigious Furman University. However, the news we received from there was not reassuring. The political and security shadows of the September 11 events were still looming over everything and every aspect of life in America. We were very worried about our beloved daughter, especially since she was about to leave my brother-in-law's house to live in the university dormitory, which would expose her to danger far from our eyes after hearing about many incidents that occurred after September 11.

We internally rejected the idea that our daughter had grown up and became a young woman. I admit that her mother and I succumbed to our emotions and decided to bring her to Amman. We told her to come and spend the rest of the summer with us before university started, and she was very happy about it. She indeed came, and our intention was not to send her back to America. Lara spent her days with us until it was time for her to return. I sat with her and told her about our decision that she should stay in Amman, continue her studies at the University of Jordan, and remain with us. Her severe crying, protesting, and pleading to return was to no avail, as our decision was final.

I admit today that this decision was a huge mistake, and I now consider it one of the dumbest decisions I have ever made in my life. It later cost me a lot, both in terms of my relationship with my daughter and financially. However, the Eastern man's nature that has accompanied me throughout all phases of this life still dominates despite my repeated attempts to get rid of its remnants.

Life goes on, surpassing what happens in our lives, whether joy or sorrow, as long as God has bestowed upon us the blessing of forgetfulness.

Without forgetfulness, the significant intervals in this life, with their sweetness and bitterness, which occur are like stop signs forcing you to pause and reflect on what is on your right and left so you can proceed and move forward with fewer disturbances and less shakiness, ultimately allowing you to pass without putting your life in danger.

Additionally, rebuilding the company's structure, which I tried hard to pull out of the deep pit that almost destroyed it and us, was not easy after starting to feel the difficulties of mending all the wounds and repercussions, especially the liquidity issue I had exhausted to remove my previous partner from the company.

Also, the issue of my daughter weighed heavily on me, trying to find an educational environment that suited her intellectual level, as well as worrying about my other children.

But in the end, I am the head of this family and the captain of its ship. I must be strong and not weaken so as not to lose its helm and find all solutions to all the problems we face. I have no option but strength and hope.

The Quest for a Permanent Home

One of the most important problems at that time was that the lease of the house we rented in Al-Rabieh was about to expire. We started seriously considering buying a house since we had settled in Amman, instead of moving from one house to another, even though our financial situation was not favorable and did not help at that moment. However, my faith in God, my reliance on Him, and my belief that He makes things easier for us pushed us to move forward in searching for a house.

It's true to say that the credit for the house goes to my wife, as she had been striving to buy a house ever since we set foot in Amman. I was opposed, thinking like a businessman, not wanting to tie up a large amount of money in a house when that money could be invested in business and multiplied. I used to tell her that as a renter, I owned all the houses; I could change the house I lived in whenever I no longer needed it, meaning there was no binding tie to those rented houses. This is what happened when we moved several times, especially since I never intended to settle in Jordan permanently. I did not want anything to hinder my movement, and I overlooked the fact that owning a house could be a psychological factor that helps in stability and achieving self-actualization, providing a launchpad.

One of the advantages of living in Amman is that you get to meet many people and can choose friends whose ideas and inclinations match yours. One such person was a young man named Abdulsalam, in his early twenties, from a large family that owned most of the land in the Um Al-Summaq area. This was the area we decided to settle in because it was upscale and centrally located in western Amman, close to everything we needed, especially our company's office. It was also the first area we lived in when we came to Amman, and we loved it.

I met Abdulsalam through a real estate broker, Abdullah, who also became one of the people whose opinions I valued. Abdullah found us our first house, and quickly, Abdulsalam and I became friends despite the age difference. Despite his young age, he owned a housing company.

Although we were living in the Al-Rabieh area at that time, which we did not like very much, we were looking forward to returning to the Um Al-Summaq area if we wanted to buy a house. I asked Abdulsalam to keep me in mind for a ground-floor apartment if he decided to build a building in the Um Al-Summaq area.

Not long after, Abdulsalam called me and said that he would start building a building at the beginning of the month and would start digging soon in an area adjacent to and close to Mecca Street, the most expensive commercial street in Amman. I agreed with Abdulsalam to visit the site together, and when we arrived, he grabbed a long stick he kept in the back of his luxurious car and began marking the ground in an undeveloped area where the paved road had not yet reached. He said, "This is where the building will be, and this will be your house, completely separate from the rest of the building."

I liked the location a lot, but what concerned me was that the plot on which the building would be constructed was very close to Mecca Street, one of the busiest streets in Amman. I told him I liked the location but thought it might be a bit noisy. However, he assured me that the house would face away from Mecca Street and that my apartment would be at the front of the building, with Mecca Street behind it, away from the noise, on a completely separate street.

I said, "In God's name, I have bought it from you," and we shook hands. He said, "It's yours!" I didn't know its size or even its price yet; Abdulsalam was only 23 years old at that time!

A week later, I went to the site with my wife and children and found the equipment digging at the site. I told them, "This will be the site of our house here; I have bought it." Everyone looked at me with signs of astonishment and said, "But where is the house?" I said, "It will be here, God willing."

Less than a month later, I visited Abdulsalam's office and said, "I bought a house from you without knowing its size or price, and you haven't written me a contract or taken any payment from me. How is that possible? I want to confirm that I have indeed purchased it." He laughed and said, "No need; we shook hands, and that's enough." However, with my insistence, he wrote a contract detailing all the specifications, including the garden and garage space, since it was a ground-floor apartment connected to a garden. We agreed to determine the price later, and he assured me I would be completely satisfied. He even said if I wasn't happy, it would be a gift from him. I said, "God bless you, but I insist on paying something upfront to solidify our agreement." He said, "Fine, write a check for a thousand dinars," which I did, thus concluding the house deal.

We followed the excavation and construction, watching our house grow day by day, stone by stone. Abdulsalam, as the project owner, had instructed the engineers and contractors that this was the house of the Abu Faras family, and if any of them wanted anything or any changes, even if they were against the design, they should implement them without consulting him. His instructions were clear, and we actively participated in designing and shaping our home the way we wanted it.

We had to extend the lease of the house we were currently living in because the house wasn't completed yet. Perhaps fate wanted to increase our longing to finish it and move into our dream home. Finally, after these months, it turned out just as we dreamed and hoped, with all the improvements and additions we included.

It was our first house in Amman, so it had to be special. We resolved to make it so despite the significant challenges, especially financial ones, we faced. Abdulsalam played a major role in making convenient arrangements for us after we agreed on the price, even giving me an additional discount after we signed the final contract. Of course, I had a plan for the garden, which I sketched on a piece of white paper. I brought in a gardener from Jerash who got me everything I asked for, making it my favorite spot in the house, maintaining and watering it until it became lush and green, pleasing to the eyes.

We planned for this house to be a nest for the family, where everyone would grow and prosper. The children would go to their schools and universities, and I would go to my work. We brought in a maid from Indonesia to help my wife with the household essentials.

The Fleeting Beauty of Life: A Tribute to Abdul-Salam

I return to my friend Abdulsalam, and it seems that beautiful things do not last and that good people are taken from us without us realizing what happened. Our relationship remained strong; we would meet not in our offices but outside of work. He introduced me to many of his colleagues, owners of housing companies, as he would gather them at his farm and host feasts for them. He was so full of life; I had never seen anyone who loved life and was as optimistic as this person.

One day, I received the news of Abdulsalam's death. Oh my God, someone shot him in the stomach with three bullets, and he didn't last long, even after being taken to the hospital. He died.

It doesn't matter what happened or how it happened, but the man died at a young age, not even thirty years old.

I was struck by complete silence and deep sadness as I made all the calls, and everyone we knew confirmed what had happened: Abdulsalam had passed away, leaving behind a small family.

In the face of all this, all I could say was, "There is no god but God. With death, you have conquered every living being. All creatures will die," as promised by God in the scripture:

"Every soul will taste death." (Surah Al-Anbya - 35 in footnotes) The face of His Majesty remains, conquering His servants with this truth. No one can escape this end.

The causes vary, but the result is the same. This is the truth that makes us lose those dear to our hearts, those who fall around us like leaves from a tree.

Those we know, laugh with and keep company with fall.

Some fall ill first and then die, and in such cases, fate sends us a signal to prepare for their loss. But those who leave suddenly, without warning, leave a sudden wound that is hard to heal. But when the moment comes, nothing can stop it.

In such moments, laughter disappears, and tears choke. But we stand helpless, knowing that the God who created and gave is the only one who takes when He deems it appropriate. We cannot change anything destined, no matter how insignificant. We can only wait for our turn, which is inevitably coming. But at what moment and how, we do not know.

It seemed as if the deceased had a feeling he wouldn't live long, so he tried to seize as many moments of happiness, joy and smiles from this life as he could. The thing that made him happiest was to bring a smile and satisfaction to someone's face.

The King

The Royal Encounter: A Milestone in a Journey

Everyone settled into their places. After much effort and struggle, my daughter Lara joined the parallel program at the University of Jordan, which was very expensive in terms of fees. After her grades were adjusted and she achieved a high average, she chose to study Spanish and English. She enrolled at the University of Jordan despite the reluctance and bitterness she felt about not returning to the United States.

The rest of the children continued attending their respective schools, making things somewhat stable. This allowed me to focus heavily on my work and my attempts to promote it. My goal and vision were to make Avon catalogs famous in every household in Jordan and to make every woman in Jordan familiar with this prestigious name.

I participated in all exhibitions and festivals, placing an advertisement in a local newspaper every week. Then, the American embassy offered us the opportunity to participate in and support the American Products Exhibition, which was to be held at the Zara Exhibition Center for a week. We agreed immediately and selected our booth at the exhibition. They informed us that His Majesty King Abdullah would inaugurate the exhibition, but we waited for his arrival on the opening day. They also told us that there was an urgent matter preventing him from coming.

However, the next day of the exhibition, we were informed that the King would come within fifteen minutes, and we should prepare ourselves. Nobody was to speak to him or shake his hand; he would just pass by and acknowledge us from a distance. So, the King came and passed by the exhibitors, greeting us from afar. When he passed by our booth, he looked at us and smiled. After I smiled back and returned the greeting, I couldn't contain myself and said to him, "Your Majesty, we are Avon!"

He didn't hesitate for a moment and walked towards us, greeting me. "I know it from the United States; it's a big name," he said. I thanked him while still holding his hand, trying to explain a little about it to him. However, the guard accompanying him tried to pull my hand away from his in a trained manner. Yet, I continued talking to him, and he smiled with utmost grace.

The photographers weren't even ready as they didn't expect him to stop with the exhibitors. My wife stood beside me, and His Majesty shook her hand while the photographers took the picture. I continued conversing with him while he shook hands with everyone after me.

Meeting King Abdullah II of Jordan

In Conclusion

It took me more than 30 years to cross to that stage, from the first moment I stood bewildered at the Abdali Car Park in Amman, spanning the bridge over the Jordan River from the West Bank where I was born to the East Bank, carrying a small bag and a sum of 17 dinars. Seventeen Jordanian dinars were all I owned in those days, and I was lost. Where do I go?

To become the president, director, and owner of a company, shaking hands with the head of state? His Majesty the King? Those years that passed, where tears and smiles mingled. Moments of joy and triumph and many moments of disappointment. The ascent to the summit and the fall to the abyss, intense sweat, fatigue, and deep sadness. Migration, separation, and constant movement between these distant countries. Many miles traveled, sometimes as an immigrant, sometimes as a visitor in airports, standing in passport lines. And the intense scrutiny, being different with my name and nationality, seeking a land to shelter me and embrace me.

For more than 30 years that passed, I tried through them to gather these scattered parts of a big dream, born and nurtured within me, which I was determined to assemble, even though these parts were scattered, broken, and not connected. I thank God very much that my son Firas urgently asked me to write about what I went through and experienced during these years, despite his young age at that time and at the appropriate time, with a vivid memory and a living age, because with time these memories begin to fade, disappear, and dissolve, just as the years of life do, and even the timing was sufficient to ignite and revive what we went through and experienced.

Human nature is to forget, especially with the passage of time and the crowding of events and years and tries to pick up bits and pieces from here and there in order to ultimately build this foundation upon which our lives as a family were built.

I can only say thank God for everything, time, and circumstances that allowed me to live this and allowed me to see my grandchildren.

Thank you.

About The Author

Younes Freajah is a distinguished writer and storyteller, known for his vivid narratives and deep understanding of cultural and historical contexts. Born and raised in Palestine, Younes experienced firsthand the challenges and triumphs of life in a region marked by conflict and resilience. His journey took him from the heart of the Middle East to various parts of the world, enriching his perspective and inspiring his writing.

With a passion for capturing the essence of human experience, Younes has dedicated his life to sharing stories that resonate with readers across generations. His autobiography, "Echoes of Exile," is a testament to his remarkable life, chronicling his personal and professional milestones, as well as his profound reflections on identity, displacement, and the enduring spirit of his homeland.

Younes's work has not only contributed to the literary world but also served as a bridge between cultures, fostering understanding and empathy. Through his eloquent prose and compelling storytelling, he invites readers to explore the depths of his experiences and the rich tapestry of his heritage.